THE WAY OF MYSTICISM IN ISLAM

THE WAY OF MYSTICISM IN ISLAM

A R Khan

MD PUBLICATIONS PVT LTD
NEW DELHI
www.mdppl.com

Published by :

MD Publications Pvt Ltd
"MD House", 11, Darya Ganj,
New Delhi - 110 002
Phone : +91-11-45355555
E-mail : contact@mdppl.com
Website: www.mdppl.com

ISBN: 978-81-7533-281-2

Published and Printed by Mr. Pranav Gupta on behalf of **MD Publications Pvt Ltd** at Mohit Enterprises, Delhi.

Preface

Sufism or tasawwuf also spelled as *tasavvuf* and *tasavvof*, is generally understood to be the inner, mystical dimension of Islam. A practitioner of this tradition is generally known as a sûfî though some adherents of the tradition reserve this term only for those practitioners who have attained the goals of the Sufi tradition. Another name used for the Sufi seeker is dervish.

Classical Sufi scholars have defined Sufism as "a science whose objective is the reparation of the heart and turning it away from all else but God." Alternatively, in the words of the renowned Darqawi Sufi teacher Ahmad ibn Ajiba, "a science through which one can know how to travel into the presence of the Divine, purify one's inner self from filth, and beautify it with a variety of praiseworthy traits."

Sufism was considerably influenced by the Hindu discipline of Yoga in such areas as physical postures (asanas) and breath control (pranayama).During the primary stages of Sufism, Sufis were characterised by their particular attachment to *dhikr* "remembrance [of God]" and asceticism. Sufism arose among a number of Muslims as a reaction against the worldliness of the early Umayyad Caliphate (661-750 CE).

This is one of the most misunderstood terms in any language or culture. That is because of the extreme materialistic, rationalistic tendency that is in vogue. We believe in reason, materialistic reason. Reason that can deal only with reality through the five senses. That can deal only with the measurable. The immeasurable is outside its sphere. But let us look at human life: friendship, smiles, love of children, admiring a flower, hate of enemy, all of these is intangible. The materialistic mind cannot deal with it. Therefore it does not exist.

Mysticism is also one of these things that the materialistic mind cannot deal with, therefore it has maligned it. It has discredited it completely. It has been associated in the modern mind with hocus-pocus or magic. Mysticism in Arabic is Tassawuf. It comes from the root word "Suf" meaning wool. Donning of woolen clothes was a sign of withdrawing from the luxury of the world, not renunciation of the world. (compare silk which stands for luxury).

There is always a thin line dividing Islamic Mysticism from a lot of heresies that are anti-Islamic. Islamic Mysticism does not shun the world or renounce it, it simply withdraws from some of its luxuries. Islamic mystics have all three components. Islamic mystics have to live all religious experiences of all the religions - then the final flowering is not union with God, but better knowledge of God. Not becoming part and parcel of God. There is always a gap or field where interaction occurs. Knowledge based on Love. The more you know Him, the more you love him, the better you know Him. Knowledge here is not Union, - Wahidat Wujud, and Unity of Being. But Wahidat Ash-shuhud, Unity of Consciousness. To many Muslim mystics wahidat wujud- or union would be heretical, moving outside Islamic orthodoxy. In Islam it would be more of a consciousness of God not a union. It is a psychological not an ontological condition.

I am very grateful to Mr. Pranav Gupta, Director of MD Publications Pvt Ltd, New Delhi, for his kind cooperation and support for this book.

A R Khan

Contents

1

The Way of Mysticism in Islam
An Introduction

Sufism, the religious philosophy of Islam, is described in the oldest extant definition as 'the apprehension of divine realities,' and Mohammedan mystics are fond of calling themselves *Ahl al-Haqq*, 'the followers of the Real.' In attempting to set forth their central doctrines from this point of view, I shall draw to some extent on materials which I have collected during the last twenty years for a general history of Islamic mysticism -a subject so vast and many-sided that several large volumes would be required to do it anything like justice. Here I can only sketch in broad outline certain principles, methods, and characteristic features of the inner life as it has been lived by Moslems of every class and condition from the eighth century of our era to the present day.

Difficult are the paths which they threaded, dark and bewildering the pathless heights beyond; but even if we may not hope to accompany the travellers to their journey's end, any information that we have gathered concerning their religious environment and spiritual history will help us to understand the strange experiences of which they write. In the first place, therefore, I propose to offer a few remarks on the origin and historical development of Sufism, its relation to Islam, and its general character. Not only are these matters interesting to the student of comparative religion; some knowledge of them is indispensable to any serious student of Sufism itself. It may be said, truly enough, that all mystical experiences ultimately meet in a single point; but that point assumes widely different aspects according to the mystic's religion, race, and temperament, while the converging lines of approach admit of almost infinite variety.

Though all the great types of mysticism have something in common, each is marked by peculiar characteristics resulting from the circumstances in which it arose and flourished. Just as the Christian type cannot be understood without reference to Christianity, so the Mohammedan type must be viewed in connection with the outward and inward development of Islam. The word 'mystic,' which has passed from Greek religion into European literature, is represented in Arabic, Persian, and Turkish, the three chief languages of Islam, by 'Sufi.' The terms, however, are not precisely synonymous, for 'Sufi' but has a specific religious connotation, and is restricted by usage to those mystics who profess the Mohammedan faith. And the Arabic word, although in course of time it appropriated the high significance of the Greek-lips sealed by holy mysteries, eyes closed in visionary rapture-bore a humbler meaning when it first gained currency (about 800 A.D.). Until recently its derivation was in dispute.

Most Sufis, flying in the face of etymology, have derived it from an Arabic root which conveys the notion of 'purity'; this would make 'Sufi' means 'one who is pure in heart' or 'one of the elect.' Some European scholars identified it with *sophós* in the sense of 'theosophist.' But Nöldeke, in an article written twenty years ago, showed conclusively that the name was derived from *suf* (wool), and was originally applied to those Moslem ascetics who, in imitation of Christian hermits, clad themselves in coarse woollen garb as a sign of penitence and renunciation of worldly vanities.

The earliest Sufis were, in fact, ascetics and quietists rather than mystics. An overwhelming consciousness of sin, combined with a dread-which it is hard for us to realise-of Judgment Day and the torments of Hell-fire, so vividly painted in the Koran, drove them to seek salvation in flight from the world. On the other hand, the Koran warned them that salvation depended entirely on the inscrutable will of Allah, who guides aright the good and leads astray the wicked. Their fate was inscribed on the eternal tables of His providence, nothing could alter it.

Only this was sure, that if they were destined to be saved by fasting and praying and pious works-then they would be saved. Such a belief ends naturally in quietism, complete and unquestioning submission to the divine will, an attitude characteristic of Sufism in its oldest form. The mainspring of Moslem religious life during the eighth century was fear-fear of God, fear of Hell, fear of death, fear of sin-but the opposite motive had already begun to make its influence felt, and produced in the saintly woman Rabi'a at least one conspicuous example of truly mystical self-abandonment.

So far, there was no great difference between the Sufi and the orthodox Mohammedan zealot, except that the Sufis attached extraordinary importance to certain Koranic doctrines, and developed them at the expense of others which many Moslems might consider equally essential. It must also be allowed that the ascetic movement was inspired by Christian ideals, and contrasted sharply with the active and pleasure-loving spirit of Islam. In a famous sentence the Prophet denounced monkish austerities and bade his people devote themselves to the holy war against unbelievers; and he gave, as is well known, the most convincing testimony in favour of marriage. Although his condemnation of celibacy did not remain without effect, the conquest of Persia, Syria, and Egypt by his successors brought the Moslems into contact with ideas which profoundly modified their outlook on life and religion. European readers of the Koran cannot fail to be struck by its author's vacillation and inconsistency in dealing with the greatest problems. He himself was not aware of these contradictions, nor was they a stumbling-block to his devout followers, whose simple faith accepted the Koran as the Word of God. But the rift was there, and soon produced far-reaching results.

Hence arose the Murjites, who set faith above works and emphasised the divine love and goodness; the Qadarites who affirmed, and the Jabarites who denied, that men are responsible for their actions; the Mu'tazilites, who built a theology on the basis of reason, rejecting the qualities of Allah as incompatible with His unity, and predestinarianism as contrary to His justice; and finally the Ash'arites, the scholastic theologians of Islam, who formulated the rigid metaphysical and doctrinal system that underlies the creed of orthodox Mohammedans at the present time. All these speculations, influenced as they were by Greek theology and philosophy, reacted powerfully upon Sufism.

Early in the third century of the Hegira-the ninth after Christ-we find manifest signs of the new leaven stirring within it. Not that Sufis ceased to mortify the flesh and take pride in their poverty, but they now began to regard asceticism as only the first stage of a long journey, the preliminary training for a larger spiritual life than the mere ascetic is able to conceive.

The nature of the change may be illustrated by quoting a few sentences which have come down to us from the mystics of this period.

"Love is not to be learned from men: it is one of God's gifts and comes of His grace." "None refrains from the lusts of this world save him in whose heart there is a light that keeps him always busied with the next world."

"When the gnostic's spiritual eye is opened, his bodily eye is shut: he sees nothing but God."

"If gnosis were to take visible shape all that looked thereon would die at the sight of its beauty and loveliness, goodness and grace, and the brightness would become dark beside the splendor thereof." {Compare Plato, Phaedrus (Jowett's translation): "For sight is the keenest of our bodily senses; though not by that is wisdom seen; her loveliness would have been transporting if there had been a visible image of her."}

"Gnosis is nearer to silence than to speech."

"When the heart weeps because it has lost, the spirit laughs because it has found."

"Nothing sees God and dies, even as nothing sees God and lives, because His life is everlasting: whoever sees it is thereby made everlasting."

"O God, I never listen to the cry of animals or to the quivering of trees or to the murmuring of water or to the warbling of birds or to the rustling wind or to the crashing thunder without feeling them to be an evidence of Thy unity and a proof that there is nothing like unto Thee."

"O my God, I invoke Thee in public as lords are invoked, but in private as loved ones are invoked. Publicly I say, 'O my God!' but privately I say, 'O my Beloved!'"

These ideas-Light, Knowledge, and Love-form, as it were, the keynotes of the new Sufism, and in the following chapters I shall endeavour to show how they were developed.

Ultimately they rest upon a pantheistic faith which deposed the One transcendent God of Islam and worshipped in His stead One Real Being who dwells and works everywhere, and whose throne is not less, but more, in the human heart than in the heaven of heavens. Before going further, it will be convenient to answer a question which the reader may have asked himself-Whence did the Moslems of the ninth century derive this doctrine?

Modern research has proved that the origin of Sufism cannot be traced back to a single definite cause, and has thereby discredited the sweeping generalisations which represent it, for instance, as a reaction of the Aryan mind against a conquering Semitic religion, and as the product, essentially, of Indian or Persian thought. Statements of this kind, even when they are partially true, ignore the principle that in order to establish an historical connexion between A and B, it is not enough to bring forward evidence of their likeness to one another, without showing at the same time (1) that the actual relation of B to A was such as to render the assumed filiations possible, and (2) that the possible hypothesis fits in with all the ascertained and relevant facts. Now, the theories which I have mentioned do not satisfy these conditions.

If Sufism was nothing but a revolt of the Aryan spirit, how are we to explain the undoubted fact that some of the leading pioneers of Mohammedan mysticism were natives of Syria and Egypt, and Arabs by race? Similarly, the advocates of a Buddhistic or Vedantic origin forget that the main current of Indian influence upon Islamic civilisation belongs to a later epoch, whereas Moslem theology, philosophy, and science put forth their first luxuriant shoots on a soil that was saturated with Hellenistic culture. The truth is that Sufism is a complex thing, and therefore no simple answer can be given to the question how it originated. We shall have gone far, however, towards answering that question when we have distinguished the various movements and forces which moulded Sufism, and determined what direction it should take in the early stages of its growth.

Christianity

It is obvious that the ascetic and quietistic tendencies to which I have referred were in harmony with Christian theory and drew nourishment there from. Many Gospel texts and apocryphal sayings of Jesus are cited in the oldest Sufi biographies, and the Christian anchorite (*rahib*) often appears in the role of a teacher giving instruction and advice to wandering Moslem ascetics. We have seen that the woollen dress, from which the name 'Sufi' is derived, is of Christian origin: vows of silence, litanies (*dhikr*), and other ascetic practices may be traced to the same source. As regards the doctrine of divine love, the following extracts speak for themselves:

"Jesus passed by three men. Their bodies were lean and their faces pale. He asked them, saying, 'What hath brought you to this plight?' They answered, 'Fear of the Fire.' Jesus said, 'Ye fear a thing created, and it behoves God that He should save those who fear.'

Then he left them and passed by three others, whose faces were paler and their bodies leaner, and asked them, saying, 'What hath brought you to this plight?' They answered, 'Longing for Paradise.' He said, 'Ye desire a thing created, and it behoves God that He should give you that which ye hope for.' Then he went on and passed by three others of exceeding paleness and leanness, so that their faces were as mirrors of light, and he said, 'What hath brought you to this?' They answered, 'Our love of God.' Jesus said, 'Ye are the nearest to Him, ye are the nearest to Him.'"

The Syrian mystic, Ahmad ibn al-Hawari, once asked a Christian hermit:

"'What is the strongest command that ye find in your Scriptures?' The hermit replied: 'We find none stronger than this: "Love thy Creator with all thy power and might."'"

Another hermit was asked by some Moslem ascetics:

"'When is a man most persevering in devotion?' 'When love takes possession of his heart,' was the reply; 'for then he hath no joy or pleasure but in continual devotion.'"

The influence of Christianity through its hermits, monks, and heretical sects (*e.g.* the Messalians or Euchitae) was twofold: ascetic and mystical. Oriental Christian mysticism, however, contained a Pagan element: it had long ago absorbed the ideas and adopted the language of Plotinus and the Neo-platonic school.

Neo-platonism

Aristotle, not Plato, is the dominant figure in Moslem philosophy, and few Mohammedans are familiar with the name of Plotinus, who was more commonly called 'the Greek Master' (*al-Sheykh al-Yaunani*). But since the Arabs gained their first knowledge of Aristotle from his Neo-platonist commentators, the system with which they became imbued was that of Porphyry and Proclus. Thus the so-called *Theology of Aristotle*, of which an Arabic version appeared in the ninth century, is actually a manual of Neo-platonism.

Another work of this school deserves particular notice: I mean the writings falsely attributed to Dionysius the Areopagite, the convert of St. Paul. The pseudo-Dionysius-he may have been Syrian monk-names as his teacher a certain Hierotheus, whom Frothingham has identified with Stephen Bar Sudaili, a prominent Syrian gnostic and a contemporary of Jacob of Saruj (451-521 A.D.). Dionysius quotes some fragments of erotic hymns by this Stephen, and a complete work, the *Book of Hierotheus on the Hidden Mysteries of the Divinity*, has come down to us in a unique manuscript which is now in the British Museum.

The Dionysian writings, turned into Latin by John Scotus Erigena, founded medieval Christian mysticism in Western Europe. Their influence in the East was hardly less vital. They were translated from Greek into Syriac almost immediately on their appearance, and their doctrine was vigorously propagated by commentaries in the same tongue. "About 850 A.D. Dionysius was known from the Tigris to the Atlantic." Besides literary tradition there were other channels, by which the doctrines of emanation, illumination, gnosis, and ecstasy were transmitted, but enough has been said to convince the reader that Greek mystical ideas were in the air and easily accessible to the Moslem inhabitants of Western Asia and Egypt, where the Sufi theosophy first took shape.

One of those who bore the chief part in its development, Dhu 'l-Nun the Egyptian, is described as a philosopher and alchemist-in other words, a student of Hellenistic science. When it is added that much of his speculation agrees with what we find, for example, in the writings of Dionysius, we are drawn irresistibly to the conclusion (which, as I have pointed out, is highly probable on general grounds) that Neo-platonism poured into Islam a large tincture of the same mystical element in which Christianity was already steeped.

Gnosticism

Though little direct evidence is available, the conspicuous place occupied by the theory of gnosis in early Sufi speculation suggests contact with Christian Gnosticism, and it is worth noting that the parents of Ma'ruf al-Karkhi, whose definition of Sufism as 'the apprehension of divine realities' was quoted on the first page of this Introduction, are said to have been Sabians, *i.e.*

Mandaeans, dwelling in the Babylonian fenland between Basra and Wasit. Other Moslem saints had learned 'the mystery of the Great Name.' It was communicated to Ibrahim ibn Adham by a man whom he met while travelling in the desert, and as soon as he pronounced it he saw the prophet Khadir (Elias). The ancient Sufis borrowed from the Manichaeans the term *siddiq*, which they apply to their own spiritual adepts, and a later school, returning to the dualism of Mani, held the view that the diversity of phenomena arises from the admixture of light and darkness.

"The ideal of human action is freedom from the taint of darkness; and the freedom of light from darkness means the self-consciousness of light as light." {Shaikh Muhammad Iqbal, *The Development of Metaphysics in Persia* (1908).}

The following version of the doctrine of the seventy thousand veils as explained by a modern Rifa'i dervish shows clear traces of Gnosticism and is so interesting that I cannot refrain from quoting it here:

"Seventy Thousand Veils separate Allah, the One Reality, from the world of matter and of sense. And every soul passes before his birth through these seventy thousand. The inner halves of these are veils of light: the outer half, veils of darkness.

For every one of the veils of light passed through, in this journey towards birth, the soul puts off a divine quality: and for every one of the dark veils, it puts *on* an earthly quality. Thus the child is born weeping, for the soul knows its separation from Allah, the One Reality. And when the child cries in its sleep, it is because the soul remembers something of what it has lost. Otherwise, the passage through the veils has brought with it forgetfulness (*nisyan*): and for this reason man is called *insan*. He is now, as it were, in prison in his body, separated by these thick curtains from Allah.

"But the whole purpose of Sufism, the Way of the dervish, is to give him an escape from this prison, an apocalypse of the Seventy Thousand Veils, a recovery of the original unity with The One, *while still in this body*. The body is not to be put off; it is to be refined and made spiritual-a help and not a hindrance to the spirit. It is like a metal that has to be refined by fire and transmuted. And the sheikh tells the aspirant that he has the secret of this transmutation. 'We shall throw you into the fire of Spiritual Passion,' he says, 'and you will emerge refined.'" {*"The Way" of a Mohammedan Mystic*, by W. H. T. Gairdner (Leipzig, 1912)}

Buddhism

Before the Mohammedan conquest of India in the eleventh century, the teaching of Buddha exerted considerable influence in Eastern Persia and Transoxania. We hear of flourishing Buddhist monasteries in Balkh, the metropolis of ancient Bactria, a city famous for the number of Sufis who resided in it. Professor Goldziher has called attention to the significant circumstance that the Sufi ascetic, Ibrahim ibn Adham, appears in Moslem legend as a prince of Balkh who abandoned his throne and became a wandering dervish-the story of Buddha over again.

The Sufis learned the use of rosaries from Buddhist monks, and, without entering into details; it may be safely asserted that the method of Sufism, so far as it is one of ethical self-culture, ascetic meditation, and intellectual abstraction, owes a good deal to Buddhism. But the features which the two systems have in common only accentuate the fundamental difference between them. In spirit they are poles apart.

The Buddhist moralises himself, the Sufi becomes moral only through knowing and loving God. The Sufi conception of the passing-away (*fana*) of individual self in Universal Being is certainly, I think, of Indian origin. Its first great exponent was the Persian mystic, Bayazid of Bistam, who may have received it from his teacher, Abu 'Ali of Sind (Scinde). Here are some of his sayings:

"Creatures are subject to changing 'states,' but the gnostic has no 'state,' because his vestiges are effaced and his essence annihilated by the essence of another, and his traces are lost in another's traces."

"Thirty years the high God was my mirror, now I am my own mirror," *i.e.* according to the explanation given by his biographer, "that which I was I am no more, for 'I' and 'God' is a denial of the unity of God. Since I am no more, the high God is His own mirror."

"I went from God to God, until they cried from me in me, 'O Thou I!'"

This, it will be observed, is not Buddhism, but the pantheism of the Vedanta. We cannot identify *fana* with Nirvana unconditionally. Both terms imply the passing-away of individuality, but while Nirvana is purely negative, *fana* is accompanied by *baqa,* everlasting life in God. The rapture of the Sufi who has lost himself in ecstatic contemplation of the divine beauty is entirely opposed to the passionless intellectual serenity of the Arahat. I emphasise this contrast because, in my opinion, the influence of Buddhism on Mohammedan thought has been exaggerated. Much is attributed to Buddhism that is Indian rather than specifically Buddhistic: the *fana* theory of the Sufis is a case in point. Ordinary Moslems held the followers of Buddha in abhorrence, regarding them as idolaters, and were not likely to seek personal intercourse with them. On the other hand, for nearly a thousand years before the Mohammedan conquest, Buddhism had been powerful in Bactria and Eastern Persia generally: it must, therefore, have affected the development of Sufism in these regions.

While *fana* in its pantheistic form is radically different from Nirvana, the terms coincide so closely in other ways that we cannot regard them as being altogether unconnected. *Fana* has an ethical aspect: it involves the extinction of all passions and desires. The passing-away of evil qualities and of the evil actions which they produce is said to be brought about by the continuance of the corresponding good qualities and actions. Compare this with the definition of Nirvana given by Professor Rhys Davids:

"The extinction of that sinful, grasping condition of mind and heart, which would otherwise, according to the great mystery of Karma, is the cause of renewed individual existence. That extinction is to be brought about by, and runs parallel with, the growth of the opposite condition of mind and heart; and it is complete when that opposite condition is reached." Apart from the doctrine of Karma, which is alien to Sufism, these definitions of *fana* (viewed as a moral state) and Nirvana, agree almost word for word. It would be out of place to pursue the comparison further, but I think we may conclude that the Sufi theory of *fana* was influenced to some extent by Buddhism as well as by Perso-Indian pantheism.

The receptivity of Islam to foreign ideas has been recognised by every unbiased inquirer, and the history of Sufism is only a single instance of the general rule. But this fact should not lead us to seek in such ideas an explanation of the whole question which I am now discussing, or to identify Sufism itself with the extraneous ingredients which it absorbed and assimilated in the course of its development. Even if Islam had been miraculously shut off from contact with foreign religions and philosophies, some form of mysticism would have arisen within it, for the seeds were already there. Of course, we cannot isolate the internal forces working in this direction, since they were subject to the law of spiritual gravitation.

The powerful currents of thought discharged through the Mohammedan world by the great non-Islamic systems above mentioned gave a stimulus to various tendencies within Islam which affected Sufism either positively or negatively. As we have seen, its oldest type is an ascetic revolt against luxury and worldliness; later on, the prevailing rationalism and skepticism provoked counter-movements towards intuitive knowledge and emotional faith, and also an orthodox reaction which in its turn drove many earnest Moslems into the ranks of the mystics.

How, it may be asked, could a religion founded on the simple and austere monotheism of Mohammed tolerate these new doctrines, much less make terms with them? It would seem impossible to reconcile the transcendent personality of Allah with an immanent Reality which is the very life and soul of the universe. Yet Islam has accepted Sufism. The Sufis, instead of being excommunicated, are securely established in the Mohammedan church, and the *Legend of the Moslem Saints* records the wildest excesses of Oriental pantheism.

Let us return for a moment to the Koran, that infallible touchstone by which every Mohammedan theory and practice must be proved. Are any germs of mysticism to be found there? The Koran, as I have said, starts with the notion of Allah, the One, Eternal, and Almighty God, far above human feelings and aspirations-the Lord of His slaves, not the Father of His children; a judge meting out stern justice to sinners, and extending His mercy only to those who avert His wrath by repentance, humility, and unceasing works of devotion; a God of fear rather than of love. This is one side, and certainly the most prominent side, of Mohammed's teaching; but while he set an impassable gulf between the world and Allah, his deeper instinct craved a direct revelation from God to the soul. There are no contradictions in the logic of feeling. Mohammed, who had in him something of the mystic, felt God as far and near, both as transcendent and immanent. In the latter aspect, Allah is the light of the heavens and the earth, a Being who works in the world and in the soul of man.

"If My servants ask thee about Me, lo, I am near" (Kor. 2.182); "We (God) are nearer to him than his own neck-vein" (50.15); "And in the earth are signs to those of real faith, and in yourselves. What! Do ye not see?"

It was a long time ere they saw. The Moslem consciousness, haunted by terrible visions of the wrath to come, slowly and painfully awoke to the significance of those liberating ideas. The verses which I have quoted do not stand alone, and however unfavourable to mysticism the Koran as a whole may be, I cannot assent to the view that it supplies no basis for a mystical interpretation of Islam. This was worked out in detail by the Sufis, who dealt with the Koran in very much the same way as Philo treated the Pentateuch.

But they would not have succeeded so thoroughly in bringing over the mass of religious Moslems to their side, unless the champions of orthodoxy had set about constructing a system of scholastic philosophy that reduced the divine nature to a purely formal, changeless, and absolute unity, a bare will devoid of all affections and emotions, a tremendous and incalculable power with which no human creature could have any communion or personal intercourse whatsoever. That is the God of Mohammedan theology. That was the alternative to Sufism. Therefore, "all thinking, religious Moslems are mystics," as Professor D. B. Macdonald, one of our best authorities on the subject, has remarked. And he adds: "All, too, are pantheists, but some do not know it."

The relation of individual Sufis to Islam varies from more or less entire conformity to a merely nominal profession of belief in Allah and His Prophet. While the Koran and the Traditions are generally acknowledged to be the unalterable standard of religious truth, this acknowledgment does not include the recognition of any external authority which shall decide what is orthodox and what is heretical. Creeds and catechisms count for nothing in the Sufi's estimation. Why should he concern himself with these when he possesses a doctrine derived immediately from God? As he reads the Koran with studious meditation and rapt attention, lo, the hidden meanings-infinite, inexhaustible-of the Holy Word flash upon his inward eye.

This is what the Sufis call *istinbat*, a sort of intuitive

deduction; the mysterious inflow of divinely revealed knowledge into hearts made pure by repentance and filled with the thought of God, and the outflow of that knowledge upon the interpreting tongue. Naturally, the doctrines elicited by means of *istinbat* do not agree very well either with Mohammedan theology or with each other, but the discord is easily explained. Theologians, who interpret the letter, cannot be expected to reach the same conclusions as mystics, who interpret the spirit; and if both classes differ amongst themselves, that is a merciful dispensation of divine wisdom, since theological controversy serves to extinguish religious error, while the variety of mystical truth corresponds to the manifold degrees and modes of mystical experience.

In the chapter on the Gnosis I shall enter more fully into the attitude of the Sufis towards positive religion. It is only a rough-and-ready account of the matter to say that many of them have been good Moslems, many scarcely Moslems at all, and a third party, perhaps the largest, Moslems after a fashion. During the early Middle Ages Islam was a growing organism, and gradually became transformed under the influence of diverse movements, of which Sufism itself was one. Mohammedan orthodoxy in its present shape owes much to Ghazali, and Ghazali was a Sufi. Through his work and example the Sufistic interpretation of Islam has in no small measure been harmonised with the rival claims of reason and tradition, but just because of this he is less valuable than mystics of a purer type to the student who wishes to know what Sufism essentially is.

Although the numerous definitions of Sufism which occur in Arabic and Persian books on the subject are historically interesting, their chief importance lies in showing that Sufism is undefinable. Jalaluddin Rumi in his *Masnavi* tells a story about an elephant which some Hindoos were exhibiting in a dark room. Many people gathered to see it, but, as the place was too dark to permit them to see the elephant, they all felt it with their hands, to gain an idea of what it was like. One felt its trunk, and said that the animal resembled a water-pipe; another felt its ear, and said it must be a large fan; another it's leg, and thought it must be a pillar; another felt its back, and declared that the beast must be like an immense throne. So it is with those who define Sufism: they can only attempt to express what they themselves have felt, and there is no conceivable formula that will comprise every shade of personal and intimate religious feeling. Since, however, these definitions illustrate with convenient brevity certain aspects and characteristics of Sufism, a few specimens may be given.

"Sufism is this: that actions should be passing over the Sufi (*i.e.* being done upon him) which are known to God only, and that he should always be with God in a way that is known to God only."

"Sufism is wholly self-discipline."

"Sufism is, to possess nothing and to be possessed by nothing."

"Sufism is not a system composed of rules or sciences but a moral disposition; *i.e.* if it were a rule, it could be made one's own by strenuous exertion, and if it were a science, it could be acquired by instruction; but on the contrary it is a disposition, according to the saying, 'Form yourselves on the moral nature of God'; and the moral nature of God cannot be attained either by means of rules or by means of sciences."

"Sufism is freedom and generosity and absence of self-constraint."

"It is this: that God should make thee die to thyself and should make thee live in Him."

"To behold the imperfection of the phenomenal world, nay, to close the eye to everything imperfect in contemplation of Him who is remote from all imperfection-that is Sufism."

"Sufism is control of the faculties and observance of the breaths."

"It is Sufism to put away what thou hast in thy head, to give what thou hast in thy hand, and not to recoil from whatsoever befalls thee."

The reader will perceive that Sufism is a word uniting many divergent meanings, and that in sketching its main features one is obliged to make a sort of composite portrait, which does not represent any particular type exclusively. The Sufis are not a sect, they have no dogmatic system, the *tariqas* or paths by which they seek God "are in number as the souls of men" and vary infinitely, though a family likeness may be traced in them all.

Descriptions of such a Protean phenomenon must differ widely from one another, and the impression produced in each case will depend on the choice of materials and the prominence given to this or that aspect of the many-sided whole. Now, the essence of Sufism is best displayed in its extreme type, which is pantheistic and speculative rather than ascetic or devotional. This type, therefore, I have purposely placed in the foreground. The advantage of limiting the field is obvious enough, but entails some loss of proportion. In order to form a fair judgment of Mohammedan mysticism, the following chapters should be supplemented by a companion picture drawn especially from those moderate types which, for want of space, I have unduly neglected.

The Arabs had commercial relations with southern India long before Islam, and their commerce by sea continued - along with missionary activity - after the appearance of the Holy Prophet. The Muslim Arabs first settled on the Malabar Coast about fifty years after the Hijrah, toward the end of the seventh century A.D., at a time when South India was agitated by religious conflicts and political instability. Islam, with its simplicity of faith and clarity of doctrine, made a tremendous impression on the Hindu mind, and within the first twenty-five years many of the people, including the King of Malabar, had accepted the new religion. Although the commerce by sea continued, the main route by which Islam came to India was overland through Iran and Central Asia. During the Caliphate of Umar the land approaches to India were explored, but Umar's policy did not countenance expansion into India. It was under the Umayyads that the first efforts were made to invade India.

For convenience in discussing the rise of Muslim culture in Pakistan and India we may divide the history into four periods: the period before the Mughals; the Mughal rule of almost two centuries; the period of disintegration; and the past century, which includes the British rule and the creation of Pakistan. The first Muslim invasion of India took place during the reign of the Umayyad Caliph Walid (87-97; A.D. 705-15) who sent Muhammad Ibn Qasim on an expedition into Sind, the area which then included most of what is now the Punjab. Although Sind was at that time governed by Brahman f amily, the religion of the common people was Buddhist. The Buddhists were suffering serious religious, social, and economic disabilities under the Brahman rule, as is shown by their petition to Qasim for the right to worship in their Buddhist temples as they used to do. Muhammad Ibn Qasim treated the Hindus very generously, keeping Hindu ministers and police inspectors in his service, but he was soon recalled and after his departure many of the Hindu feudal princes revolted against the Caliph's authority.

The first Abbasid Caliph sent an army into Sind to oust the Umayyad governor, and the second Caliph, Mansur, sent another expedition which founded the garrison town of Mansura. During the time of the Abbasid Caliph Mamun (198-218; A.D. 813-33) many Arab families migrated to Sind, founding a large Arab colony. Later, as the power of the Abbasid Caliphs declined, Sind became a neglected province governed by petty princes who acknowledged the Caliph only as their spiritual head. The two principal Muslim kingdoms of Sind were at that time Multan and Mansura.

The real history of Muslim India begins with Mahmud of Ghazna, ruler of a small Turkish kingdom in Afghanistan which had become independent when the Samanid Empire collapsed. Mahmud led seventeen expeditions into India from 391 to 417 (A.D. 1000-1026). The rule of the Arabs in Sind came to an end in 396 (A.D. 1005) when Mahmud of Ghazna sent an army of Turks and Hindu mercenaries under Abdu'r Razzaq to uproot the power of the Qarmati Ima'ilis, who seem to have gained considerable influence there. The Punjab was annexed to the Ghaznavid Empire and ruled from Ghazna, but Mahmud's successors, faced with the rising power of the Seljuq Turks, could not hold it.

The dynasty which laid the permanent foundations of Muslim rule in North India was that of the Ghorids, rulers of a small mountainous state in Afghanistan. Ghori conquered Mukan in 572 (A.D. 1176), defeated the last Ghaznavid king of the Punjab, and in 588 (A.D. 1192) gave a crushing blow to the remnants of the Rajput Hindu princes. His Turkish slaves who served as leaders of his armies carried on his work and consolidated the Muslim power with the conquest of Banaras and Bengal, carrying Muslim rule to the east coast of India. After the death of Ghori, one of the Turkish slaves, Qutbuddin Aibak, assumed supreme power and became the first real Indian Muslim Emperor and the founder of what was called the Slave Dynasty.

The Slave Dynasty was an oligarchy of Turks which jealously kept the doors shut against the non-Turks. They were replaced by the Khilji Turks who came to power in Delhi in 689 (A.D. 1290). Under the Khiljis the distinction between Turks and non-Turks vanished, and all avenues to power and office were open to Indianized Muslims, converts and no converts. They extended Muslim power much farther into southern India than ever before. The farthest southern extension of Muslim rule came under the Tughluqs, who held power from 720 to 815 (A.D. 1320-412) and pressed their invasion almost to the southern tip of the continent. It was during their dynasty that Timur invaded northern India in 801 (A.D. 1398) and created chaotic conditions which weakened the control from Delhi. The Sayyids ruled for a time after the Tughluqs, only to be supplanted by the Lodhis, an Afghan tribe which exercised authority until they were ousted by the Mughal invader, Babar, who defeated the last of the Lodhis at the famous battle of Panipat in 933 (A.D. 1526).

The Muslim culture in Sind did not receive much influence from its Arab rulers since the center of the Arab Empire was in Damascus and then in Baghdad, so far from the Sind that the Arabs paid little attention to their distant eastern provinces. The chief Arab influence centered in the garrison towns established after the departure of Qasim in an effort to retain some measure of control over the local rulers. The Arab tribes which settled there left some influence on the language of Sind, but little is known about them. After the establishment of the Fatimid rule in Egypt, toward the end of the third century (A.D. 909), Isma'ili preachers began to enter Sind and established a particularly active following. A family of these Isma'ilis, perhaps of the same blood as the Druzes of Syria, founded a separate Kingdom near modern Thatta. Later the Isma'ilis gained a foothold in Multan, which had long been under Sunni rule. The name of the Fatimid rulers was recited in the Friday addresses at Multan and in other centers of Isma'ili influence.

There were several Sindhi Muslim scholars of note in this period, men whose influence extended to Iraq where the people thought highly of their learning. Their judges were also noted for their mastery of Hadith. The school of Hanafi came to dominate the whole province of Sind to the exclusion of all other systems of jurisprudence. Two Sindhi poets, Abul Ata and Abu Zila, attained great fame. The Arab poets were generally bilingual, writing in both Sindhi and Arabic. Some of the poetic compositions of the Sind were transmitted throughout the Arab Empire, and it is related that famous Arab poets visited Sind or sent their poems to the governors there. The development of literature and poetry in India was quickened by the coming of many scholars who were driven from their homes in Iran and Transoxiana by the Mongol invasions. Outstanding among the immigrant scholars was the famous historian al-Biruni, author of the epoch-making *Kitabul Hind*.

Under the Arabic rule the official language used for governmental and commercial dealings in Sind was Arabic. The educated classes used both Arabic and Sindhi, but the common people spoke only their own mother tongue. With the rise of Persian power, the Persian language gained a firm footing in Sind along with Arabic, with the result that modern Sindhi, written in Arabic script, contains more than fifty per cent Arabic and Persian words.

Since no schools are mentioned in the accounts of travelers of that time, it is assumed that there was no regular system of education in Sind other than the mosques which served as centers of learning, as they did in other parts of the Muslim world. Uchh, however, seems to have been a busy center of educational activity, for when it was conquered in 614 (A.D. 1217) it is recorded that the conqueror carried away to Delhi a large number of Sindhi scholars.

The kings of Delhi before the advent of the Mughals were absolute autocrats. Some of them even defied the Shari'a which placed limitations on the absolutism of rulers. Most of them, however, respected the religious law and some, like Firuz Tughlaq, went to unreasonable lengths in their orthodoxy. Their relations with the Abbasid Caliphs varied according to the inclinations of individual rulers. Even when the power of the Abbasid Caliph was reduced to a shadow the Indian rulers maintained their allegiance, as is shown by the fact that the Caliph's name was struck on the coins and prayers were offered for him in the Friday services in the mosques.

There were usually two religious departments under the pre-Mughal rulers, each of them headed by an officer of the highest rank whose authority came directly from the monarch. One department dealt with the administration of mosques, the supervision of waqf funds, and financial aid to schools and Sufi lodges. The other was the department of the judiciary, in which the judges followed the provisions of Islamic law with complete freedom from the encroachment of executive authority.

The Sufis generally were favored over the ulama because they kept aloof from politics, while the religious scholars sometimes could set limits to the authority of the rulers. Most of the kings of Delhi were ardent devotees of the Sufis. Two great Sufis, Salar Masud Ghazi and Shaikh Isma'il, came to India in the fifth century (eleventh century A.D.) and won thousands to Islam in spite of the fact that there was as yet no Muslim ruler in India. Another great mystic was Moinuddin Chishti who was born in Samarkand and came to India sometime before the establishment of the Ghorid dynasty. There he laid the foundation of the Chishti order of Sufis, which is even today the most popular Sufi order in Pakistan and India. His tomb in Ajmer is visited annually by hundreds of thousands of Muslims and many Hindus.

The Suhrawardi order of Sufis which was founded in this period differed from the Chishtis in laying greater stress on the observance of religious law. It disapproved of the particular type of music and dancing usually sanctioned by the other Sufis. Two other orders, the Qadiri and Naqshbandi, also gained widespread influence in India in pre-Mughal times.

The impact of Islam on Hinduism made itself felt in the reform movements it inspired among the Hindus in the third to the sixth century (ninth to twelfth century A.D.). These movements, associated with the names of Sankara and Ramanuja and their followers, appeared first in South India as a result of early contacts with Muslims who came to India as travelers and merchants, before there were any Muslim conquests in southern India. It was only later that the reform movements spread to the north where the rulers were Muslim. The early influence of Islam on Hinduism seems to have come chiefly from observing the Sufi practices and the rites and customs of Muslims in their daily life.

The Mughal period begins with the battle of Panipat in 933 (A.D. 1526), in which Babar's decisive victory over the Lodhis made it possible for him to establish his rule at Delhi. Babar, who was descended from Timur, was a Turk and proud of his lineage. He spoke both Persian and Turkish, but since the Mughals were already saturated with Persian culture before they came to India, it was Persian rather than Turkish which was the vehicle of literary expression. Many scholars and poets from Khurasan and neighboring lands settled in India after the invasion of Babar, and soon the Mughal court became the center of intense literary and cultural activity.

When Babar died in 937 (A.D. 1530) he was succeeded by his son Humayun, a man of taste, of learning in astronomy and mathematics, and the founder of the first schools and colleges in Mughal India. But Humayun's rule was brief, for he was driven out by Pathan forces and compelled to take refuge in Iran. He later returned and reconquered northern India with the help of the Iranian monarch.

The real history of Mughal India begins in 963 (A.D. 1555) when Akbar, son of Humayun, came to the throne. His Persian teacher and guardian, Bairam Khan, consolidated Mughal rule in India while Akbar was still in his teens. Akbar had the genius to attach to himself many native Hindus of administrative experience, one of whom created the Mughal revenue system which continued with some modifications under the British rule. At the beginning of the eleventh century (seventeenth century A.D.) the territory governed by Akbar was one of the best administered in the world and cultural pursuits flourished as never before.

After fifty years of rule Akbar was followed by Jahangir, who reigned from 1014 to 1038 (A.D. 1605-28). Shah Jahan, famous as the builder of the Taj Mahal, was emperor from 1038 until 1070 (A.D. 1628-59), when the control of the government was taken over by his son Aurangzeb, the last of the great Mughal emperors, who died in 1119 (A.D. 1707). Although the Mughal rule continued after Aurangzeb, it was a prolonged period of disintegration, which lasted until the Mutiny of 1274 (A.D. 1857).

It was under the Mughals that Muslim rule in India was finally consolidated. Although some fresh conquests were made in southern India, the main center of Mughal power remained in the north. Since they came from Central Asia, where they were within the range of Turko-Iranian culture, the Mughals had imbibed many Iranian influences. Babar called himself *Padishah,* an Iranian title for king which implied that he was not the democratic chief of a few Turkish tribes but was an autocratic Iranian sovereign. The Mughal power structure rested on a heterogeneous Muslim aristocracy composed of newcomers from Transoxiana (where Bukhara and Samarkand had long been centers of Arabic Islamic culture), of Iranian noblemen seeking careers in the newly conquered country, and of the Turkish and Afghan aristocracy who were already entrenched in India but now removed from supreme power. The Mughals themselves were a microscopic minority, but were able to maintain their control. For long time immigration from Central Asia and Iran continued - until the foreign Muslim aristocracy in India became Indianized, and then foreigners were no longer welcome.

The Muslim aristocracy was feudal in character, depending on levies enlisted from the middle and lower classes of Muslims, usually of the same nationality as the feudal leader. Thus Afghans would never enlist themselves in the feudal levies commanded by the Iranian Shi'a nobles. In this way separatist and sectarian trends were fostered among the other members of the Muslim minority of India, the people on whom the Mughal power ultimately depended. The Mughal emperor who ruled over this mixed population was an autocrat bound by no law and admitting only the slight restraint imposed by the Islamic Shari'a which was never allowed full sway. The emperor could take the life and property of his nobles whenever he was displeased with them, a thing which would never have been possible under the rule of the Shari'a. Thus the Mughal state was in no sense an Islamic state. It was primarily an Iranian autocracy with a few Mongol and Turkish features added.

The Mughal system of administration was patterned on the Abbasid government as adapted to Indian needs. The emperor was the spiritual as well as the temporal head of the state. He had a Vizier, or Chief Minister, aided by secretaries, but no cabinet of ministers. The chief of the religious department occupied an important position as the guardian of Islamic law. He awarded lands and stipends to religious scholars, schools, and college s and was charged with the duty of helping the needy. The chief judge was the highest judicial officer, overseeing the Qadis and Muftis who tried and decided the civil and criminal cases of the Hindus and Muslims. They were chiefly concerned with the administration of sacred law based on the interpretations of the four Muslim schools of law.

Literature and poetry were assiduously cultivated under the patronage of the Mughal court. Mughal rulers such as Babar and Jahangir were themselves literary men of high distinction, and their courtiers included men of great learning and collectors of large libraries. Persian poetry under the Mughals reached a high degree of perfection with famous Indian poets who could stand comparison with the best poets of Iran.

The use of the Persian language has left a permanent influence on Indian languages and gave birth to Urdu, one of the great languages of India and Pakistan today. Historians of this period wrote works which are immensely valuable sources of information to scholars of modern times. Many translations from Indian languages into Persian were made under the patronage of the Mughal emperors, notably the translation of the Mahabharata and Ramayana under Akbar. Akbar's interest in religion was so extensive that he had the Bible translated into Persian for the first time.

The Mughal period was marked by the rise of new religious movements in Islam. At the time when the Hindus were taking to new ways of religious thought, the Muslims were shaken out of their lethargy by the Mahdavi and Roshni movements. Sayyid Muhammad of Jaunpur, who was born about 982 (A.D. 1574), claimed to be the Mahdi, the Expected One. The followers of this movement organized a brotherhood in which all members enjoyed equal rights. At the same time the Roshni movement arose in Afghanistan.

Although both of these movements created militant groups in which the leader claimed temporal and spiritual power, they did not leave any appreciable marks on Muslim religious thought. The Mahdavi sect still exists in India and Pakistan as an insignificant minority group.

Much more important were the consequences of the religious controversy created by the emperor himself and some of his courtiers. Akbar believed that he needed closer social contacts with the Hindus, for he was of the opinion that Mughal rule in India could not rest for long on the strength of the Muslim minority unless it had the active support of the Hindus.

This led him to adopt many Hindu customs and abolish the customary poll-tax on non-Muslims. Muslim orthodoxy, however, was firmly entrenched and Akbar's new policy started a religious struggle whose effects outlasted him. After about 983 (A.D. 1575) Akbar began to show unusual interest in religious discussions, largely as a result of association with some of his courtiers who were free-thinkers. Akbar erected a special hall where religious discussions were held with scholars of all views and schools. The controversies could not, of course, be restricted to the differing views of the Sunnis and Shi'as, or the conflicts of the various schools of law.

Soon the fundamentals of religion came under discussion and Akbar felt dissatisfied with the existing state of religion. He then began to invite people of all religions to take part in the discussions. Even the Christian fathers from Goa, represented by Aquaviva and Monserrate, came to join this debate, but they failed to influence Akbar. Gradually he was led to assume the mantle of a religious leader. He issued a decree of infallibility which made him the supreme arbiter in matters of religion and then went a step further by promulgating a new religion compounded of Muslim, Hindu and Christian elements. In the new religion Akbar required the followers to prostrate themselves before the emperor and forbade circumcision, prohibited the use of beef, and discouraged the growing of beards. Eighteen of his courtiers joined the new religion but all the rest kept aloof. In the end, Akbar achieved only the exasperation of the ulama.

Akbar's religion died with him, but some of its ideas lived and found an echo during the next two generations. Dara Shikoh, the son of Shah Jahan, was in his early life influenced by the liberalism of the Sufis, as distinct from the orthodoxy of the ulama, and later began to take increasing interest in the Hindu religion. Under his inspiration, several of the Hindu scriptures were translated into Persian, and he was himself the author of many books on religion, including a biography of Sufis and saints, and a treatise on the technical terms of Hindu pantheism and their equivalents in Sufi theology. He also tried, under the influence of the Sufis, to arrive at a synthesis which would reconcile the opposition between Islam and Hinduism. The Sufis, though many of them were orthodox in their practices, verged more and more toward pantheistic ideas congenial to the Indian mind. Their theology provided *a* common ground between Islam and Hinduism.

Such tendencies spurred the orthodox party to muster enough strength to play a leading role in the defeat and assassination of Dara Shikoh at the hands of his brother Aurangzeb, who was his rival for the throne. Aurangzeb was largely influenced by the religious ideas of Shaikh Ahmad of Sirhind, who played a prominent part in reestablishing Muslim orthodoxy and combating Sufi deviations from Islam. Shaikh Ahmad's son was a close associate of Aurangzeb. The reaction which set in following the appearance of Shaikh Ahmad inspired Aurangzeb to order a codification of Muslim law by bringing together the scattered elements of Hanafi law found in the legal decisions of the Muftis. This stress on the juristic aspect of Islam is plainly a reaction against the deviating Sufis and Muslim free-thinkers whose attitude toward Muslim law had loosened the bonds of social and religious discipline.

The ideas and teachings of Shaikh Ahmad Sirhindi are important in the history of Islam, for he has left a permanent impression on Indian Muslim thought. Shaikh

Ahmad, now called the Twelfth Renovator, was born in the Punjab in 1002 (A.D. 1593). After completing his religious education he joined the Suhrawardi and Chishti orders of the Sufis, but later he became a member of the Naqshbandi order. Shaikh Ahmad was quick to perceive the spiritual degeneration which had overtaken his contemporaries, the Sufis as well as the ulama. While the Sufis, under the influence of Ibn Arabi's philosophy, had come to believe in the doctrine of the unity of existence and were prone to abolish all distinction between God and man, the ulama were under the spell of a narrow legalism which led to interminable disputes on minor points of law. Both, according to Shaikh Ahmad, had lost the moral fervor of Islam.

Shaikh Ahmad regarded the Sufis as more dangerous than the ulama for he clearly perceived that all the commandments of religion are based on a distinction between God and His creation. If creation was unreal and God alone had existence, as Ibn Arabi maintained, then the need for religion and law vanish, and, what is more important, life and existence would become matters of little moment. No wonder that the Sufis sought refuge in the doctrine of annihilation in God, leaving mundane matters to be attended to by worldly-minded men. Therefore, Shaikh Ahmad set himself to disprove the philosophy of Ibn Arabi and put forward the contention that the mystic experience of the unity of God and the world is an illusion. He affirmed the existence of the world as a separate entity which is the shadow of a Real Being. This philosophy was directed against the pantheistic ideas of the Sufis, which were influenced by Ibn Arabi and drew largely upon Hindu sources.

Shaikh Ahmad's writings gained for him a considerable following, both at the Mughal court and in the army. Jahangir for a time took strong steps to check his pervasive influence but, faced with an uprising by one of his army chiefs who was an adherent of Shaikh Ahmad, came to terms with him. It was agreed that all of the non-Islamic practices adopted by Akbar, such as prostration before the emperor and the prohibition of beef, should be stopped at once. Jahangir afterward became a devoted follower of Shaikh Ahmad, and thus Muslim orthodoxy was able to reassert itself after a brief eclipse.

Under the Mughals education depended on private initiative. The emperors and their nobles encouraged education by grants of land and money to mosques, to lodges which served as residences for religious training, and to individual saints and scholars. The mosques invariably had primary schools attached to them. Jahangir promulgated a regulation that whenever a rich man or traveler died without heir his property would go to the crown to be used for repairing madrasas and lodges. Shah Jahan founded an imperial college at Delhi and Aurangzeb founded numberless colleges and schools. He gave extensive grants of land and money to develop a flourishing center of learning at Lucknow. Female education under the Mughals seems to have been confined to rich and learned families, especially the ladies of the royal house, some of whom were famous for the high literary quality of their writings. Babar brought with him the Byzantine architectural style, for the Turks and Turkish offshoots of the disintegrated Timurid Empire had long been in touch with the Greek states and the Balkan Peninsula.

The pupils of Sinan, the Albanian architect famous in the Ottoman Empire, found their way into the kingdoms of the Timurid rulers. But Babar employed Indian stonemasons chiefly. Akbar adhered to the Persian ideas of art which he inherited from his mother and his father, who had lived in Persia, but his Rajput marriages attracted him to Hindu art traditions. Thus the Jahangir Mahal in Agra Fort and many of the buildings of Fatehpur Sikri, his projected capital, show unmistakable blending of Persian and Indian art types. Since craftsmen even from the Far East are said to have been drawn to the Mughal court and some acquaintance with Indonesian architectural styles through overseas pilgrim traffic and trade survived in the time of the Mughals, it is not improbable that Indian and Indonesian Buddhist survivals left their stamp on Mughal architecture.

The palaces and forts constructed by the Mughals are a mixture of Indian and Muslim styles, but the mosques and mausoleums are chiefly Islamic in conception and execution, with the dome and the pointed arch as their most characteristic features. Of all the Mughals, Shah Jahan holds the preeminent position in the history of Muslim architecture. His Special Hall (Diwan-i-Khas) and the Taj Mahal, which is the mausoleum of his wife, are the finest achievements of Mughal architecture. Among the characteristics of this architecture are the lavish use of marble and the decoration of walls and roofs with multi-coloured carved and inlaid lacework.

The art of calligraphy received great encouragement from the Mughals, who had many famous calligraphers attached to the court. Even greater favor was shown to painters. When Babar conquered India, the popularity of the great Persian painter Bihzad was at its zenith. His style of miniature painting was the standard which Mughal painters chose to follow. After the return of Humayun from his enforced exile in Persia, the Mughal nobles took the Persian style of painting for their model, thus making Bihzad and his school the example as Persian art was engrafted on Indian painting.

Miniature painting is characterized by its intense individualism which shows no interest in masses and crowds or the interrelation of forms in their infinite multiplicity. It looks at every detail of the individual figure. Since this art form was born in the courts of Genghis Khan and Timur it naturally depicts scenes of battles and the hunt

- but chivalry and romance, youths and maidens dallying in gardens, and gorgeous receptions in princely courts are also represented, and of piety and mysticism there is no lack. The king and the beggar were the two poles around which the individual moved. The Sultan of today may be the darwish of tomorrow - hence the frequency of the scenes showing the darwish living in the wild forest or the lonely cave, the darwish as the miraculous master leading fierce animals as if they were lambs, and the darwish dancing in the ecstasy of mystic joy. The supernatural was represented in the figures of Jinn, goblins, monsters, and fairies.

After the death of Aurangzeb in 1119 (A.D. 1707) the Mughal Empire went into a sharp decline. The various provincial governors became semi-independent, and the extent of Mughal rule shrank to Delhi and the adjoining areas. The anarchic conditions created by warfare among the provincial governors were further complicated by the rise of the Maratha power m the Deccan. The Marathas were militant Hindus in the Bombay province, led at first by the able Hindu leader Sivaji, who formed a small kingdom along the coast. During the period of anarchy following Aurangzeb's death their kingdom was extended by a succession of able Maratha rulers until it became a formidable empire in the Deccan and threatened to engulf the warring Muslim leaders and their nominal sovereign, the Mughal emperor himself. Their power was crushed by the Afghan invader Ahmad Shah Abdali, in 1175 (A.D. 1761).

Meanwhile the English, along with the Portuguese, the Dutch, and the French, had entered India as traders and obtained many commercial concessions from the Mughal emperors. As the Mughal authority declined, the Europeans' factories became fortified settlements to protect their trading operations from the prevalent anarchy and disorder. The acquisition of Bengal by Clive after the battle of Plassey in 1117 (A.D. 1757), in which the independent Mughal Governor of Bengal was defeated, transformed the position of the British in India. They became then one of the many local powers contending for ultimate sovereignty. After the Mutiny of 1274 (A.D. 1857), in which the remnants of Muslim nobility rallied under the last Mughal Emperor of Delhi and suffered total defeat, the British rule was firmly established. The East India Company then gave way to the direct exercise of control by the British Parliament, and India became the brightest jewel in the British crown.

The disintegration of the Mughal Empire after the death of Aurangzeb went on rapidly, but the Muslim literature of this period shows no consciousness of the fate that was overtaking the Muslims. Age-old methods of education and the cultivation of established sciences went on as before because of the large endowments which learned scholars had received at the hands of the Mughal emperors. A significant feature of this period was the rise of the Urdu language and the creation of Urdu literature which took its place side by side with Persian literature. The new language was a combination of Hindi, Arabic, and Persian, its grammar and syntax being based on Sanskrit while its vocabulary was largely Arabic and Persian. Persian still retained its predominance as late as the period of the last Mughal emperor, when Ghalib, one of the most brilliant Urdu poets, still prided himself on his Persian odes and looked upon his Urdu poetry with shame.

Although it was a time of disintegration, the age of decline produced one thinker and scholar of great profundity, Shah Walliyulla (died 1180; A.D. 1766), rated by some as superior to Ghazali and Lbn Rushd (Averroes). Shah Walliyulla left an abiding impression on the development of Muslim thought. Both politically and intellectually the idea of Pakistan owes much to him because from his theories and practical activities arose the tides which were to lead to the Muslim struggle for independence. Alone among his contemporaries Shah Walliyulla was conscious of the period of disintegration through which Muslim culture was passing and recognized the need for a mental transformation to cope with the changing situation. He was quick to realize that the age of kings and monarchs had passed and the age of masses and democracy was within sight. He was conscious of the economic breakdown in Muslim society caused by the luxurious living of the rulers and upper classes among the Muslims. His writings contain unmistakable hints of his antimonarchical and socialistic tendencies.

His first work was the Persian translation of the *Quran* with commentary. Up to that time the *Quran* had not been accessible to the average educated man in his own language. This was a daring innovation in the light of the ultraconservative temper of the times and Walliyulla had to face the full brunt of the public fury excited by the ulama. He followed his translation of the *Quran* with a work on the principles of Quranic exegesis, the first attempt made at the scientific study of the *Quran*. In an attempt to popularize the scientific study of the Hadith, Walliyulla wrote two commentaries on the works of Imam Malik, choosing him because in his opinion Malik's work was the foundation on which the superstructure of Hadith had been reared. His object was to simplify the unwieldy and complex material of the Hadith and thus reduce the conflicts among the recognized schools of Muslim law. Since Malik's writing takes account only of the traditions which bear on legal matters, Walliyulla seems to confine genuine Hadith to purely legal traditions and to treat the rest of the corpus with all its complexities as of subsidiary importance.

In the realm of jurisprudence, Walliyulla's main work was concerned with reconciling the conflicts and differences among the four recognized schools of jurisprudence. In a tract on *The Differences Among the Jurists* Walliyulla shows that the supposed differences are more apparent than real if they are referred to the main source of Muslim jurisprudence, the science of Hadith. In drawing attention to Hadith as the accepted modes of juristic deductions, but also gave a new impetus to the science of Hadith and paved the way toward the formation of a new school of thought, known as the People of the Hadith, a school which rejected the authority of the jurists and sought direct guidance from the Hadith in matters concerning Islamic law.

At the same time Walliyulla attempted to reconcile the two rival schools of mysticism, the one pantheistic under the influence of Ibn Arabi and the other which followed Shaikh Ahniad Sirhindi in maintaining the transcendentalism of Islam. The pantheistic school believed in the identity of the Creator and the created, while the rival school held to the generally accepted view that the relation between the two was one of opposites. Walliyulla showed that these differences were trivial and at a deeper level there was much in common between the two schools. It is obvious that he was distressed by the growing disunity of the schools, both juristic and mystical, and by the sectarian conflicts to which Muslim society had fallen prey. He was in search of a unity that could make the Muslims what they were intended to be - a compact body of believers inspired by the unity of spiritual ideals.

The same urge for unity led Walliyulla to write a work in which he deals with the political theory of Islam and refutes the doctrines of the Shi'a sect. The significance of the book lies in its insistence that Islam is not a matter of personal loyalties but a movement in which loyalty to ideals is the decisive factor. This point was emphasized because Walliyulla seems to have felt that the Shi'as had from the outset given a highly personal turn to religion by taking their stand on loyalty to the house of Au, which logically involved a condemnation of all those members of the Islamic community who did not believe that the succession to the holy Prophet was an exclusive privilege of his family.

Shah Walliyulla's most important work contained, for

the first time, the germs of a theory of natural religion which was to be developed later by Sir Sayyid Ahmad Khan, and the beginnings of a revolutionary socialism which was to be used by Ubaidulla Sindhi, who was a tireless commentator on Walliyulla and a great revolutionary leader at the time of the Pakistan movement.

Here for the first time is presented an evolutionary concept of Islam. Walliyulla begins with the primitive social organization as the primal unit of social life and goes on to develop four stages of civilization, each rising upon the other and growing out of it. In the first stage man rises above animal life by adopting the use of tools to provide for his basic needs. When he has learned to provide for his primary economic needs he rises to the second stage of social organization, with markets and villages.

The third stage is that of city life, which requires a higher form of social organization and brings into existence law and order and government which applies moral and legal sanctions to protect the social organization. Thus morality replaces custom. But the growth of independent cities and small kingdoms leads to frontier disputes, intercity rivalries, and warfare. This leads to the fourth stage, when man is forced to develop international law and international agencies to solve his difficulties.

It is in the fourth stage that religion comes into prominence because city life exposes men to all kinds of temptations arising from the ample leisure and wealth of the richer classes. As the social evils multiply and the exploitation of the lower classes increases, the need for religious morality is recognized and the penal laws of religion come into force. According to Walliyulla, Islam made its appearance in the fourth stage of human evolution at the opportune moment, when the Roman and Persian civilizations had crushed the natural equality of mankind and the exploitation of the poorer classes by the rich had become almost unbearable for large masses of mankind. The entire life mission of the Prophet of Islam was the destruction of the Roman and Persian ways of life and the substitution of a juster social and economic order.

Thus Walliyulla builds his concept of Islam on ideals rather than on personalities. In his writings Islam becomes a social and religious movement arising out of the natural needs of man. At the same time he shows signs of a universalism remarkable for a man of his times and surroundings. He says that the permissible and the forbidden in Islam are equally matched by similar commands and prohibitions in all other societies, for the innate moral sense of man is the same in all religions and societies. He also explains the penal laws of Islam as arising from the needs of Arabian tribal society, and as based on the national sentiments of the Arabs. He repudiates the common misunderstanding that the laws of religion have nothing to do with man's natural reason or needs. Walliyulla likens a moral and religious preceptor to a physician who enforces restrictions in diet on his patients to cure them of their maladies.

Walliyulla's political and intellectual outlook bore fruit in what is incorrectly known as the Wahhabi movement. The leader of this movement was Sayyid Ahmad of Bareli (died 1246; A.D. 1831) who started as a disciple of the Walliyulla family and soon assumed the role of spiritual and temporal leadership. With members of the Walliyulla family as his supporters he toured northern India and attracted large masses of Muslims. Although he traveled to Mecca he does not seem to have made contact with the Wahhabis there, for they were under a ban at that time. He fought against the prevailing practices among the Muslims, such as the worship of saints and other social customs which had no religious sanction.

The Punjab was then under the rule of the Sikhs who made life impossible for the Muslims there. Sayyid Ahmad and his follower, Shah Isma'il, who was a prominent member of the Walliyulla family, fired the Muslims of northern India with a burning zeal to overthrow the Sikh power which was suppressing the Muslims and interfering with their religion. After some phenomenal successes with the help of the frontier tribesmen of Peshawar and adjoining districts, the movement suffered a serious defeat due to the betrayal of Sayyid Ahmad by his tribal followers and the disunity of the party caused by minor religious and juristic differences. He and his disciples were killed in 1246 (A.D. 1831), but the movement spread to other parts of India, particularly to Bengal where it led to a clash with the British. Though suppressed by force of arms and economic pressure, the memory of this great upsurge lived for a long time.

After the Mutiny, when the Muslim freedom movement was finally crushed by the British, the remnants of the defeated party sought to revive the Walliyulla tradition and build up a fresh movement for the freedom of Islam. They established the famous religious and educational institution at Deoband which produced many distinguished religious leaders and scholars and still carries on a precarious existence in India. Deoband was really the recruiting ground for a new movement for freedom, with educational activity secondary to their main purpose. In later years it served as a center of Muslim orthodoxy, but it also created religious leaders who did not hesitate to make common cause with the Hindus in an effort to wrest power from the British. Muslim orthodoxy, in general, remained so firmly anti-British in outlook that it could not reconcile itself to the Muslim League politics which it suspected of being pro-British. However, under the growing menace of Hindu communalism a not inconsiderable section of the religious leadership came forward to support the Pakistan movement.

While the Walliyulla School gravitated more and more toward religious conservatism in sharp contrast to its original stand - largely because of its anti-Western bias - and soon became merged in the general Muslim conservatism, a pro-Western group of Muslims was taking shape under the leadership of Sir Sayyid Ahmad Khan.

Throughout the early British period, the Muslims of India suffered a terrible economic, educational, and political loss, as they were suspect in the eyes of their new rulers and much too conscious of their erstwhile political, intellectual, and cultural superiority to be able to accept their new position. While the Muslims lost in the economic, political, and educational spheres, the Hindus made corresponding gains all around due to their realistic acceptance of the new order and their freedom from a false sense of pride. The British also favored the Hindus at the expense of the Muslims.

A new era of Muslim cooperation with the British was inaugurated by Sir Sayyid Ahmad Khan, the founder of Aligarh Muslim University. Muslims began to turn increasingly toward Western education and the acceptance of Western ideas, even though they had to face the full opposition of conservative Muslims, to whom modernism was anathema. The Hindus, who had become by this time economically very powerful and educationally much more advanced than the Muslims, were not slow to enlist the support and sympathies of the Muslim conservative classes in the political struggle which they were beginning to launch against the British with the aim of gaining political power for themselves. But a large majority of the Muslims, under the leadership of Sir Sayyid, were suspicious of Hindu motives, particularly because of their communal and revivalistic outlook. Sir Sayyid, for that reason, discouraged Muslim participation in the Indian National Congress which was agitating for home rule under the British.

The Balkan wars, the invasion of Tripoli, and the dismemberment of Turkey after the First World War, however, dealt a severe blow to the concept of British - Muslim cooperation envisaged by Sir Sayyid. Muslim feeling was so embittered by the British attitude toward the Turks and Arabs that they increasingly turned away from their own political organization, the Muslim League, and joined the Hindu National Congress in large numbers. With the support and sacrifices of the Muslims, the Indian National Congress emerged as the most powerful political organization and was able finally to obtain self-government in the provinces.

In 1937 the Congress formed its own ministries in seven of the eleven Indian provinces, but the Muslim supporters of the Congress were so disillusioned by the short period of Congress rule and its attempts to destroy Muslim culture and the separate sense of nationhood that they began to support the Muslim League.

When the Muslims found that the constitutional safeguards against the encroachment of the majority on the minority rights were of no avail against the formidable power of Hindu communalism, they became vigorous supporters of the Pakistan idea, which envisaged separate homelands for the Muslims in the northeast and northwest of India where Muslims had a clear majority. From the idea of Pakistan to its realization the way seemed difficult, but the justice of the claim was based on such strong grounds that when the British left India they were forced, despite the opposition from all Hindu parties and their own unwillingness, to accede to the demand for Pakistan, which became a reality on the fourteenth of August, 1367 (A.D. 1947).

The appearance of the West on the Indian scene some two centuries ago brought a new force with which both the Hindus and the Muslims had to reckon. Hinduism had already been influenced by Islamic monotheism, giving rise to such eclectic schools as the Sikh religion which sought to unite the Hindus and Muslims. To the impact of Islam was now added that of Christianity and the West. Among the Hindus this led to the rise of the Brahmo Samaj School led by Ram Mohan Roy. Like the Hindus, the Muslims also felt the impact of the new forces. Ram Mohan Roy had his Muslim counterpart in Sir Sayyid Ahmad Khan. Just as Ram Mohan Roy had established a Hindu college in Calcutta, Sir Sayyid established a Muslim college at Aligarh in 1292 (A.D. 1875) which played a prominent role in the struggle for Pakistan. Free-thinking had its start at both institutions. Again, like Mohan Roy, Sayyid Ahmad entered into controversy with Christian missionaries and writers and developed in the process a naturalistic view of religion which earned for him the accusation by conservative Muslim leaders that he worshiped nature rather than God. Sir Sayyid gathered around him at Aligarh some leading Muslim intellectuals who sought to defend Islam not only against Christian missionaries but also against the conservative Muslim outlook which provided the occasion for Christian attacks on Islam.

Sir Sayyid's chief work was his series of addresses written in reply to Sir William Muir's *Life of Mohammad.* In his first address he says that some scholars have likened religion to the prescriptions of a doctor who does not create any properties in the medicines but only points to such as nature has putin them. Shah Walliyulla, he regrets, has rejected this view, but he himself believes in the truth of this simile. He also expressed the opinion that the term Islam should not be applied to those juristic decisions which have been accepted by the Muslim community. Real Islam consists of those clear and specific injunctions of the Holy Prophet which do not admit of differing interpretations. These injunctions are of two kinds - those which constitute the inner core of religion and are in full accord with the laws of nature, and others which form a protective cover to the original commands.

In the sixth address Sir Sayyid clarifies his stand concerning Hadith. He says that authentic Hadith is of three kinds: that which accords well with the *Quran*, that which explains Quranic verses, and that which consists of commands which are not mentioned in the *Quran*. Concerning the last category he says that the Prophet himself made it clear that except for the *Quran* no part of his speech should be treated as a divine inspiration. The divine inspiration, he says, is limited to those matters which relate to the Prophet's religious mission, such as ethical rules and descriptions of Heaven and Hell. Lest this should be taken as a wholesale rejection of Hadith, Sir Sayyid advocates closer scrutiny of the Hadith relating to the personal habits and social circumstances of the Holy Prophet, as well as the Hadith bearing on political and administrative matters. He says that unless there is sufficient reason for the acceptance of such Hadith, we are not bound by any of them.

Sir Sayyid urged the Muslims to develop a new science of dialectics to counter the atheistic trends produced by Western civilization, and in 1292 (A.D. 1875) he wrote a commentary on the *Quran* in which he rejected the conception of Islam as a code of rules and regulations which, he said, cannot stand the test of scientific scrutiny. He claimed that the *Quran* cannot be disproved by any fresh development in the field of knowledge. His commentary produced a sharp reaction from the conservative sections of the Muslim community and spurred them to produce their own rival commentaries.

Ahmad Khan was also involved in a controversy with the Christian missionaries which led him to write a commentary on the Bible, in which he showed that many Muslim religious scholars, such as Bukhari, did not believe that the words of the Old Testament and the New Testament had suffered from interpolation at the hands of the Jews and the Christians. This again produced a storm of indignation among the conservatives, who held to the dogma that the words of the Bible had been changed. They were particularly antagonized because Sayyid was attempting to prove that true Christianity did not differ materially from true Islam. But the Christian missionaries also did not like the book because it repudiated the doctrine of the Trinity and condemned the Christians for their rejection of the Prophet of Islam.

Thus Sir Sayyid created a trend in Muslim thought toward the rejection of Hadith and toward a theology based exclusively on the *Quran*, a trend which ultimately resulted in the formation of the school of thought which rejects all other sources of authority than the *Quran*. Walliyulla had already turned Muslim attention to the Hadith as the real source of Islamic jurisprudence as opposed to the decisions of the jurists. Sayyid went further and brought Muslims direct to the *Quran*. He also made a great contribution toward understanding between Muslims and Christians by writing articles which dealt with the lawfulness of Muslims taking Christian food and associating with them in social affairs. It was rather bold on his part to indulge in such writing at a time when the Muslim sense of pride had been so deeply wounded by Western supremacy. Although Sayyid could not prevail against Muslim orthodoxy, he set in motion a trend of thought which produced free-thinkers like Ameer Ali, whose *The Spirit of Islam* expresses similar sentiments. It is significant that Ameer Ali calls himself a neo-Mu'tazilite, one who believes that there is no inherent conflict between reason and revelation.

Among the colleagues and disciples of Sir Sayyid one of the most outstanding was the historian Shibli, who wrote scholarly biographies of the Holy Prophet and of several other religious leaders such as the Caliph Umar, Abu Hanifah, and Ghazali, thus awakening the Muslims of India to a sense of their glorious past. He laid the foundation of the Nadva, a rival educational institution at Lucknow, because he felt that Sir Sayyid was taking the Muslims much too far from their proper religious outlook, and because he felt that religious education should be combined with secular education. Although it was a religious institution, English and some modern subjects were also taught at Nadva, but it could not rival Deoband which was founded earlier by Walliyulla's followers. It was much less conservative than Deoband, because of the slight secular bias of its curriculum.

Among the disciples of Shibli was Abul Kalam Azad, who soon rose to prominence as a writer of great power. He was a profound scholar of Arabic and Persian who developed a highly ornate style of Urdu prose and edited two weekly papers from Calcutta. This was the period of the Balkan Wars and the invasion of Tripoli by Italy, before the First World War The atmosphere was charged with anti-Westernism due to the attitude of the European powers toward Turkey and the crusading zeal of the Christian powers. It was natural, therefore, for the Muslims of India to turn away from the pro-Western attitude fostered by the writings of Sir Sayyid and his colleagues. Even Aligarh, the center of Muslim freethinking, succumbed to the religious frenzy of the day. In Azad, the Education Minister of the Government of India until his death in 1377 (A.D. 1958), the Muslims found an exponent of the pan-Islamic doctrine. Azad's early writings exercised great influence on the minds of Indian Muslims. He created a lively interest in the study of the *Quran* and became the earliest exponent of political concepts based on it. He was also responsible for the later anti-intellectual trends in Muslim thought and the religious emotionalism of the Muslims of India which was not always healthy in its effects. Although he later abandoned his pan-Islamism and became a vigorous champion of Indian nationalism and secular politics, his earlier writings had so deeply influenced the Muslim mind that he could not turn the Muslims away from the paths into which he had led them.

Azad's last work was an incomplete commentary on the Holy *Quran* in which his literary style bloomed in full vigor. But unlike his previous writings, the commentary added further to his unpopularity because he attempted to find a common ground between Islam and other religions. This was offensive to Muslim sentiment because it brought Islam to a level with other religions.

Among those who came under the influence of Abul Kalam Azad was Sir Muhammad Iqbal (died 1357; A.D. 1938), the only philosopher of modern times produced by the Muslim world. It is strange that while Azad, the product of religious •education, became an ardent nationalist and moved toward a secular outlook, Iqbal, the product of Western education, grew to be a fiery pan-Islamist and advocated a return to the religious and political ethics of early Islam.

Iqbal's poetry is full of the religious emotionalism which characterized the Muslim thought of this period. He wrote his poems both in Urdu and Persian, particularly in Persian because he sought to address his appeal to the entire Muslim world. Among his Persian poems, *The Secrets of the Self* and *The Mysteries of Selflessness* are the most thought-provoking. In these two poems he presents a theory of the self which is plainly a reaction against the doctrine of self-annihilation developed by Muslim mystics under the influence of non-Muslim religious thought.

Iqbal seemed to attribute the decline of Muslim culture to the enervating philosophy of self-annihilation which had led the Muslims to despise the conquest of material forces. He argued from the *Quran* and early Muslim history that Islam is a doctrine of self-assertion which teaches man to work for the attainment of worldly power and to attempt the conquest of the self and the non-self. This power philosophy led him to formulate the ideal of the superman. His idea of the superman is obviously derived from the philosophy of Nietzsche, but it is given a new form by Iqbal who called his superman the Man of Belief. This Man of Belief was armed both with spiritual and material power. Iqbal stood for the fusion of the material and the spiritual and criticized Nietzsche because his superman accepted no moral or spiritual limits to his power. The same union of the spiritual and temporal characterizes Iqbal's concept of the state and, on the same ground, he opposed the concept of Indian nationalism and the secular philosophy of the state associated with it.

Iqbal's thesis was that the spirit is dynamic, not earth-rooted. The spiritual view of life, therefore, repudiates nationalism for nationalism is earth-rooted and is opposed to the principle of movement which is one of the fundamentals of Islamic teachings. The migration of the Holy Prophet to Medina typifies to Iqbal the dynamic nature of Islam, with its freedom from geographical and racial limitations.

Iqbal's only prose work is a series of lectures entitled *Reconstruction of Religious Thought in Islam.* From Bergson and Nietzsche he derives much of his anti-intellectualism, giving primacy to will and conation over reason, while his philosophy of the self is largely based on McDougall's psychology. In giving primacy to love over reason, Iqbal follows in the footsteps of the Muslim Sufis whom he nevertheless opposes for their self-denying and self-annihilating trends. In claiming for intuition a higher place than reason, Iqbal defends revelation, on which all religion is based. However, Iqbal does not repudiate reason in its entirety and even criticizes Bergson for his antiintellectualism. He stands for the fusion of the heart and mind.

Iqbal was not unaware of the fact that the Muslims of his age were going through the same process of mental transformation that had taken place in Europe during the Age of Reformation. He therefore welcomed the advent of liberal ideas but warned that "Liberalism has a tendency to act as a force of disintegration." In the same lectures he cautioned the Muslims against the rising tide of Muslim Protestantism. "A careful reading of history shows that the Reformation was essentially a political movement, and the net result of it in Europe was a gradual displacement of the universal ethics of Christianity by systems of national ethics." He also moderated his anti-nationalistic views in those lectures when he said, "It seems to me that God is slowly bringing home to us the truth that Islam is neither nationalism nor imperialism but a league of nations."

Iqbal not only prepared the necessary intellectual atmosphere for the Pakistan movement but also played a leading role in the agitation for Pakistan. He was the first leader to realize that no amount of constitutional safeguards would avail against the menace of Hindu communalism and that the only solution of the Hindu-Muslim problem was the partition of India into predominantly Muslim and Hindu areas. Mr. Muhammed Ali Jinnah, hitherto a nationalist, was so much impressed by his discussions with Iqbal that he took up the cause for Pakistan and made it a live issue from then on.

While thinkers like Sir Sayyid and Iqbal were dealing with the problem posed by the impact of the West, a religious conflict was in progress because of the activities of the Christian missionaries and militant Hindu movements like the Arya Samaj, both of them trying to win Muslims to their own faith. Out of the religious and theological discussions between Muslims and the Christian and Hindu missionaries was born the Qadiani movement, founded by Mirza Ghulam Ahmad, who was born in 1251 (A.D. 1835) at Qadian in the Punjab. He proved his mettle in discussions with the Christian and Hindu Arya Samaj missionaries and as a result gained many followers and admirers. Emboldened by his success he claimed at first to be the double of the Christian Messiah, and later - about

1311 (A.D. 1893) - he said that he was the Christ whose second coming had been promised. At the same time he maintained that he was still a follower of the Prophet of Islam and a non-lawgiving prophet, and since he brought no new law and adhered to the law of Islam as interpreted and codified by the jurists, he claimed to be a good Muslim. He also denied that Muhammad was the last prophet, a basic article of faith with the Muslims. As he gained a strong and well-organized following he went further and claimed that a true Muslim must believe that he, Mirza Ghulam Ahmad, was a prophet.

Among the doctrines which caused conflict between the Qadianis and the general body of Muslims was Ghulam Ahmad's rejection of jihad, holy war, as one of the principles of Islam. He stood for cooperation with the British power and would not countenance any attempt to undermine in the name of Islam the British hold on India. The doctrine that the holy war was not necessary was, of course, pleasing to the British since those were the days when the Indian Muslims were carrying on agitation to restore the Caliph of Turkey to his temporal power. Because Britain was considered to be responsible for the dismemberment of Turkey and the overthrow of the Caliphate, the Muslims of India were calling for jihad. But the pro-British attitude made the Qadiani movement unpopular and its adherents remained largely a local group confined to the Punjab.

The opposition to the Qadianis was often most virulent. Even Dr. Muhammad Iqbal joined the fray in his last days when Pandit Jawaharlal Nehru, the leader of the Indian national movement, entered the lists and sought to defend the Qadianis. Iqbal wrote a long letter to the Pandit in which he made out a case against the Qadianis, the main charge being that the Qadianis did not look to Mecca as their spiritual home but to Qadian. They were, therefore, opposed to the spirit of international Islam and belonged to a purely

Indian religion. The growing unpopularity of the Qadianis resulted in their social segregation, which led them to adopt an increasingly exclusive attitude toward Muslims in general, sometimes even declaring them pagans. The moderate Qadianis, however, treat Muslims as people of the book, just as Muslims look upon the Christians and Jews. They are now a minority of less than half a million people.

The unpopularity of the movement led to a split among the Qadianis when a group called the Lahoris seceded under the leadership of Maulana Muhammad Ali and Khwaja Kamaluddin. Those two men founded the Ahmadiyyah Association to preach Islam, an organization which is still active. The Lahoris do not believe in the prophethood of Ghulam Ahmad, maintaining that he was a Renovator - but the general body of Muslims does not notice much difference between the Qadianis and the Lahoris, both of whom refuse to intermarry with Muslims. The main service of the Qadianis to Islam consists of their defense of Islam against Christians and the Arya Samaj Hindus and their vigorous missionary activity in Western countries. The Lahoris had a mission in Berlin before the Second World War The mosque in London also achieved some notable results. In the United States the Qadianis have succeeded in getting a few Negro converts. The Qadiani organization is at present controlled from Ribwa, a small town in the Punjab which is peopled exclusively by the followers of Ghulam Ahmad, whose successor, known as the Second Messiah, is the head of the organization.

In the triangular conflict between Muslim modernism, Indian secular nationalism, and communism, another religious and political movement was born, led by Maulana Ab'ul A'la Maudoodi (born 1322; A.D. 1904). Islam was being subjected to the two-pronged attack of the communists and the Indian secularists. The communists prophesied the downfall of all religions; the secularists reduced religion to a few private beliefs and rituals and denied that any social order could be built on the basis of religion. In his autobiography Pandit Nehru declared that there is no such thing as a Muslim culture distinct from modern international culture. What distinguish the Muslim from the Hindus, he said, is a particular kind of dress and a few remnants of Mughal refinements which will soon be swept away by the scientific and international culture of the modern age. At the same time a few Muslim freethinkers, led by one Niaz Fatehpuri, were attacking traditional Islam and concentrating their criticism on the Hadith and medieval jurisprudence.

Maudoodi took up the cudgels on behalf of Islam. He had been an editor of a Muslim Congress magazine and was recognized as a polished writer, even though he had neither the formal scholastic training of a religious seminary nor the Western training of an English school. He began by publishing a monthly Urdu magazine from Hyderabad in the Deccan. Hyderabad, under the Muslim dynasty of the Nizams, had become a center of Muslim culture and Urdu literature and poetry after the establishment of Usmania University, the first institution to use Urdu as the medium of instruction in higher education. In his magazine articles Maudoodi developed a dialectic which, though it could not silence the triple attack of communism, secularism, and modernism, was yet able to meet them face to face. None of those three schools had produced as able an exponent of their doctrines as Maudoodi. His articles over a period of years exercised great influence on youthful minds and made many converts from the modernists and Muslim communists - but very few from the Muslim nationalists, since they belonged to religious orthodoxy and were not inclined to listen to the young Maudoodi.

Iqbal himself was impressed with the dialectical ability of Maudoodi; it is said that he called him to the Punjab, where Maudoodi settled in 1357 (A.D. 1938). Soon after he arrived Iqbal died and Maudoodi moved to Lahore where he continued to edit his magazine and write books and pamphlets in his popular, lucid style. While still in Hyderabad he had written a book on *Holy War in Islam,* a comparative study of Islamic laws on war and modem international law. He also had written a series of articles on Islam and nationalism in which he denounced nationalism as contrary to Islam, maintaining that the Muslims are not a nation but an international party with a universal creed and a definite social and economic programmeme.

Maudoodi entered the lists against the Muslim wing of the Indian National Congress by writing a book on *Muslims and the Present Political Struggle,* in which he argued so forcefully against the stand taken by the Muslim Congress that the Muslim Leaguers hoped he would come over to support the Pakistan movement. But Maudoodi maintained his opposition to all kinds of nationalism, whether Indian or Muslim. He wanted a true Islamic state, not a mere displacement of Hindus by Muslims. He maintained that unless the Muslims developed a truly Islamic outlook and underwent a great mental transformation, Pakistan would not be Islamic in the real sense of the word. He charged that the programme of the Muslim League did not differ from that of the Indian nationalists except that the Muslim League stood for the material uplift of the Muslims while the Indian nationalists worked for the uplift of the Hindus. Muslim nationalism, he said, was no better than Hindu nationalism because its values, outlook, and programme were drawn from the Western concept of nationalism and had nothing to do with the international creed of Islam.

In a tract on *The Process of Islamic Revolution* Maudoodi said that a true revolution must be preceded by a great mental transformation and be led by men who believed and practiced Islamic ethics and stood for equal rights for all human beings, who did not exploit the basic emotional side of man's nature for their immediate ends, who did not preach national hatred and economic rivalry, who exemplified in their daily lives the Islamic virtues of piety and God-consciousness. He charged that the Muslim League leaders were utterly lacking in those virtues and that their outlook was purely nationalistic and Western. The Muslim League made the fight with the Hindus a struggle for power, office, and economic and commercial interests. But Islam requires preaching, suffering, and struggle. Unless the issues at stake were ideological and spiritual, rather than territorial and political, the Hindus would feel no attraction for Islam.

A considerable number of Muslim intelligentsia, particularly those who had no deep acquaintance with Western civilization, were so much influenced by Maudoodi's writings that he was able to form a party of his own in 1360 (A.D. 1941). Only those were admitted who fulfilled the minimum requirements of Islamic doctrine and practice, and they had to go through a probation period. Not many joined, but a considerable number came forward as sympathizers.

During the last years of the British rule in India another religious thinker, Maulana Ubaidulla Sindhi, came into prominence. He was born in 1289 (A.D. 1872) in a Sikh family, but early in life he left his birthplace in the Punjab and accepted Islam. He received his education at Deoband and then was sent to Kabul, where he founded the Kabul branch of the Indian National Congress and maintained contacts with Indian fighters for independence who had gone into exile in Moscow and Berlin. He spent some time in Russia and then moved to Turkey, where he greatly admired the work of the Turkish revolutionaries. For a considerable time he lived in Mecca, devoting himself to the study of Walliyulla. Through the intercession of the Indian National Congress he was permitted to return to India while the British were still in power, but he was not popular with the Congress because he objected to the Hindu revivalism which characterized the work of Mr. Gandhi.

He believed that India should be a multinational country in which the people should be given the largest possible amount of cultural, linguistic, and political freedom. This was contrary to the one nation creed of the Indian National Congress and its policy of centralization.

Ubaidulla's main contribution lies in popularizing the philosophy of Shah Walliyulla, whom he believed to be the greatest thinker of Islam. Ubaidulla did not gain much following because he was torn between opposing forces and tried to reconcile too many conflicting doctrines. By nature a revolutionary, by training an orthodox Muslim, he yet admired international communism and Turkish secularism and tried to combine them with Walliyulla's programme of a religious revolution based on the true teachings of the *Quran*, a revolution which would follow the model of the international revolutionary party built by the Prophet of Islam.

A significant movement which came into prominence some time before the partition was the Khaksar movement led by Inayatulla Khan Mashriqi of Lahore. This was a militant organization which seems to have been influenced by Iqbal's philosophy of power. Its object was to create military discipline among the Muslims, looking back to the early Islamic tradition when every Muslim was a soldier of God. The movement was very popular because of its religious color, military discipline, the habits of simple living it inculcated, the unconditioned obedience to leaders which it enjoined upon its followers, and its utter disregard of rank and riches in the enforcement of its discipline. But the leader, Mashriqi, seemed to have no clear objectives.

The Khaksars first interfered in the conflict between the Sunnis and Shi'as at Lucknow. Lucknow had long been the seat of a Shi'a ruling dynasty before the coming of the British and was noted for Shi'a fanaticism which was much more pronounced than that found among the other Indian Shi'as. Some of their practices, such as their public condemnation of the first two successors of the Holy Prophet, injured the feelings of the Sunnis. The Sunnis retaliated by publicly praising the deeds of the first four Caliphs. This agitation, known as the praise of the Companions, created much Shi'a-Sunni bitterness. The Khaksar leader threatened both parties, urging them to stop the senseless agitation, and pitched his semimilitary camp at Lucknow, whereupon the Congress government of the province put Mashriqi in jail for a time. After he was released it was discovered that a member of the Khaksar party had been involved in an attempted assassination of Mr. Jinnah, which caused a great wave of resentment among the Muslims. The British government suppressed the movement because of their suspicion of its Nazi affiliations, and thereafter the movement died a natural death. Mashriqi passed into obscurity for a time but recently has staged a comeback in Pakistan as leader of a small party which is shorn of all militant aspects.

One of the most influential religious leaders in Sind today is the present Pir Pagaro, head of a branch of the Qadiri order of Sufis. In the past century, when Sayyid Ahmad led his followers against the Sikhs in the Punjab, the Pir Pagaro of that time offered him men and money. This party of warriors came to be known as the Hurs and developed martial traditions. Originally they were staunch followers of the shari'a but later they developed heretical tendencies - they believed that their leader was divinely inspired, that his word had the same authority as the Word of God. The rest of Pir Pagaro's followers remained true to the shari'a. There are about a quarter of a million followers of Pir Pagaro in Pakistan today.

Pakistan was created by the Muslims of India who believed that they should form a separate nation because of their history, religion, and culture. To the Hindu objection that religion could not be the basis of separate nationhood the Muslim League replied that Islam is not a religion in the usual sense of the word but it is at the same time a religion and a social order with a distinct culture of its own. Those religious leaders among the Indian Muslims who supported Pakistan did so on the understanding that it would be an Islamic state where the social and economic principles of Islam would be implemented.

The party of Maudoodi at first opposed Pakistan on the ground that the Muslim League leadership, since it was composed of people who accepted Western concepts of social and political life, could not create a true Islamic state. After the establishment of Pakistan, however, they joined with some of the leading conservatives of the ulama and took up agitation for the promotion of a state which they could recognize as truly Islamic. The Maudoodi School by and large agreed with the time-honored concept of Islam as a complete social system with detailed rules and regulations which do not allow legislative freedom to the Muslims except in such matters as were not expressly touched upon by the *Quran* and the Hadith. The Muslim League and Mr. Muhammad Ali Jinnah, the founder of Pakistan, were not altogether clear in their statements as to what an Islamic state should be in the modern world. Sometimes they spoke in purely secular terms and sometimes they expressed the view that Pakistan was created in order to enable the Muslims to live according to the Islamic principles of life.

The Objectives Resolution of the Pakistan Constituent Assembly, passed in 1368 (March, A.D. 1949), stated that all sovereignty belongs to God and that the Constitution of Pakistan would be framed in accordance with the principles of democracy as enunciated by Islam. The Resolution promised that the Muslims would be able to live their lives in accordance with the principles of the Holy *Quran* and the Sunnah, and the religious minorities would enjoy full and equal rights of citizenship.

The Islamic concept of the state has been defined and interpreted in various ways, not all of which are easily reconciled. The religious classes, and particularly the followers of Maudoodi, seem to have a clear idea of the kind of social structure the Islamic state would create, but the secular elements raise several objections to their interpretation. They say that the Islamic state would be a theocratic state dominated by the Mullahs - the conservative religious leaders - and that the shari'a cannot be enforced under modern conditions because the very attempt to enforce it would undermine the economic structure of the state based on modern finance and banking.

They object that such an Islamic state would reduce the non- Muslims to a secondary position in the society and would introduce sectarianism in the body politic. It would also, they object, lead to a highly complicated and unwieldy legal system, since not only each religious community but also each sect within the community would have to be allowed full freedom to follow its own laws.

The initial popularity of Maudoodi's party was greatly lessened when he said that the war in Kashmir could not be a jihad, a holy war, because no specific declaration of war against India had been made and all treaties with that country were still unabrogated. A considerable section of the Muslims was alienated from the Maudoodi group when he came forward in support of feudalism. He quoted the *Quran* and the Hadith in support of his contention that Islam never tampers with the rights of individual property in land or industry and therefore the state was not allowed, on religious grounds, to appropriate the lands of the big landholders. His opponents charged him with feudalism. Maudoodi, however, stuck to his concept of a highly individualistic capitalist economy and opposed all tendencies toward the nationalization of property as being against Islamic principles. Meanwhile the communists had given up open attacks on Islam and encouraged many writers to vindicate socialistic and communistic principles on the basis of quotations from the *Quran* and the Hadith and the actions of the Companions of the Holy Prophet.

Although progressive Muslims in Pakistan differ from Maudoodi, only one group has emerged with a clear-cut school of thought. This group is led by Ghulam Ahmad Parvez, a retired Under-Secretary of the Government of Pakistan, who before the partition published in Delhi a monthly magazine dedicated to popularizing the philosophy of Iqbal. Parvez rejects the Hadith, claiming that it is binding only on those who lived in the time of the Prophet but not on other Muslims. The *Quran* is the final and only authority after the time of the first four Caliphs. The interpretation of the *Quran* must be made by the ruler of the state. "The revival of Islam," says Parvez, "would mean the re-establishment of a central authority, a ruler, who would deduce detailed regulations from the *Quran* in accordance with modern needs and conditions and would enforce the collective obedience of the people."

Parvez combines with this concept of the Islamic state the principles of a socialistic state. He denies that the *Quran* sanctioned individual rights in property. According to him, the *Quran* expressly declares that all land and property belongs to God, and God, in Islamic terminology, is the state. The denial of Hadith exposes this school to the charge that it breaks up the historical continuity of Islam. By giving the ruler the sole authority to interpret the *Quran* it would bring Islam under an infallible leader who would be, in effect, a Pope. This runs counter to the popular conception of Islam as a democracy in which ijma, or the consensus of opinion of the leading religious scholars, is the final authority on all questions. The Maudoodi School, on the other hand, accepts only the *Quran* and the Hadith as the infallible sources of law and does not regard the decisions of the medieval jurists as binding in all cases. Such legal decisions were, after all, made by fallible men and the community can revise them in the light of the *Quran* and the Hadith. The other ulama and conservative scholars, while accepting the *Quran* and the Hadith, retain their allegiance to the legal schools to which they belong and are guided by the legal decisions handed down by recognized jurists. They do not believe in the right of ijtihad, that is, of individual judgment.

In addition to these influential schools in Pakistan there are prominent individuals who have their own interpretations of Islam which are accepted by their admirers scattered over the whole country. Among them is Dr. Khalifa Abdul Hakim, Director of the Institute of Islamic Culture at Lahore. The Institute has published many books on Islamic ideology and the Islamic solution of the economic and social problems of the country. Dr. Khalifa holds that only the fundamental principles of Islam are eternal, while its specific commands are subject to readjustment. Islam has only set certain goals and pointed the direction for mankind to follow. In the modern world Islamic principles will have to be applied in new ways. The social and economic structure of the Muslim world was largely conditioned by the stage of social development in which it appeared. He also believes in the coexistence of religions.

Another such individual is Vice-Chancellor Allama I. I. Kazi of Sind University, a man of profound learning who spent a large part of his life in England. He has written a very good book on comparative religion called *Adventures of the Brown Girl in Her Search for God.* He believes in the evolutionary concept of religion. Islam, as the latest product of religious evolution, he says, has displaced all other religions, which exist today only as fossils.

He also holds very firmly that Western civilization is essentially Islamic since the West has adopted most of the leading principles of Islam and made them an integral part of the structure of modern civilization. He is opposed to nationalism because Islam is, in his opinion, outgoing and expansionist, unconfined by geographical, natural, or racial frontiers.

The clash of Islam with modern secularism is replete with big consequences out of which may come a new synthesis. In Pakistan secularism lacks the attraction which it possessed for the Western mind for it has not grown from within; it has not produced any thinker or intellectual school with a clear-cut secular philosophy. The past hundred years have been the years of secular rule and the religious classes have been out of power.

There is no organized church or religious order in the Muslim world which could inspire men with the fear of a religious priesthood. There is much dislike of conservatism and dogmatism in the Muslim educated class, but none of that hatred which led to the Protestant revolt in Europe. Secularism is, therefore, unable to harness the emotional loyalties of the people. At best, secularism is a negative doctrine in Pakistan which can offer freedom from the possibility of the Mullah Raj, the rule of the Mullahs, and liberation from sectarian feuds. Beyond that it has no positive content comparable to that offered by either Islam or communism.

In a country where the last hundred years of foreign rule have destroyed the concept of social equality and intensified class stratification, where a foreign system of education has created a wide gulf between the educated class and the masses, the prevailing mood of the people is to recover their lost dignity and equality. Islam or communism, with their positive programmes, can attract them, but secularism cannot.

Even so, the future of Islam is beset with difficulties. Unless the religious leadership gives up its medieval ways of thinking, its rigidity and conservatism, it is difficult to see how the modern educated class will accept its conception of Islam. The conflict must continue until the secular and religious groups arrive at a compromise which accepts the best in both points of view, but this will require a sustained effort to liberalize the popular concept of Islam.

In East Pakistan, where the average Muslim is more religiously inclined than in West Pakistan, the influence of Islam has been very strong. The political-religious movement led by Sayyid Ahmad of Bareli lasted much longer in Bengal than elsewhere, but with the consolidation of the British power things began to change. The Muslims of Bengal suffered economically and educationally even more than other Muslims, and the influence of the Hindus increased until they practically monopolized all education, culture, government services, and respectable means of livelihood. The Bengali language also was infiltrated more and more by Hindu mythology and all art and literature was deeply permeated with Hindu ideas.

When the Muslims began to develop political consciousness some forty years ago, they attempted to Islamize their language and literature, aided by such leaders as the poet Qazi Nazrul Islam, who popularized Islamic ideas. However, these attempts could not change the literary and artistic trends overnight. It needed the creation of an independent Pakistan to rouse the consciousness of Bengali Muslims. The progress of liberal Islamic ideas is impeded in East Pakistan today by the presence of a powerful minority of the Hindus, the existence of communist fifth columnists, and, above all, by the hold of the conservative ulama, who are wedded to medieval scholastic notions about Islam.

The Muslims of India, after the initial frustration and demoralization which followed partition, have recovered their poise and are gradually gaining in self-confidence. Some competent observers even hold the opinion that Islamic religious life has better prospects in India than in Pakistan. Certainly the religious life of the people has become more intensified. There is a feeling among the Indian Muslims that they have not lived up to Islamic ideals and this has been the cause of their suffering and persecution. Their persecution has created new energy, but it is regrettable that they are still in the grip of narrow orthodoxy.

The agitation for the recognition of Urdu as a regional language in India has so far met with little success. It was once hoped that Urdu might become the national language of India, but since it was a product of Muslim culture the Hindus, under the leadership of Mr. Gandhi, took their stand for Sanskritised Hindi as the future national language. This alienated a large number of Indian Muslims and added force to the Pakistan movement. With the partition of the country, the cause of Urdu naturally suffered a great setback, but the Muslims of North India are very active in popularizing their language and have been able to secure for it at least a regional status. Urdu still serves as a social link between Indian and Pakistani Muslims; poetic competitions are held both in India and Pakistan and Urdu poets from both countries take part in them.

Of the various religious movements in India mention should be made of the Indian counterpart of the Maudoodi School in Pakistan. This party has been very active in post-partition India. Recently its activities aroused the suspicion of the Indian government, leading to a few arrests.

The Tabligh movement was started before partition by Maulana Iliyas and continues to be very active in India. By his exemplary life and preaching the Maulana converted many Hindus to Islam, and today his followers concentrate on preaching Islamic virtues and urging their followers to observe prayers, fasts, and the other injunctions of Islam. They organize preaching groups which visit the villages and go from door to door asking the people to become God-conscious and to offer their prayers with a spirit of inner devotion. One of the most prominent leaders of this group is Abul Hasan of Lucknow who is an able writer and head of the Nadva, the educational institution founded by Shibli.

There is a small group of religious leaders who regard Ashraf Ali, a man with mystic leanings, who was a prominent religious figure before partition, as their spiritual progenitor and the foremost renovator of Islam. This group defends mysticism and is opposed to the Maudoodi School for its anti-mystical attitude. The Ferangi Mahal School at Lucknow, which was originally founded by Qutbuddin in the time of Aurangzeb and which produced many distinguished ulama, is losing its influence, but the Deoband continues its precarious existence. Many of the ulama of Deoband were vigorous supporters of the Indian National Congress and arch-opponents of Pakistan. Their leader, Maulana Husain Ahmad Madani, is still alive but is no longer as active and influential as before. Some of the post-partition policies of the Indian government have antagonized a large section of those Muslims who supported the Indian national movement against Pakistan.

The Association of Ulama of India, originally a political organization of the religious leaders and firmly wedded to Indian nationalism, is the most active religous party in Muslim India. It has lately come forward with a definite programme for the economic uplift of the Muslims, realizing that a healthy religion can exist only on sound economic foundations. Through its leadership it wields great influence in the Indian government.

It is estimated that about ten percent of the Muslims of India and Pakistan are Shi'as and the rest Sunnis. Shi'a-Sunni relations in India and Pakistan have not been uncordial on the whole. Intermarriages between Sunnis and Shi'as were usual in the past. The Sunnis are as much devoted to Ali and Husain as the Shi'as. There is even a group of Sunnis which believes that Ali was superior to all other Companions, although it holds them all in deep reverence. On most matters the Shi'as and Sunnis agree. However, the Shi'as differs on certain matters relating to ceremonial worship. For example, they consider it lawful to combine the noonday prayers with the evening and night prayers - but this is a practice which is sanctioned by some jurists among the Sunnis as well. The Shi'as has their own criteria of judgment concerning Hadith since they attach greater authenticity to the Hadith transmitted by Ali and his descendants and followers.

A distinctive practice of the Shi'as is called *taqiya,* that is, the art of concealing one's religious views, for the Shi'as hold that they can lawfully pretend to be other than what they are if they find themselves in hostile circumstances. The Shi'as' condemnation of the first three Caliphs has been a source of friction with the Sunnis, for the Sunnis believes that excellence belonged to the first four Caliphs in the order of their succession. But the majority of the Sunnis agree with the Shi'as in the condemnation of Yazid, the son of Mu'awiya and murderer of Imam Husain. It is a general Sunni accusation that on special occasions the Shi'as indulges in condemnation of the first three Caliphs, whom they regard as usurpers.

The act of condemnation is a necessary religious duty of the Shi'as, but whether it is real abuse or only unfavorable comment, it is difficult to say. The more fanatical Shi'as may go to extremes, but the cultured Shi'as hold that the condemnation is no more than what it literally means, the declaration of one's total dissociation from the acts of injustice done to the house of Mi. Modern education seems to have had little effect in breaking down sectarian barriers between Shi'as and Sunnis since, as with all minority religions, the Shi'as take special interest in the religious training of their children.

Even more than Ali, Imam Husain holds the highest place in the affection of the Shi'as of Pakistan and India, while their attitude toward his elder brother Hasan is lukewarm, as he is said to have compromised with Mu'awiya. The tragedy of Karbala, where Husain and his family suffered martyrdom at the hands of the Umayyad general, is annually commemorated by the Shi'as with great religious devotion and has become the central feature of Shi'a religious practice. The celebrations take place during the first ten days of Muharram, the first month of the Muslim lunar year. While the more orthodox Sunnis refrain from participation in these celebrations, the illiterate Sunni masses join in large numbers. Wealthy Shi'a families set apart a special building for the annual performance of the Muharram celebrations, usually decorated with fanciful representations of the tombs of the martyrs, often handsome and costly structures of wood and paper on which great artistic skill is lavished.

The celebrations begin with large gatherings held in the homes of the well-to-do and middle-class Shi'a families. A preacher narrates in dramatic detail the story of Karbala, working up the passions of the audience by dwelling on the most gruesome features of the tragedy and bringing into prominence the cruelties of Yazid and his generals. The audience goes wild with lamentations and shrieks, the more sober confining themselves to shedding silent tears - for weeping is considered to be a meritorious act. This is followed by regular beating of the breasts which is sometimes done so violently that it causes bleeding. Cultured people, however, just pat the breasts with their hands. Women also take a prominent part in these lamentations.

The ten days of the Muharram celebrations are all days of lamentation, but on the seventh day there is a procession to commemorate the marriage of Qasim, son of Husain. The next day lances are paraded on the streets to represent the standards of Husain, and on the ninth day the representations of the tombs of the martyrs are carried through the streets with much drumming and shouting. On the last day the interment in the local Karbala is enacted.

The two religious festivals sanctioned by Islam and observed by the Sunnis are the Id al-Fitr, the Little Festival, which comes at the end of Ramadan, the month of fasting, and the Id al-Adha, the Great Festival, which comes after the pilgrimage. Although many Muslims do not practice fasting, public opinion is generally sensitive to the sanctity of the month. Eating, drinking, or smoking in public during the month of Ramadan is sure to bring heavy censure and in some regions, such as the Northwest Frontier and the tribal areas of Pakistan, it may even lead to physical violence. The festival which comes at the end of the month of fasting is celebrated with great pomp after the public prayers have been offered in the morning.

The festival which comes after the conclusion of the annual pilgrimage is accompanied by animal sacrifice. Recently there has been great agitation in Pakistan about the enormous wastage involved in animal sacrifice and suggestions have been made that the money spent on slaughtering animals should be spent on social and philanthropic activities, but the conservative groups remain unconvinced. On the occasion of both festivals the rich as well as the poor put on their best clothes and exchange greetings with their friends and relatives.

Another important occasion celebrated by Muslims is the Prophet's birthday, although this seems to be a late innovation. It is not sanctioned by religion and was not observed in the early centuries of Islam. However, most people observe the occasion by holding meetings in public and in private homes where poems are recited in praise of the Holy Prophet and speeches are made in praise of his life, manners, character, and work. When the speaker describes the birth of the Holy Prophet and the stories of miraculous events associated with it, the audience stands up as a mark of reverence. There has been some difference of opinion concerning the lawfulness of this practice because the Prophet prohibited his Companions from standing up when he appeared in public. Some hold that the Prophet's commands should be obeyed, but others believe that reverence is more essential.

Another recent Sunni innovation, probably as a reaction to Shi'a practices, is the commemoration of the birthdays of the Companions of the Prophet. However the Companions do not call forth the same amount of devotion as do some of the saints, notably the highest saint, Abdu'l Qadir Jilani of Baghdad, who lived in the fifth century (eleventh century A.D.). He is considered to be a patron saint by a large number of the Sunnis, who invoke his help in case of difficulty. His birthday falls on the eleventh of the month Rabi Awwal. At that time prayers are offered over specially prepared food, which is then distributed among relatives and the poor. This is not as universal a practice as the observance of the birthday celebrations of the Holy Prophet.

A large number of illiterate and semi-educated - and some of the educated - Muslims are also great believers in prayers for the souls of dead ancestors. On the anniversary of death special food is prepared, and after the recitation of prayers it is distributed within the family, to relatives, and to the poor. Preoccupation with the dead is a marked social phenomenon among the general body of Muslims. Those who can afford it build costly sepulchres for their dead relatives and observe the fortieth day of death with great ceremony, preparing rich food and inviting friends and relatives to partake of it. Some of these practices are falling into disuse with the spread of modern education.

While the emphasis on the external observances and rites of Islam is palpably decreasing, Western culture seems to have had little effect on the cult of saints. Even highly educated people, persons who are otherwise skeptical of religion in general, are devoted admirers of saints and believe literally in the miracles ascribed to them.

The saints are believed to retain effective power after their death and are credited with the power to heal diseases, to avert calamities, and to bring material prosperity and promotions to their devotees. Most, but not all, of the worship of saints is associated with Sufism. Among the tombs of great saints which attract large crowds are those of Shah Abdul Latif Bhittai in Bhit Shah in the Sind, Data Ganj Bakhsh in Lahore, Khwaja Moinuddin Chishti in Ajmer, Hajji Waris Ali Shah in Dewan in Uttar Pradesh, Yousuf Sharif Shah in Hyderabad, Deccan, and Nizamuddin Auliya in Delhi - as well as those of many other famous saints and thousands of lesser local saints. It is interesting to see skeptics who ordinarily laugh at the externals of religion offer their homage to saints in the hope and expectation of rapid success in their worldly ventures.

There is usually an annual function held at each of the tombs of the saints, sometimes accompanied by fairs. At these functions a number of ceremonies are carried out, such as laying wreaths on the sepulchers, covering them with costly drapes, and burning candles before them. A particularly interesting feature of these functions is the musical party in which professional singers perform to the accompaniment of drums and other musical instruments. Female singers are not excluded, but only one type of music is allowed - music which is considered lawful in Sufi circles.

The people visit the tombs of the saints and invoke their help in their daily needs. Sometimes written requests are hung by the side of the sepulchre, and some extreme devotees offer prostration at the grave - and religious authority does not want to support such practices. The more orthodox Muslims, however, condemn such practices as non-Islamic and limit themselves to offering prayers for the dead; and the extremely orthodox Muslims would never visit a tomb, for they believe that once a man is dead his connection with the living is ended forever. Those Muslims who lack devotion to the saints are dubbed Wahhabis by the large mass of the people.

The mosques have ceased to attract worshipers. Only the poor and the illiterate among the people frequent the mosques at the daily services. The educated people, if they pray at all, offer their prayers at home. This is because the religious leadership of the Muslims has passed into the hands of people whose knowledge even of the purely religious sciences is highly inadequate. The educated classes find their age-old arguments and preaching dull, insipid, and unconvincing. The prayers and addresses are conducted in Arabic in a stereotyped form and can no longer provide inspiration to a generation which has no knowledge of Arabic and the traditional sciences. The Imams and religious preachers do not discuss the problems which are agitating the minds of the educated people; they are even ignorant of the very existence of such problems. For them the world is still the old medieval world with its scholasticism.

Muslim youth also is skeptical and finds no guidance from the Imams and the mosque preachers. It is only on the occasion of the two great annual festivals that the people visit the mosques in large numbers and offer their prayers there. It has been suggested from time to time that the mosques should be converted into centers of social and educational activity guided by properly trained and educated Imams, but so far these ideas have not been put into practice because there is no proper organization to look after the mosques and their keepers. At present the mosques exist on purely private contributions and the Imams are paid by the local community - and very poorly paid, with an income less than that of the lowest paid clerk.

Still, the mosques hold great possibilities. No social reform of the future can dispense with the need for this institution where prayers can be combined with instruction. Left to themselves the mosques will remain centers of fanaticism and obscurantism.

The government has been afraid to touch this problem lest it be exposed to the criticism of the people who distrust official activity in this area, but some means must be found to organize the support of the mosques and to give proper education to the Imams who are responsible for their care. The strength and vitality of Islam springs from its social and institutional ideals.

Islam started as a social order with a definite social and economic structure, but it has become a highly individualistic religion. At this time, when the people are moved by a strong urge for social equality and economic and political justice, there is a great need for a country-wide agency to look after their religious needs and to guide them to an understanding of the principles of Islam.

2

The Path

Almost fourteen hundred years ago Muhammad, born in Mecca and raised as an orphan by an uncle and receiving little or no formal education, began in middle age to experience what he believed to be Divine Revelations which were recorded through the services of a scribe who later became a disciple. Muhammad began to expound religious and social teachings based upon these revelations and was obliged to flee from Mecca in what the western world regards as the year 622 A.D. as his teachings had alienated powerful local interests.

The Islamic world has its own calendar which counts up from this year of Muhammad's flight from Mecca. After an eight year absence in the city of Medina, where his teachings had won many converts, Muhammad and a band of Muslim faithful thousands strong proceeded to Mecca where the existing idolatrous religious forms were overthrown and the local populations were persuaded, more by the clemency shown rather than by the force used, to profess Islam themselves. Islam had appeal by virtue of the strength of its message and also by virtue of demonstrably regarding all persons as being morally equal under God. It was seen by its Prophet Muhammad as a completion of the tradition of faith which also encompasses Judaism and Christianity. Christians and Jews are regarded, alike with Muslims, as being "People of the Book".

In order to present key insights about spirituality sourced from Islamic Mysticism a number of quotations from the Masnavi, attributable to the remarkable mystical poet Rumi, are related here. Rumi was born in Afghanistan some eight hundred years ago but his family moved to Anatolia soon thereafter in order to escape the depradations of the Mongols. Rumi is considered as having been a member of the mystical Sufi tradition within Islam. Mystics of every race and creed have described the progress of the spiritual life as a Journey or a pilgrimage. Other symbols have been used for the same purpose, but this one appears to be almost universal in its range. The Sufi who sets out to seek God calls himself a 'traveller' (*salik*); he advances by slow 'stages' (*maqamat*) along a 'path' (*tariqat*) to the goal of union with Reality (*fana fi 'l-Haqq*). Should he venture to make a map of this interior ascent, it will not correspond exactly with any of those made by previous explorers. Such maps or scales of perfection were elaborated by Sufi teachers at an early period, and the unlucky Moslem habit of systematising has produced an enormous after crop.

The 'path' expounded by the author of the *Kitab al-Luma'*, perhaps the oldest comprehensive treatise on Sufism that we now possess, consists of the following seven 'stages', each of which (except the first member of the series) is the result of the 'stages' immediately preceding it:

1. Repentance,
2. Abstinence,
3. Renunciation,
4. Poverty,
5. Patience,
6. Trust in God,
7. Satisfaction. The 'stages' constitute the *ascetic and ethical* discipline of the Sufi, and must be carefully distinguished from the so-called 'states' (*ahwal*, plural of *hal*), which form a similar *psychological* chain. The

writer whom I have just quoted enumerates ten 'states'- Meditation, nearness to God, love, fear, hope, longing, intimacy, tranquillity, contemplation, and certainty. While the 'stages' can be acquired and mastered by one's own efforts, the 'states' are spiritual feelings and dispositions over which a man has no control:

"They descend from God into his heart, without his being able to repel them when they come or to retain them when they go."

The Sufi's 'path' is not finished until he has traversed all the 'stages,' making himself perfect in every one of them before advancing to the next, and has also experienced whatever 'states' it pleases God to bestow upon him. Then, and only then, is he permanently raised to the higher planes of consciousness which Sufis call 'the Gnosis' (*ma'rifat*) and 'the Truth' (*haqiqat*), where the 'seeker' (*talib*) becomes the 'knower' or 'gnostic' (*'arif*), and realises that knowledge, knower, and known are One.

Having sketched, as briefly as possible, the external framework of the method by which the Sufi approaches his goal, I shall now try to give some account of its inner workings. The present chapter deals with the first portion of the threefold journey -the Path, the Gnosis, and the Truth by which the quest of Reality is often symbolized.

The first place in every list of 'stages' is occupied by repentance (*tawbat*). This is the Moslem term for 'conversion,' and marks the beginning of a new life. In the biographies of eminent Sufis the dreams, visions, auditions, and other experiences which caused them to enter on the Path are usually related. Trivial as they may seem, these records have a psychological basis, and, if authentic, would be worth studying in detail. Repentance is described as the awakening of the soul from the slumber of heedlessness, so that the sinner becomes aware of his evil ways and feels contrition for past disobedience. He is not truly penitent, however, unless:

1. He at once abandons the sin or sins of which he is conscious, and
2. Firmly resolves that he will never return to these sins in the future. It he should fail to keep his vow, he must again turn to God, whose mercy is infinite. A certain well-known Sufi repented seventy times and fell back into sin seventy times before he made a lasting repentance. The convert must also, as far as lies in his power, satisfy all those whom he has injured. Many examples of such restitution might be culled from the *Legend of the Moslem Saints*.

According to the high mystical theory, repentance is purely an act of divine grace, coming from God to man, not from man to God. Some one said to Rabi'a:

"I have committed many sins; if I turn in penitence towards God, will He turn in mercy towards me?" "Nay," she replied," but if He shall turn towards thee, thou wilt turn towards Him."

The question whether sins ought to be remembered after repentance or forgotten illustrates a fundamental point in Sufi ethics: I mean the difference between what is taught to novices and disciples and what is held as an esoteric doctrine by adepts. Any Mohammedan director of souls would tell his pupils that to think humbly and remorsefully of one's sins is a sovereign remedy against spiritual pride, but he himself might very well believe that real repentance consists in forgetting everything except God.

"The penitent," says Hujwiri, "is a lover of God, and the lover of God is in contemplation of God: in contemplation it is wrong to remember sin, for recollection of sin is a veil between God and the contemplative."

Sin appertains to self-existence, which itself is the greatest of all sins. To forget sin is to forget self. This is only one application of a principle which, as I have said, runs through the whole ethical system of Sufism and will be more fully explained in a subsequent chapter. Its dangers are evident, but we must in fairness allow that the same theory of conduct may not be equally suitable to those who have made themselves perfect in moral discipline and to those who are still striving after perfection.

Over the gate of repentance it is written:

"All *self* abandon ye who enter here!"

The convert now begins what is called by Christian mystics the Purgative Way. If he follows the general rule, he will take a director (Sheykh, Pir, Murshid), *i.e.* a holy man of ripe experience and profound knowledge, whose least word is absolute law to his disciples. A 'seeker' who attempts to traverse the 'Path' without assistance receives little sympathy. Of such a one it is said that 'his guide is Satan,' and he is likened to a tree that for want of the gardener's care brings forth 'none or bitter fruit.' Speaking of the Sufi Sheykhs, Hujwiri says:

"When a novice joins them, with the purpose of renouncing the world, they subject him to spiritual discipline for the space of three years. If he fulfils the requirements of this discipline, well and good; otherwise, they declare that he cannot be admitted to the 'Path.' The first year is devoted to service of the people, the second year to service of God, and the third year to watching over his own heart. He can serve the people, only when he places himself in the rank of servants and all others in the rank of masters, *i.e.* he must regard all, without exception, as being better than him, and must deem it his duty to serve all alike.

And he can serve God, only when he cuts off all his selfish interests relating either to the present or to the future life, and worships God for God's sake alone, inasmuch as whoever worships God for any thing's sake worships him, not God. And he can watch over his heart, only when his thoughts are collected and every care is dismissed, so that in communion with God he guards his heart from the assaults of heedlessness. When these qualifications are possessed by the novice, he may wear the *muraqqa'at* (the patched frock worn by dervishes) as a true mystic, not merely as an imitator of others."

Shibli was a pupil of the famous theosophist Junayd of Baghdad. On his conversion, he came to Junayd, saying:

"They tell me that you possess the pearl of divine knowledge: either give it me or sell it." Junayd answered: "I cannot sell it, for you have not the price thereof; and if I give it you, you will have gained it cheaply. You do not know its value. Cast yourself headlong, like me, into this ocean, in order that you may win the pearl by waiting patiently."

Shibli asked what he must do.

"Go," said Junayd, "and sell sulphur."

At the end of a year he said to Shibli:

"This trading makes you well known. Become a dervish and occupy yourself solely with begging."

During a whole year Shibli wandered through the streets of Baghdad, begging of the passers-by, but no one heeded him. Then he returned to Junayd, who exclaimed:

"See now! You are nothing in people's eyes. Never set your mind on them or take any account of them at all. For some time" (he continued) "you were a chamberlain and acted as governor of a province. Go to that country and ask pardon of all those whom you have wronged." Shibli obeyed and spent four years in going from door to door, until he had obtained an acquittance from every person except one, whom he failed to trace. On his return, Junayd said to him:

"You still have some regard to reputation. Go and be a beggar for one year more."

Every day Shibli used to bring the alms that were given him to Junayd, who bestowed them on the poor and kept Shibli without food until the next morning. When a year had passed in this way, Junayd accepted him as one of his disciples on condition that he should perform the duties of a servant to the others. After a year's service, Junayd asked him:

"What think you of yourself now?" Shibli replied: "I deem myself the meanest of God's creatures." "Now," said the master, "your faith is firm."

I need not dwell on the details of this training- the fasts and vigils, the vows of silence, the long days and nights of solitary meditation, all the weapons and tactics, in short, of that battle against one's self which the Prophet declared to be more painful and meritorious than the Holy War. On the other hand, my readers will expect me to describe in a general way the characteristic theories and practices for which the 'Path' is a convenient designation.

These may be treated under the following heads: Poverty, Mortification, Trust in God, and Recollection. Whereas poverty is negative in nature, involving detachment from all that is worldly and unreal, the three remaining terms denote the positive counterpart of that process, namely, the ethical discipline by which the soul is brought into harmonious relations with Reality.

The fatalistic spirit which brooded darkly over the childhood of Islam-the feeling that all human actions are determined by an unseen Power, and in themselves are worthless and vain-caused renunciation to become the watchword of early Moslem asceticism. Every true believer is bound to abstain from unlawful pleasures, but the ascetic acquires merit by abstaining from those which are lawful. At first, renunciation was understood almost exclusively in a material sense. To have as few worldly goods as possible seemed the surest means of gaining salvation. Dawud al-Ta'i owned nothing except a mat of rushes, a brick which he used as a pillow, and a leathern vessel which served him for drinking and washing. A certain man dreamed that he saw Malik ibn Dinar and Mohammed ibn Wasi being led into Paradise, and that Malik was admitted before his companion. He cried out in astonishment, for he thought Mohammed ibn Wasi had a superior claim to the honour. "Yes," came the answer, "but Mohammed ibn Wasi possessed two shirts, and Malik only one. That is the reason why Malik is preferred."

The Sufi ideal of poverty goes far beyond this. True poverty is not merely lack of wealth, but lack of desire for wealth: the empty heart as well as the empty hand. The 'poor man' (*faqir*) and the 'mendicant' (*dervish*) are names by which the Mohammedan mystic is proud to be known, because they imply that he is stripped of every thought or wish that would divert his mind from God. "To be severed entirely from both the present life and the future life and to want nothing besides the Lord of the present life and the future life-that is to be truly poor."

Such a *faqir* is denuded of individual existence, so that he does not attribute to himself any action, feeling, or quality. He may even be rich, in the common meaning of the word, though spiritually he is the poorest of the poor; for, sometimes, God endows His saints with an outward show of wealth and worldliness in order to hide them from the profane.

No one familiar with the mystical writers will need to be informed that their terminology is ambiguous, and that the same word frequently covers a group, if not a multitude, of significations diverging more or less widely according to the aspect from which it is viewed. Hence the confusion that is apparent in Sufi text-books. When 'poverty,' for example, is explained by one interpreter as a transcendental theory and by another as a practical rule of religious life, the meanings cannot coincide. Regarded from the latter standpoint, poverty is only the beginning of Sufism. *Faqirs,* Jami says, renounce all worldly things for the sake of pleasing God. They are urged to this sacrifice by one of three motives:

a. Hope of an easy reckoning on the Day of Judgment, or fear of being punished;
b. Desire of Paradise;
c. Longing for spiritual peace and inward composure. Thus, inasmuch as they are not disinterested but seek to benefit themselves, they rank below the Sufi, who has no will of his own and depends absolutely on the will of God. It is the absence of 'self' that distinguishes the Sufi from the *faqir*.

The straight path of Islam requires submission to the will of God as revealed in the *Quran*, and recognition of Muhammad as the Messenger of God who in his daily life interpreted and exemplified that divine revelation which was given through him. The believer who follows that straight path is a Muslim.

The word *Islam* literally means "peaceful submission to the will of God - without resistance." This complete submission presupposes as an acceptable minimum a firm belief in the truth and justice of all that God has revealed in human history. In the *Quran* it is made clear that from most ancient times the word *Islam* has been used by all divine messengers and their followers as the name for their religion. Islam is thus the generic term applicable to every revealed religion so long as that religion is not altered by men. The *Quran* assures us of the intimate relation of its revelation to the previous revelations: "God has ordained for you that religion which He has already commended to Noah, Abraham, Moses, and Jesus".

Thus it is that Noah declared, "I was commanded to be among the Muslims" (Surah X, 73). Abraham and Ishmael, (Isma'il), when they were constructing the Ka'ba as a place of worship at Mecca, addressed God in these words: "Our Lord! Make us Muslims unto Thee and of our seed a nation of Muslims unto Thee" (Surah II, 128). Jacob gave his sons this counsel: "... and die only as good Muslims" (Surah II, 132). His sons reassured him with their reply, "We do worship thy Lord, the unique God, the God of thy fathers Abraham, Ishmael, Noah, and Isaac, and we are good Muslims" (Surah II, 133). When Moses was instructing his people, he said, "Trust yourselves to God if you are true Muslims" (Surah X, 85). The disciples of Jesus avowed, "We have believed and you can be witness that we are Muslims" (Surah V, 111).

The *Quran* makes it clear that Islam is the only religion acceptable to God when it says, "Lo! Religion with God is Islam" (Surah III, 19). That is, religion is submission to God's will and guidance. Again the *Quran* says, "And who seeketh as religion other than Islam, it will not be accepted from him" (Surah III, 85). Thus there has been but one true religion on earth, the religion of God, to which believing men have belonged at all times and places. Each of the holy messengers of God who has taken part in revealing the nature of the religion of God has been a stone in the building of that edifice. For the *Quran* this unity of believing humanity is not only a fact, it is above all an essential part of religious belief.

The prophets are required to show mutual recognition and acknowledgment of each other. The believers must accept and respect all revealed books and all messengers of God without distinction between them. To show preference among the revelations of God is to be guilty of a mortal sin which destroys the very basis of our belief. "Those who wish to separate God from his envoys, those who say we believe in some and do not believe in others, those are all the true infidels, and we have prepared for the infidels a terrible torture" (Surah IV, 150- 51). Showing preference among the revelations of God is infidelity because it makes our own desire, our own passion and fanaticism, a criterion and principle of belief; because it resists the will of God which has been authenticated by the divine signs which appear with each one of His messengers.

The fundamental mission of the messengers of God has been to teach true belief about the one God and to establish justice among men. The unity of this belief springs from the one God and creates a union of the prophets and of their followers, who together form a unique spiritual nation, Islam. Thus, after enumerating the prophets from Noah to Jesus, the *Quran* says, "Here is your nation, one and united, and I am your Lord. Worship me, then" (Surah XXI, 92).

The belief in the divine revelation and in the spiritual peace which comes from submission to God is expressed in daily life by obeying His commandments and avoiding that which is forbidden. A humble obedience to the divine commandments is a second essential part of Islam, completing the act of faith - which is belief in God's revelation - by obeying God's commandments in practical affairs. For example, in our personal life we are commanded in the *Quran* to act with righteousness, to be straightforward in speech, to control our passions, and to purify our souls. In family life, we are commanded to treat women kindly, with full regard for their rights, and to be generous in our dealings with them.

In social life, God commands that all cases shall be judged with equity; justice and charity are required; no injustices shall be done to people because of hatred toward them; all life is made sacred by God and may not be ended except through justice. In spiritual life, the Muslims must have always present in their minds the idea of God and must never despair of the forgiveness of the Lord; it is in God that believers must put their trust.

"The Muslim," said Muhammad "is he who spares others all his bad words and evil deeds." Thus, Islam is external peace and internal peace, peace with God and peace with all creatures, the peace which comes through submission to God. It is noteworthy, however, that historically speaking the meaning of the term *Islam* has undergone a continuous and gradual evolution in the successive divine revelations. Each new book and each new prophet constitutes a new element to be added to our creed. The most complete revelation has naturally been reserved for the latest revelation which summarizes and confirms all the others. It is thus justified to consider those who accept the last revelation as the Muslims. It is in that spirit that *Quran* calls them not only Muslims, but *the* Muslims. God's latest revelation is given in the *Quran;* therefore, it is necessary to know the *Quran* in order to follow the straight path of Islam. The message of the *Quran,* however, is better understood by those who know the Prophet Muhammad who was the Messenger of God, the interpreter of the *Quran* and its living example.

Muhammad, the son of an illustrious Arab family known for its religious accomplishments and political activities, was born in Mecca on Monday, the ninth of the month Rabi Awwal (April 20, A.D. 571), in the fifty-third year before the beginning of the Muslim Era. His father died before the child was born. When Muhammad lost his mother in his sixth year he was taken into the house of his grandfathers who foresaw for him a splendid future. The grandfather died two years later, leaving him to be cared for and educated by his uncle Abu Talib who had always shown a fatherly interest in him.

The affectionate bond between the young lad and his uncle was so strong that he often traveled with him on caravan journeys. Tradition says that when he was twelve he accompanied his uncle on a commercial journey to Syria, where they met a Syrian monk called Bahira who recognized in the young man the characteristics of a prophet. He advised the uncle to take good care of Muhammad always, and to mistrust especially the Jews who might wish him ill if ever they learned of the prophetic mission he would be called to fulfill. Muhammad spent his youth in humble circumstances, much of the time working as a shepherd. As he later pointed out, herding sheep was also the occupation of many other prophets, Moses and David in particular.

As a young man he distinguished himself by his refined manners, his extreme shyness, his absolute chastity, and his avoidance of the easy pleasures pursued by other young men of his community. All those who knew him showed complete confidence in him for he fully deserved the name by which he was called, al-Amin, which means the true and reliable one. When he was only twenty years old he was called to sit with the most venerable shaikhs of the Fudul league, an association which cared for the weak and helpless and sought to assure peace between the tribes. At the age of twenty-five he married the rich and virtuous Khadijah, and in his married life he revealed to his family and the community his excellent human qualities. The trade which he carried on with his wife's funds kept them in comfortable circumstances, but he used his resources only as a means of spreading happiness. For instance, in order to repay his uncle for having taken care of him in his youth, he took responsibility for the education of Abu Talib's son, Ali.

Muhammad remained a faithful, loving husband during the quarter-century of his marriage to Khadijah, and after her death he was so fond of recalling the sweet memories of their married life that he caused not a little naive jealousy in his second marriage. He was an excellent father and grandfather, showing an ideal tenderness toward his children and grandchildren. He allowed them to hang on his neck or to mount on his back, even while he was praying; he interrupted his speeches in order to greet them and made them sit with him on his chair. Some Bedouins, seeing him kiss one of his grandchildren, said, "You kiss the children? We never do that." To which the Prophet replied, "What can I do if God has deprived your hearts of all human feeling? God does not grant His mercy to those who are not merciful".

His most famous action between the time of his marriage and his prophetic calling came when he was thirty-five years old. The sacred shrine in Mecca, the Ka'ba, was being rebuilt, and when the time came to place the Black Stone (the revered angular stone of the traditional monument), there was a furious competition among the Arab tribes for the honor of lifting it into position. The controversy was about to break out into a fight, with swords drawn, when Muhammad was seen to enter. The crowd started shouting, "al-Amin, al-Amin!" and all submitted to the arbitration of the true and reliable one. With his remarkable presence of mind and the impartiality which he always showed, Muhammad spread his coat on the ground, put the Black Stone on it, and asked the chiefs of the principal tribes to grasp the edges of the coat and together lift the stone to the required height. Then he took the stone and placed it with his own hands, thus resolving the dispute and restoring harmony among the tribes.

By this time Muhammad was physically, intellectually, and morally a mature person, endowed with those characteristics which made him a leader throughout the rest of his life. His figure was taller than average, solidly built, with a large chest and shoulders. He had a noble and always serene countenance, a large mouth with white, slightly separated teeth, black eyes set in a somewhat bloodshot background, a white, rosy skin, and black, wavy hair falling just below his ears. His walk was lively yet dignified. He wore simple clothes which were always clean and well-groomed.

He was very sober and normally restrained; he talked little, but always agreeably and with good humor. His sweet temperament and extreme delicacy would never allow him to force the pace of a conversation with anyone, nor would he ever show a desire to finish a discussion. He never withdrew his hand first from a handshake. While he was inflexible and impartial in applying justice to others, he was indulgent and yielding when his personal rights were involved. When he later became sole master of the state he was not tempted by earthly wealth but remained as simple and frugal as he had always been, deliberately avoiding all luxury and pomp for his family as well as for himself. After his death his few possessions were not inherited by his relatives but were distributed among the poor. In his fortieth year he approached the decisive event which wrought a complete change in his life and in the history of mankind.

The first sign of his prophetic vocation, according to his own words, was the discovery that everything which he dreamed happened in his waking hours precisely as he had foreseen it. After some time he felt a strong inclination to seek solitude and withdrew to Mount Hira, or the Mount of Light, north of Mecca.

This was a spiritual withdrawal, broken only occasionally by visits to the town for food. Muhammad received his first revelation on the seventeenth day of Ramadan (February, A.D. 610) in the thirteenth year before the beginning of the Muslim Era. This revelation took the form of a discussion between teacher and pupil, between the Archangel Gabriel and Muhammad.

"Read!" commanded Gabriel. "I am not of those who know how to read," replied Muhammad. "Read!" Gabriel repeated. "What shall I read?" asked the astonished pupil. "Read!" insisted Gabriel. "But how shall I read?" asked the solitary hermit. The Archangel then recited the first five verses of Surah XCVI:

- *Read:* In the name of thy Lord who createth,
- Createth man from a clot.
- *Read:* And thy Lord is the most Bounteous,
- Who teacheth by the pen?
- Teacheth man that which he knew not.

This is the first fragment of the *Quran*. The Angel then disappeared and Muhammad, completely overcome, was starting to leave the grotto when he heard a voice calling to him. He lifted up his head and saw the Angel filling the entire horizon in its immensity, and heard the Angel tell him, "O Muhammad: Really, you are the messenger of God, and I am Gabriel." After that, Muha-mmad saw nothing else.

When he reached home he told Khadijah of these happenings and expressed his fears. His devoted wife reassured him with wise and consoling words, "No," she said, "do not worry. God would surely not do you any harm, or heap shame upon you, for you have never done harm. You always speak the truth, you help the feeble, and you always assist those who suffer for a just cause." To comfort him further she accompanied him on a visit to her cousin, Waraqa Ibn Nawfal, who said to him, "This is good news which should fill you with rejoicing. I declare that you are the prophet announced by Jesus. Oh, that I could live until your countrymen will chase you, Muhammad, from your country." "How is it," cried Muhammad, "that they will chase me from here?" "Of course," replied Waraqa, "never has a man brought his fellow-men what you brought with you without becoming the object of persecution and hostility."

Muhammad often returned to the grotto where he had received his first message to seek another revelation. He placed himself in the same condition, he walked the mountains, he turned his eyes in all directions. Days passed, weeks went by, month followed month, one year was gone, another began, and according to the account of al-Cha'bi even a third year came without another revelation. His only comfort was that each time when he felt himself on the brink of despair he heard, "O Muhammad, you are the messenger of God, and I am Gabriel," but without hearing the message he so ardently expected.

By this time Muhammad was forty-three years old. He continued to wake up almost every night in the hope of hearing this "heavy and grave" promised word. Each year he withdrew to Mount Hira in the month of Ramadan. Finally one day, when he had finished his retreat and was descending to the town, he heard someone calling him. He looked around, to the right, to the left, and behind him, but saw no one. Then he lifted his eyes toward heaven and recognized the Angel whom he had seen at Mount Hira. The suddenness of the apparition, the majestic immensity of the heavenly being, struck him so strongly that he could not remain standing. The sublime visitor then gave him the decree which invested him with his second responsibility: "Oh you, who cover yourself carefully, get up, and spread your announcement" (Surah LXXIV, 1-2).

Thus Muhammad must not only receive his divine knowledge, he must also transmit it to the people. To his role of Prophet was added that of Apostle. After this second message, the revelations succeeded each other without the long interruption which came between the first and second. Muhammad's career as the Messenger of Islam lasted for twenty years, with ten years in Mecca before the Hijrah (the move from Mecca to Medina in A.D. 622, which is the starting date for the Muslim Era) and ten years at Medina before his death.

He began his preaching in Mecca by discreetly speaking only in his most intimate circles. Abu Bakr was the first man to be converted to Islam and Khadijah the first woman; All was the first young man. The first foreigners were Zaid Ibn Haritha, the Yemenite; Bilal Ibn Rabah, the Abyssinian; and Sohaib Ibn Sinan, the Roman. Islam spread slowly in Mecca, privately at first, and then, in the tenth year before the Hijrah the calling to Islam became public. At first it was kind and courteous and evoked no animosity among the unbelieving. But when the message became reproachful of paganism the Arabs rose in opposition and showed their hatred.

The opposition of the Arabs was at first directed mainly toward the Prophet. It was relatively mild toward those of his believers who had a distinguished family or tribal position, but tended to be cruel toward the humble and the powerless. Therefore, in the middle of the ninth year before the Hijrah the Prophet allowed eleven men and four women to seek refuge with the King of Abyssinia, who received them well and was himself converted to Islam. By the beginning of the eighth year before the Hijrah there were scarcely forty men and about ten women who were Muslims in Mecca, and they met in secret. The conversion of such important people as Hamzah and Umar in this year gave such strong support and encouragement to the followers that they were able to say their prayers openly near the Ka'ba, and the new religion began to spread more rapidly.

This new growth of Islam aroused the unbelieving to redouble their violence and persecutions and in the seventh year before the Hijrah a second contingent of refugees, eighty-three men and eighteen women, emigrated to Abyssinia. The Prophet himself became the target of a conspiracy but was protected by the two family branches most closely related to him, the Bani Hashim and the Bani al-Muttalib, who rallied around him in the Hashimid quarter. The other branches and tribes thereupon banded together in opposition and took a written oath to boycott the protecting quarters until Muhammad was handed over to them. They maintained their severe boycott for three years, abandoning it in the fourth year before the Hijrah.

The ending of the boycott would have been a great relief to the Prophet if it had not been that just at this time he suffered two cruel losses: the death of his uncle Abu Talib and shortly afterward the death of his wife Khadijah. The Prophet calls this year "the year of suffering." Having become a widower without the consoling intimacy of a wife, he married Sawdah, a courageous believer whose suffering during the persecution and emigration had just been crowned by the loss of her husband after their return from Abyssinia. Accordingly, this marriage must be considered more a compensation for her than for him.

When Muhammad lost the support which his uncle afforded him in Mecca, he left the town to look elsewhere for allies and adherents. He spent ten unsuccessful days with the tribe of Thaqif, at at-Ta'if, but he was received badly and returned disappointed to Mecca to devote his proselytizing efforts to the pilgrims' encampment at the Ka'ba. Toward the end of the third year before the Hijrah he saw a faint hope in six men from Medina. These good men, who had heard the message of the Prophet during a brief encounter at Mina, responded enthusiastically to his appeal and carried the holy message to Medina where they made many converts.

Toward the end of the following year, the second before the Hijrah, five of those men from Medina with seven new converts visited the Prophet and took an oath to abstain from any polytheistic cult, from all vices, and to observe strict discipline. A year later, seventy-five men from Medina came to swear allegiance, confess their faith, and declare their submission. They also promised to defend the Prophet and their Muslim brothers if they should choose Medina as their refuge. This represents the first defense treaty in Islamic history.

Immediately after receiving this promise from the men of Medina the Prophet authorized and even obliged those men among his followers who had sufficient means to settle in Medina with their new brothers. Those who insisted upon remaining in Mecca without valid reason were to be regarded as hypocrites. But the Prophet himself did not hasten to leave his post and join the community of his faithful followers. He awaited an express authorization by revelation, an authorisation which came after three months, on the day before the unfaithful had planned to carry out a plot against him.

Before the Hijrah, when Muhammad joined his followers in Medina, the Muslims did not form a nation or even a community; they did not even have a majority in Mecca. In Mecca they occupied no post of authority. They could not make a solemn call to prayer or come together for a public gathering. In Medina, however, Muslims could settle openly and Islam could develop. Communal prayer was observed solemnly even before the arrival of the Prophet. The day after his arrival in Medina the Prophet assumed full authority, started forming the state, and began the building of the great mosque.

Muhammad's authority in Medina was of an entirely new and original kind: it was at the same time absolute and consultative, theocratic and socialist. It was religious and absolute in its framework, based on revealed commandments and general rules, but socialistic and consultative in the details and the application of the rules.

The Muslim state which the Prophet created in Medina remains the model of every Muslim state worthy of the name. It is unique in human history, for although this Muslim state was fundamentally religious, it established two principles which are not found elsewhere except in a nonreligious state or in a religion which has no state government associated with it. The first is the principle of freedom of religion, a freedom which the Muslim state not only admits and authorizes but must even defend and guarantee. The second is the principle which defines the idea of fatherland or nation in the most tolerant and human sense, a principle which guarantees equality of rights and national duties for those of all races, colors, languages, and ideologies existing in the country.

The first year and a half after the Hijrah were entirely devoted to purely pacific and constructive activities, to the development of religious and social institutions such as fasting, almsgiving, fraternization of the immigrants with the original inhabitants, agreements between tribes, and the like. Thus far nothing suggested the use of force. It was only because they wanted to be indemnified for the loss of their houses and worldly goods, which had been left behind in the hands of their enemies in Mecca, and because they wanted to put an end to the persecution and violence which the enemies were inflicting upon their brethren in Mecca that the Muslims tried several times, unsuccessfully, to intercept enemy caravans passing near Medina.

In Ramadan of the second year after the Hijrah the pagans reacted to these fruitless attempts to intercept the caravans by declaring an offensive against Medina. The Muslims thereupon sought to defend themselves, in a rather improvised manner, and although inferior in numbers and weapons they obtained a decisive victory. In the month of Shawwal in the third year the Meccans took their revenge, and for the next few years actions and counteractions followed until in the sixth year a ten-year truce was concluded. This truce was very favourable for the growth of Islam. Not only did it spread among the Arabs of the Hijaz - the western side of the Arabian Peninsula - who were in frequent contact with the Muslims, but during this time the Prophet sent his messages and messengers to the Roman Emperor Heraclios, and to the kings and princes in Persia, Egypt, Bahrein, and Yemen.

In the year A.H. 8 the Meccans broke the truce, and this time the Prophet marched victoriously into the capital. The indulgent and merciful character of the Prophet, which he had always shown, was clear to all the people of Mecca after this conquest when, without repressive action or loss of life, he generously pardoned all his former persecutors.

The conversion and submission of the whole Arab peninsula came soon after the conquest of Mecca, but in the northern part of the peninsula the Romans (Byzantines) prepared themselves for a strong attack against the young religion. In A.H. 9 the Prophet himself led an expedition as far as Tabouk (halfway between Medina and Damascus) which made the Romans renounce their enterprise. When the Prophet returned to Medina he had concluded non-aggression treaties with the neighboring countries to the north.

It was also in the ninth year of the Hijrah that the Prophet ordered Abu Bakr, his closest disciple, to lead the pilgrims to Mecca and to proclaim that the approach to the Ka'ba from that time onward was to be forbidden to all pagans and polytheists.

In the tenth year after the Hijrah the pilgrimage to Mecca was led by the Prophet himself. This is known as the "farewell pilgrimage," during which the Prophet received the divine message that his mission was fulfilled and foresaw that the end of his life was near. "This day have I perfected your religion for you and completed my favour unto you, and have approved for you as religion Al-Islam" (Surah V, 3).

Those who heard his sermon on Arafa day in the tenth year recognized that they were hearing his last will and testament. With great emphasis he reminded all human beings of their brotherly love, their common origin, their equality without distinction except by means of virtue. With clear authority he commanded respect for the person, the family, and for property. With kindly compassion he recommended gentleness toward women.

With great vision he enjoined his listeners to retain and transmit his message to all those who have not heard it, for, he said, "Who knows? Maybe I shall not see you again after this year." Finally, addressing himself to the pilgrims who had come from all the surroundings countries in such numbers that they reached the horizon and spread over all the desert, he said, "God will ask you about me: did I transmit to you His message?" "Yes! Yes!" Thereupon, looking toward heaven and pointing his fingers, Muhammad prayed in a loud voice, "My God, be witness."

Less than three months after this sermon, on the twelfth day of Rabi Awwal, A.H. 11 (June 7, A.D. 632), Muhammad's soul returned to his eternal resting place.

The question of miracles in relation to Muhammad has often been debated. Did he perform miracles other than the *Quran*?

The *Quran*, revealed to the world by the voice of Muhammad, is a miracle - yes, rather THE Miracle. Everything proves it: its style, its contents, the extraordinary events by which it was revealed, taught, and written down; its constant conformity with past, present, and future truth; its transcendent character which never shows a trace of a particular man, of any one society or epoch of history or specific region of the globe.

The *Quran* is not a passing event in history which appears once and disappears the next, to be known only by more or less correct hearsay reports. No, it is a fact, stable and durable, which remains unchanged and eternally present for the admiring contemplation of all men. The *Quran* is not a temporary wonder which deceives the mind and is alien to the new knowledge which it has come to influence. It is the truth, the truth which proves itself, and while it appeals to reason it transcends reason and thus shows its divine origin.

The recognition of the *Quran* as THE Miracle does not diminish the value of other material and tangible miracles, known through our senses. These miracles, too, can very well bring us conviction; they are often the best means to reinforce our faith. That is why our earlier prophets have performed miracles. Was it the same with the Prophet of Islam? Has he performed miracles other than the transmission of the *Quran*?

There are current tendencies toward answering in the negative, pretending to find proof in the *Quran* itself. The *Quran*, it is said, tells us that the Prophet Muhammad systematically refused to satisfy those who asked him to produce miracles.

And they say: We will not put faith in thee till thou
cause a spring to gush forth from the earth for us;
Or thou have a garden of date-palms and grapes, and
cause flyers to gush forth therein abundantly...
Or thou have a house of gold; or thou ascend up into
heaven, and even then we will put no faith in thine
ascension till thou bring down for us
a book that we can read. (Surah XVII, 90-93)
And they say: Why are not signs sent down upon him
from his Lord? Say: Signs are with Allah only,
and I am but a plain warner.
Is it not enough for them that We have sent down unto
thee the Scripture which is read unto them?
Lo! herein verily is mercy, and a reminder for
folk who believe. (Surah XXIX, 50-51)

At the basis of the theory that the Prophet refused to perform miracles we find a grave misinterpretation, not only of the meaning of these quotations, but more so of the Islamic conception of the author of miracles in general. In those quotations the possibility of a miracle is not denied. Rather, they point out that miracles come from the supreme authority which alone is capable of any form of creation, and above all of creating supernatural things.

It is a matter of demarking the frontier which separates human and divine power. The man is not yet possessed of the true Islamic faith who confounds those two powers, believing that the prophets themselves created their miracles. For the prophets are only human; they cannot overcome physical laws nor can they overcome the laws of the mind. God alone does so, if and when He wants to, in order to prove the divine origins of the message which the prophets transmit.

Therefore, it was not Moses who transformed the stick into a living snake, for this transmutation took place to his great surprise. It was not Jesus, either, who by his own power revived the dead; he did it only by the authority of the Lord. And when he refused the demands of those who once asked him to produce a sign from heaven, does this mean that he no longer performed miracles? Evidently not!

It is the same with Muhammad in his refusal to comply with certain pagan requests. The answer with which he avowed his own incapability to perform miracles is the same which he gave concerning the *Quran*. It is not Muhammad, who is the author of the *Quran*, but it is "the faithful spirit"; it is the Archangel Gabriel who, on God's command, brought the *Quran* down from heaven and deposited it in Muhammad's heart so that it may guide and rejoice those who believe in it. Not only could Muhammad not modify an iota of it, he did not even expect to be its bearer and was not sure that he would continue to receive it.

Thus no miracles, material or spiritual, are of human origin, for all are exclusively within God's domain and competence. All prophets have avowed that they are subject to the same limitations.

Neither they nor the people to whom they were sent could demand a certain miracle or substitute one miracle for another according to their preferences. God gives His mandate to whomsoever He wills, in the form which He deems proper to persuade any epoch of history or any age of humanity to each epoch of its book and to each people, its guide.

And verily We sent messengers (to mankind) before thee, and We appointed for them wives and offspring, and it was not (given) to any messenger that he should bring a sign save by Allah's leave. To each epoch, its book. (Surah XIII, 38)

In Islamic terminology a miracle is most often defined as a fact contrary to general rules, opposed to the normal course of events, with a cause which escapes human comprehension; and this fact is also a challenge to anyone who doubts it.

Now the only fact which most obviously fulfills all these conditions is, of course, the *Quran*, which repeatedly and in many ways cries out its challenge to all beings visible and invisible and predicts their impotence to prove that it is not the miraculous message of God. It invites them first to imitate its text in its entirety, then to create ten Surahs similar to those in the *Quran* or to create but a single similar Surah, and finally asks but for a Surah only slightly resembling one in the *Quran*.

The question as to whether or not the Prophet performed any miracle other than the revelation of the *Quran* thus depends on the definition of a miracle. If it is required that such a challenge must have been explicitly expressed, then it must be said that in Islam there has been no miracle other than the *Quran*. But once we eliminate the arbitrary stipulation that the challenge must have been expressed, we find an uncountable number of miracles performed by the Prophet.

Some of those miracles are mentioned in the *Quran* itself:

The Prophet's journey made by supernatural means from Mecca to Jerusalem in a single moment of the night; a journey during which he saw many divine signs, and distinguished clearly all topographical details of the place, details which he later described, to the surprise of all (Surah XVII, 1). The prediction of a cleavage on the surface of the moon, a celestial phenomenon which indeed took place immediately in the presence of the crowd of people he was addressing and which was observed and confirmed by travelers (Surah LIV, z). The miraculous victory over the army of his enemies which was accomplished by a small number of faithful, poorly armed followers, but men who were assisted by divine power (Surah VIII, 17).

The fact that the society in Medina, which had been divided and eaten by hatred and civil war for dozens of years, became overnight a united group of intimate friends - a sudden change of mind which could not have been accomplished by earthly forces (Surah III, 103; VIII, 63) and its revelation by the Prophet of secret facts which had been carefully hidden from his knowledge (Surah IV, 113; LXVI, 3). Innumerable predictions fulfilled, such as the announcement of the precise date of a coming victory of the Romans over the Persians (Surah XXX, 2-6) also innumerable truthful reports of historic facts which were unknown to him and his people (Surah XI, 49; XII, 102; XXVIII, 44-46).

Among other miracles not mentioned in the *Quran* only a few can be cited here. The knowledge of these miracles, performed publicly by the Prophet, has been transmitted from generation to generation by reporters who have been identified and are known to be trustworthy historians. These examples are taken from the first chapter of al-Bukhari's *Alamate El Noboua:*

The prediction that the Roman and Persian empires would cease to exist immediately after the death of their emperors who were contemporaries of the Prophet and the announcement of the death of the King of Abyssinia on the date of his death.

The assurance he gave that, after the battle against the pagans of Mecca in the fifth year of the Hijrah, the Meccans would never again march against Medina and that Mecca would be conquered by the Muslims. The prediction that his grandson al-Hasan would re-establish unity and end the conflict between two great parties of Islam, a prediction which was fulfilled in the days of Mu'awiya, the fifth Caliph.

A miracle which was often repeated during times of drought and general thirst in the army was the production of an abundant yield of water from a little vessel which the Prophet blessed by putting his fingers in it. Fifteen hundred soldiers were able to quench their thirst, perform their ablutions, and water their animals with the water from that little vessel. During a Friday sermon, when a Bedouin complained about the continuing dry weather and the famine which would ensue, the Prophet prayed for rain, and storm-clouds gathered from all directions, bringing rain which continued until the following Friday.

The next Friday the same Bedouin complained of the destruction being caused by the rain, and after the Prophet prayed the sky above Medina cleared immediately. Once when the Prophet had been sitting on a tree stump and then abandoned it for a higher seat in order that the increased number of listeners might hear him better, all the audience heard the wailing complaint of the stump, a wailing which continued until the Prophet took the stump in his arms and consoled it as one would console a baby.

These are only a few of the many authenticated examples of miracles, other than the great miracle of receiving the revelation of the *Quran*, which were performed by the Prophet Muhammad, the Messenger of God.

The greatest miracle was the revelation of the *Quran* which was transmitted by the Prophet in passages of unequal length at different times over a period of twenty-three years. As soon as the Prophet received each inspired message he recited it to his audience and they in turn repeated it to the community, which was made up of people who were fond of literature and eagerly awaited each new message, whether they were partisans or adversaries.

As the Prophet dictated each new passage it was written down by the scribes on anything within reach, on thin white stones, pieces of parchment, wood, leather, or whatever was available. Tradition counts up to twenty-nine different persons in Medina who served as secretaries; a lesser number of scribes recorded the revelations received in Mecca. From the very beginning the faithful never failed to record the revealed messages, even during the persecutions. Among these scribes were included the first five Caliphs: Abu Bakr, Umar, Uthman, Mi, and Mu'awiya.

Thus the holy book of Islam became known in both an oral and written form. In its oral form it was called *Quran,* that is, Recital. In its written form it was called *Kitab,* or Scripture. At the beginning the written extracts were not put in order or even gathered together, for other messages were expected.

As time went on several groups of verses began to grow up and tended to become independent unities as new verses were added according to the instructions given by the Prophet, who was following the orders of the Revealer Spirit. Although the text was originally scattered in its written form, it always had a definite order in the Prophet's mind and in the minds of the faithful, with each verse or group of verses fitting into its proper place in the structure of the whole. In the Prophet's lifetime there were hundreds of his Companions, called "*Quran* bearers," who were specialists in reciting the Book and knew by heart every Surah in its proper place in the structure.

At the death of the Prophet the *Quran* was preserved in the memories of the faithful as well as in writing. While in its oral form every Surah was complete and in its proper place in the order known today, in its written form it was nothing but scattered documents written on many different materials. During the year following the death of the Prophet no one worried about the written form because there were innumerable oral witnesses among them as living copies of the *Quran* complete in its final form. But about a year after the Prophet's death seventy of the *Quran* bearers were killed in the battle with Musailima, the false prophet, and it became clear that it would be necessary to guard against the loss of the oral tradition by gathering the written documents into a book easy to handle and use for reference. The idea of preparing the book was suggested by Umar and carried out by Zaid Ibn Thabit, a *Quran* bearer who had attended the last recital of the *Quran* by the Prophet and a man known for his intelligence, integrity, and competence.

Under the guidance of Zaid Ibn Thabit the correct written form of the *Quran* was determined by including only those passages which were verified by two witnesses as having been written down at the dictation of the Prophet and as being in the oral text of the last recital by the Prophet. This official collection is distinguished from the other personal, oral versions by an absolute rigorism which excluded from the text any explanatory notes and even eliminated the Surah titles. 'When the written form was completed it was given to the first Caliph, Abu Bakr, who entrusted it to Umar when he designated him the second Caliph. Since the third Caliph had not been chosen at the time of Umar's death, he gave it to his daughter Hafsah who was one of the widows of the Prophet.

The universal authority of the written form of the *Quran* dates from its publication by the third Caliph, Uthman, who received it from Hafsah and ordered four secretaries to write as many copies of the document as there were big towns in the Islamic Empire. From that time the Uthman edition has been the only one in use in the Islamic world.

Ever since the earliest days the question has been raised as to whether the *Quran* was of divine or human origin. The explicit and implicit testimony of the *Quran* is that the author is God Himself. It is never the Prophet who speaks in the *Quran*. The Scripture either refers to him in the third person or addresses him directly - O Prophet, O Messenger, We reveal to thee, We send thee, do this, recite this; such is the language of the *Quran*.

The direct proof of the divine origin of the *Quran* is manifest all through the Scripture itself. It is also shown by the peculiar phenomena which accompanied every revelation of the *Quran*, according to the testimony of the true tradition. The Prophet's contemporaries were objective witnesses of the visible, tangible, and audible signs of the mysterious accompanying phenomena which made evident the real source of the *Quran* and opened the eyes of the truth-seekers.

In the presence of the Revealer Spirit the Prophet's inspired face was illumined, like a mirror; there was silence; conversation stopped as if in moments of absence of mind; his body relaxed as if in sleep and a mysterious buzz was heard around him - as in a telephone conversation where the one listening is the only one who can hear distinctly enough to understand. There was nothing voluntary about these phenomena, for the Prophet could neither avoid them when they came nor bring them into being when he earnestly desired to receive a message. On many occasions the Prophet sought a revelation but it was not given; then, sometimes after an interval as long as a month, the mysterious phenomena would come, appearing suddenly and vanishing abruptly, after which the people with him would listen to the wonderful text.

The literary style and contents of that text are conclusive evidence of the divine origin of the *Quran*, but before considering that evidence let us turn to the arguments by which attempts have been made to prove that the origins were human. It is to the honor of Islam that the *Quran* records all hypotheses, reasonable or absurd, by which the contemporaries of the Prophet attempted to establish human origins for the Scripture. If the origins were human, they must have come from Muhammad's environment, from other religions in that environment, or from the meditations and reasoning of the human author. Let us examine the activities of the Prophet before and during his apostolate and see what he could have learned from his surroundings or from his own meditations.

It is scarcely necessary to point out that at the beginning of Islam neither the ideas nor the practices of the people of Mecca show any resemblance to the teachings of the *Quran*. There is no relation between the pure unitarian system, the most perfect and refined ethics of the Holy Book of Islam, and the ignorance, paganism, superstitious idolatry, arrogant materialism, infanticide, prostitution, incest, dowry extortion, oppression of orphans, disregard for the poor, and scorn of the weak which were characteristics of Mecca in those times.

An effort has been made to show that the teachings of the *Quran* are similar to those of the Sabians, a sect well-known in Mecca at that time. But the Sabians were idolatrous and polytheistic, worshiping the stars and angels with a mixture of pagan, Christian, and other rites. Their pilgrimage was not to the Ka'ba, but to Harran in Iraq, and their prayers were to the stars at sunrise, at noon, and at sunset - three times when prayer is prohibited in Islam.

It was also suggested that Muhammad might have been influenced by the travelers and immigrants who came to Mecca: the Abyssinians or Romans, the laborers or wine merchants. It is clear that our Personage could not have known the vulgar class of immigrants for he lived either alone, in complete solitude, or as a shepherd, or as a big merchant in a caravan, or in the high society with the leaders of the community. Even if he had any contact with such people, their lack of religious knowledge would have been evident, and as the *Quran* points out, their foreign language would have made communication impossible (Surah XVI, 103).

It has been argued that in Muhammad's travels he became acquainted with Arab tribes which had been converted to Christianity and got his ideas from them. Many scholars, ancient and modern, have pointed out that such contact with Christianity is unlikely but that, even if it did happen, the Christianity practiced in that part of the world was so debased that it was indistinguishable from paganism. The fourth Caliph, Ali, said that the tribe Taghlib had taken from Christianity nothing but the habit of drinking wine. Wherever Muhammad traveled he found beliefs to be rectified, deviations to be brought back to the right way. Nowhere did he find a moral or religious model which could have been copied for his work of reform.

Again, it has been suggested that the Prophet gleaned his teachings from the reading of books recording previous revelations. But the *Quran* categorically denies that he knew how to read or write (Surah XXIX, 48). Furthermore, the Bible was not available in Arabic until many centuries after the Prophet's time, and the Bible in other languages was out of reach of the common people. The few biblical ideas which may have circulated among the common people were so vague and often contradictory that they cannot be the basis for the precision, extensiveness, unity, and vigor of the material in the *Quran*. Nor can it be argued that Muhammad was influenced by Jewish teachings after he came to Medina, where he was in contact with Jewish scholars. Even before the Hijrah the Holy History had been revealed in all its true details in the Meccan Surahs, and the *Quran* had condemned the believers in the Pentateuch as followers of satanic inspiration, unworthy of being accepted as teachers or examples (Surah XVI, 63).

In the revelations in Medina the *Quran* goes even further in its condemnation of the followers of the Pentateuch (Surah II, 79-80; III, 75; IV, 161). The psychological attitudes on both sides made Jewish influence on Islamic thought practically impossible. The majority of the Jewish scholars adopted an antagonistic position which was far from the benevolent attitude of teachers. Those of the Israelite scholars who were impartial enthusiastically welcomed the Prophet in Medina and declared their conversion to Islam, thereafter as disciples recognizing him as their Master. Between the two categories of the hostile or the submissive, there was no place for a third group of friendly tutors.

Thus it is clear that the teachings of the *Quran* cannot be attributed to the influence of the environment on Muhammad. There remains the question as to whether or not he could have created the *Quran* by himself through the use of meditation and reason. To a limited extent, reason could have revealed the falseness of idolatry and the senselessness of superstition, but how could it know how to replace them? It is not by mere thinking that facts can be known, that previous events can be described, yet the *Quran* was always in perfect accord with the essential data of the Bible, even those hidden from Muhammad by scholars. Mere intellect by itself could not have given such details. The *Quran* confirms that before the revelation Muhammad did not know any book nor even the meaning of faith (Surah XLII, 52).

He could not possibly have guided others, for he did not even know how to guide himself in religious matters. He was ignorant of all the legislative, moral, social, and ritual details which are included in the revelation of the *Quran*. It was not by reason, or by the study of books, but only by revelation that Muhammad could know the creative God and the divine attributes. Only as it was revealed to him could he define the relation between God and the visible and invisible worlds and specify the future reserved to man after death. We have seen that the *Quran* could not have human origins traceable either to the experience of Muhammad in the environment of his time or to his ability to construct the Holy Book by use of his reason. We have seen that the divine origin of the *Quran* is attested by the mysterious phenomena which always preceded a revelation. Now let us look further and consider the internal evidence for the divine origin in the literary form and contents of the *Quran*.

The literary form of the *Quran* is distinguished clearly from all other forms, whether they be poetry, rhythmic or non-rhythmic prose, the style of the common people, or that of the Prophet himself. The exceptional eloquence of Muhammad was always acknowledged and is known to us in countless instructions which he gave after careful thought, or dictated as non-Quranic insights. In all such passages there is not the slightest resemblance between them and the revealed messages.

We feel such ascendant power in the revealed texts that they penetrate the soul. The infidels in the time of the Prophet considered the form of the text such an extraordinary phenomenon that they used to call it magic. Even in modern times those who can understand the Arabic text recognize its sublime character without being able to explain it. In our lectures on exegesis at Al Azhar University in Cairo - the oldest university in the world - the following analysis is used to point out the ways in which the literary form of the *Quran* transcends the powers of man and defies imitation.

The form of the *Quran* reflects neither the sedentary softness of the townsman nor the nomadic roughness of the Bedouin. It possesses in right measure the sweetness of the former and the vigor of the latter.

The rhythm of the syllables is more sustained than in prose and less patterned than in poetry. The pauses come neither in prose form nor in the manner of poetry, but with a harmonious and rhythmic symmetry. The words chosen neither transgress by their banality nor by their extreme rarity, but are recognized as expressing admirable nobility.

The sentences are constructed in a dignified manner which uses the smallest possible number of words to express ideas of utmost richness.

The brevity of expression, the conciseness, attains such a striking clearness that the least learned man can understand the *Quran* without difficulty. At the same time there is such a profundity, flexibility, suggestively, and radiance in the *Quran* that it serves as the basis of the principles and rules for the Islamic sciences and arts, for theology, and for the juridical schools.

Thus it is almost impossible in each case to express the ideas of a text by one interpretation only, either in Arabic or in a foreign language, even with the greatest care. Qur'anic speech appears to be superhuman in its transcendence of the psychological law that intellect and feeling are always found in inverse proportion to each other.

In the *Quran* we find constant cooperation between the two antagonistic powers of reason and emotion, for we find that in the narrations, argum ents, doctrines, laws, and moral principles the words have both a persuasive teaching and an emotive force. Throughout the whole *Quran* the speech maintains a surprising solemnity and powerful majesty which nothing can disturb. Finally, when we pass from the structure of a sentence, or a group of sentences dealing with the same subject, to the structure of the Surah and of the *Quran* as a whole, we find an over-all plan which could not have been created by man.

We know that the *Quran* was revealed in long and short fragments over a period of twenty-three years and that they have been arranged according to neither their chronological order nor their subject matter but in an independent, complicated order which appears to be arbitrary. As each revelation appeared it was placed in its fixed place, given its number among the verses, and its place was never changed. Thus, for every revealed verse there are two different orders, the chronological order based on the date of its revelation and the architectural order which determined its place in the composition of the Book. Throughout the long period of the revelations these two orders were strictly followed for every verse, every Surah, and the whole work.

In the chronological order, every revelation meets the need of the hour and links with the previous and following ones in a gradual progress in teaching and legislation. For instance, consider the main outline of these successive stages: it begins with the simple command, "Read!" (Surah XCVI, 1); then goes on to the apostolic charge, "Preach!" (Surah LXXIV, 2); then the call at first to the near relatives only (Surah XXVI, 214), extended next to the whole town (Surah XXVIII, 59), then to the neighboring towns (Surah VI, 92), and at last to humanity (Surah XXI, 107). Consider also the general outline of the progress in teaching in its two big divisions: first the fundamental bases of the work in the Surahs of Mecca; then the codified application of those general principles in the Surahs of Medina. This long course of events continued from the day of the grotto, when Muhammad was simply warned that he would receive a divine teaching, until the day of the last pilgrimage, when he was told that his mission was accomplished and he had nothing else to do on earth. After receiving the revelations for twenty-three years, he was called back.

Nothing, therefore, has been improvised in the *Quran*. Everything was foreseen and formed as a whole and in every detail, from the beginning to the end, including the death of the Prophet. Who could have formed and carried out such a complete plan who other than God from whom come this heavenly mission? In addition to the chronological order there is the architectural order in the *Quran*. The very texts which follow in the chronological order the wisest educational plan were taken from their historical positions and fixed in the architectural order, every one in a definite frame already built to receive it, taking its place in those units of different length called Surahs. What makes it so wonderful is that once each Surah is completed from those scattered parts it is a unit faultlessly formed, artistically, linguistically, and logically. A special musical rhythm runs equally through all parts of the speech; there is a common, harmonious style, and a logical plan in the development of the ideas expressed.

It is clear that to establish such a scheme in advance the author would have had to foresee not only the problems which would arise from the events of the next twenty-three years, and their solutions, but also the literary form, the musical tone and rhythm in which it would be expressed, the appropriate structure for all the revelations yet to come, and the precise spot in that framework where each revelation would be fixed. It must be confessed that no man or any other creature is capable of knowing the future in such detail or creating such a Book. Only the Divine Omniscience could be the creator of the *Quran*.

The teachings of the *Quran* are universal, addressed to all people throughout the world regardless of their origins and revealed to mankind to enlighten man's spirit, to purify his morals, to unify his society, and to replace the domination by the powerful with justice and fraternity. As is confirmed in Surah XVI, 89, all human problems can be solved through the *Quran*, either directly or indirectly: "And we reveal the Scripture unto thee as an exposition of all things."

This revelation in the *Quran* deals primarily with the Supreme Truth and with virtue. All the rest of the contents of the text - such as knowledge of the soul, the sciences of the nature of the heavens and the earth, history, prophecy, warnings, and the like - are only means to strengthen the message of the *Quran*, to give it more weight and conviction. The great theologian al-Ghazali, who died A.H.

505 (AD 1111), pointed out in his *Pearls of the Quran* that 763 verses are concerned with knowledge, and 741 verses with guidance in virtue. For him these 1504 verses represent the most precious substance of the Book, while the remaining 5112 verses are, so to speak, the envelope or shell of the teachings.

According to the *Quran*, the act of faith must include these three elements:

- Belief in God
- Belief in His messages addressed to humanity
- Belief in the Day of Judgment.

The starting point in Islam is belief in God, the Almighty, the Benefactor, the Creator of everything, the only proper object of worship. In the attempts to persuade the polytheists to accept this pure monotheism, the chief point at issue is the question of the proper object of worship. The *Quran* in many passages points out that the pagans confess that there is but one Creator and Administrator of the universe (Surah XLIII, 9), but their mortal mistake is that in their worship they associate secondary gods with God and claim that those secondary gods are capable of interceding with Him on their behalf and winning His favour.

The *Quran* uses arguments based on reason and on tradition to bring back those who have strayed from monotheism into polytheism. In the rational arguments directed at the polytheists, the *Quran* emphasizes their agreement that creation and providence are attributed exclusively to God and seeks to persuade them to the exclusive worship of God. How can one equate the creature to the Creator? Is it conceivable that the being which has created nothing equals the One who has created everything? (Surah XVI, 17). Is it not illogical to invoke that which never answers us, which never even hears our appeal? (Surah XLVI, 5). Is it not ungrateful on our part to forget the

Benefactor who grants us our happiness, the Benefactor to whom we address all our supplications in times of disaster?

Is it not ungrateful to associate with Him in worship others who are incapable of either good or evil actions? (Surah XVI, 53-54). And finally, those polytheists who pretend that any man or saint or other being has the power of mediation or intercession with the great God must prove that it can be done (Surah II, 255; XIII, 33; XXXIX, 3). In addition to the rational arguments against polytheistic worship, the *Quran* points to the unanimous testimony of the prophetic traditions. "There has not been one previous prophet to whom We have not revealed this truth that there is no God but Me, therefore worship Me" (Surah XXI, 25). "Ask the divine messengers who preceded you: Have We allowed them to worship other gods than the Merciful?" (Surah XLIII, 45).

While the starting point of faith is belief in God as the Creator, the Benefactor, and the only object of worship, it must be recognized that God is also the Legislator. He commands our actions and our emotions. He requires our trust and obedience. This truth can be known by natural intelligence, by common sense and conscience, and also by the confirmation given in the *Quran*. God has given man the natural power to discern good and evil, justice and injustice (Surah XCI, 7-8), but the experience of all time shows that passions, work, and material and worldly preoccupations sometimes turn our minds away from the highest ideals and lead us to erroneous judgments and practical mistakes. Therefore the Divine Mercy did not abandon us to our natural intelligence alone. To check any tendency in us toward declining our responsibilities, God has reinforced our natural intelligence with revealed Truths (Surah XXIV, 35).

In order that His commandments might be known to men without dependence on reason alone, God chose among men and Angels those worthy of receiving and transmitting the divine light, sending to every nation or large tribe His warning (Surah XVI, 36). Those who refuse to believe in any spokesman of God refuse to believe in God himself, for every divine messenger has been given proof of the divine origin of his revelations (Surah LVII, 25). The first two elements in the faith of Islam - belief in God and in His messages - are not complete without the third: belief in the Day of Judgment. God is Creator, God is Legislator, and God is also the supreme Judge. He is the beginning and the end; to Him all men must turn to give an account of their deeds and to receive from Him equitable retribution according to their merits (Surah XL, 16; LVII, 3; II, 281). The doctrine of life after death includes belief in the survival of the soul and the resurrection of the body.

The belief in the survival of the soul did not give rise to difficulties, but the impious objected with irony to the doctrine of the resurrection of the body: "Give us back our fathers if you speak the truth!" (Surah XLIV, 36). The *Quran* opposed such superficial reasoning by pointing out the argument from nature, how the earth is at one time dead and dry and then living and fertile. (Surah XXII, 5-7; XXX, 50). The *Quran* establishes that resurrection is not only possible, it is certain. It is certain because God has promised it, and it is certain because it is required by wisdom and justice in order to give to each creature a just retribution for his deeds. Otherwise, the creation of man would have been in vain. "Deemed ye then that we had created you for naught, and that ye would not be returned unto us?" (Surah XXIII, 115).

Neither should it be thought that good and bad men nor would be treated in the same way, giving them similar life and death (Surah XLV, 21). In the Day of Judgment, justice will be given to all men. Belief in God the Creator, God the Legislator, and God the Judge is not enough in itself. The *Quran* teaches that a genuine believer must have that faith and must also observe the law; it requires sincere belief and laborious obedience. In giving its commandments it awakens in us a sense of good and evil, of beauty and ugliness. "God could not order indecent things" (Surah VII, z8). "Tell them: My Lord forbids only what is indecent done in public or in private; deeds of the limbs or of the heart, such as any impious action and any unjustified violence" (Surah VII, 33). "The faithful do not defame the reputation of those who are absent. Would any one of you like to eat his dead brother's flesh?" (Surah XLIX, 12). The *Quran* points out those ideals of universal duty were always taught by wise men and the saints.

The names of Abraham, Isaac, Ishmael, Jacob, Moses, and Jesus are often mentioned as having taught such virtues and the necessity for prayer, charity, fasting, and the like. Thus it is clear that the *Quran* has preciously preserved these previous teachings concerning virtue which were true, but we must notice that the *Quran* does not synthesize the sometimes divergent previous teachings; it marks out its own way by a spontaneous impulse. While it preserves the religious and moral patrimony, it adorns it more, crowning the divine building on which all the prophets have collaborated. By means of a variety of proofs convincing to the mind and attractive to the heart, the teaching concerning the divine attributes, the destiny of the soul, and the moral duties of man is much more developed in the *Quran* than anywhere else. For instance, instead of only prohibiting drunkenness, the *Quran* stops the evil at its source by strictly forbidding the use of all intoxicants.

Again, after reconciling the two apparently opposed principles of the Old and New Testaments, the principles of Justice and Charity, the *Quran* adds quite a new dimension which can be called the Code of Politeness, Discretion, and Propriety (Surah IV, 86; XXIV, 27 -28, 31, 58-62). With the Decalogue of Moses, we are still in the fundamental and elementary laws, as if on the ground floor of morality. With the Sermon on the Mount we already find ourselves on a very high level at which charity excels justice and the heavenly kingdom scorns the earthly realm. Finally, through the laws of the *Quran* we reach the summit where charity and justice are combined and there is a total disinterestedness which aims at the absolute Good which is God. It is God Himself who must be borne in mind while carrying out His will by living a virtuous life.

In the revelations of the *Quran,* as in every previous revelation, a new and original contribution is added to the earlier ones. It is the purpose of the *Quran* to "confirm and to safeguard the former books" (Surah V, 48). "Safeguard," in that verse, means to discard the alterations and false interpretations unjustly attributed to the earlier revelations (Surah XVI, 63-64). The text of the *Quran* itself is safeguarded against any additions or changes because God Himself promised to be its protector (Surah XV, 9). As for the other books, they were written by men and left to their protection (Surah V, 44). In addition to the Qur'an's primary aim of revealing religious and moral truths, there arc secondary objectives designed to strengthen faith in the Creator or to support the faithful in their hope. It is striking to discover the extent to which the explanations of the natural world, God's creation, correspond precisely with the latest discoveries of cosmology, anatomy, physiology, and the rest of the positive sciences.

For instance, consider these remarkable examples of scientific knowledge: the sphericity of the earth (XXXIX, 5), the formation of rain (XXX, 48), fertilization by the wind (XV, 22), the aquatic origin of all living creatures (XXI, 30), the duality in the sex of plants and other creatures, then unknown (XXXVI, 35), the collective life of animals (VI, 38), the mode of life of the bees (XVI, 69), the successive phases of the child in his mother's womb (XXII, 5; XXIII, 14). A constant support to the faithful in their hope is the fulfillment of prophecies. In a short passage in Surah XLIV the *Quran* predicted accurately the different stages through which the Islamic preaching would pass and the different attitudes toward it which would be taken by the first adversaries, how they would at first be heedless and careless, then conciliatory and interested, and finally opposed and obviously hostile. At the same time it was predicted that the ungrateful town of Mecca would at first endure an awful misery which would bring some of the people from incredulity to an attraction of their souls toward heaven, then it would have prosperity which would make them forget God, and finally Mecca would suffer a humiliating defeat in the first battle (Surah XLIV, 9-16).

Other verses announce the triumph of Islam, the permanence of its doctrine, the growth of the empire of young Islam, and the inability of any earthly power to annihilate Islam (XIII, 18; XIV, 24; XXIV, 55; VIII, 36). The *Quran* also predicted the eternal schism in Christendom (V, 14), the dispersion of the Israelites (VII, 168), their world (VII, 167), their everlasting need of a protecting ally (III, 112), and the dominance until the day of resurrection persecution until the end of the world (VII, 167), their everlasting need of a protecting ally(III, 112), and the dominance of the Christians over the Jews until the day of resurrection (III, 55). It must be noted that not only have the prophecies of the *Quran* been confirmed, but the *Quran* has thrown out this challenge: nothing can ever contradict the prophecies of the *Quran,* neither in the past, the present, nor the future (XLI, 42).

Who could ever give guarantees against space and time other than the Master of Space and Time Himself? The divine origin of the *Quran* is evident for all the reasons which have been considered in this discussion. The possibility of human origin has been eliminated. Nowhere in the *Quran* is the personal character of the Prophet reflected; nowhere is there an echo of his daily joys and sorrows or of his earthly surroundings. There are no indications of geographical, atmospherical, racial, tribal, or individual peculiarities in the subjects treated. Only that which is necessary for the education of humanity is found in the *Quran*. The revelations were accompanied by visible signs of their divine origin. The linguistic and stylistic form of the *Quran* gives positive signs of its divinity. The religious and moral teachings are clear evidence of its divine origin, free from the possibility of borrowing from other books. It is for this reason that the *Quran* holds the highest place in Islam.

For Muslims, the *Quran* is not only the text of prayers, the instrument of prophecy, the food for the spirit, the favourite canticle of the soul; it is at the same time the fundamental law, the treasure of the sciences, the mirror of the ages. It is the consolation for the present and the hope for the future. In what it affirms or denies, the *Quran* is the criterion of truth. In what it orders or prohibits, it is the best model for behavior. In what it judges, its judgment is always correct. In what it discusses, it gives the decisive argument. In what it says, it is the purest and most beautiful expression possible in speech. It calms or incites most effectively. Since the *Quran* is the direct expression of the divine will, it holds supreme authority for all men. The obedience due to our parents, our superiors, our community, or the Prophet himself is given only when it is based on a principle found in the Book of God. Their commands are obligations to us only so long as they transmit the divine commandment or do not contradict it. It is edifying to know how the Prophet himself regarded the text of the *Quran*.

He could not by his own will retouch it in the slightest; he interpreted it exactly as any commentator would a text which was not his own. And when he postponed carrying out any of its commandments even for a short time, in order to treat kindly the souls of the faithful and to forestall the objections of adversaries, we see the Revelation reproaching him most severely. Those reproaches he accepted with resignation and left engraved forever in the text (Surah

XXXIII, 37). This constantly humble, submissive, and reverential attitude toward the words of God is sincerely confessed in the *Quran* itself: "Recite: my prayer, my acts of devotion, my life and my death belong exclusively to God, the Ruler of the Universe, lone Ruler and without partner. Of this I received the order and I am the first of the submissives" (Surah VI, 163-64).

SUNNAH

The prophetic teachings outside the *Quran* are called the *Sunnah,* the Traditions. The base of Islam, as we have seen, is the *Quran,* and nothing is believed or commanded which is contrary to any revelation in the Holy Book. The Sunnah is the derived law of Islam which every Muslim is obliged to obey. The Prophet taught in three ways: by oral instructions; by the example of his personal behavior; and by his silence, his tacit approval of other people's actions, by letting others do as they pleased without comment or reproach. These three aspects of the Prophet's teaching - speaking, acting, and approving - are the basis for the Muslim tradition called the Sunnah, and are considered to be the second source of Islamic legislation and instruction.

The Prophet draws this triple authority from the *Quran* itself, for it commands us to obey the Messenger's orders (Surah IV, 59; XXIV, 56), tells us that he who obeys the Prophet obeys the very commandments of God (Surah IV, 80), and recommends that we follow his example (Surah XXXIII, 21). In the *Quran* the Prophet is commanded to behave in such a way that his behavior will be a model for believers (Surah XXXIII, 37). It also describes the Prophet as one who gave to mankind all good instructions and forbade all bad actions; therefore, the action he does not forbid is permitted (Surah VII, 157).

The great majority of Muslim learned men hold, with good reason, that the Prophet's teachings follow either the directive of divine, though non textual, inspiration or, if it was a personal, purely human effort, he applied the very essence or spirit of the law of the *Quran*. If in his instruction as a human being, without specific revelation, he ever was in error, he was immediately brought back to the truth through a revelation (Surah IV, 106-13; VIII, 67; IX, 43, 113). In the absence of such correcting revelations, all his orders, and permissions, judgments, and behavior are rightly considered as implicitly approved and having full legislative and educative authority, subject only to the condition that they have been transmitted through authentic and strictly verified sources. Thus the Muslim tradition in Islam is related to the *Quran* as a nation's laws are related to its constitution.

It is a significant fact that regarding our two most essential practical duties - prayer, which is our obligation to God, and alms, which is a duty to our fellow men - the *Quran* refers us directly to tradition for detailed instruction. Speaking of prayer, the *Quran* says explicitly, "Do that which God has taught you". Again, speaking of alms, it says that it is a "precise and known" right of the needy to receive a share of the possessions of pious men. And similar references are found concerning the season of pilgrimage and the sacred months. Now, in the absence in the *Quran* of any further elaboration on these subjects, any clear details as to how these duties are to be performed, it is obvious that through these references the *Quran* establishes the authority of the Sunnah, and grants to it the right to elaborate and define the general precepts of the *Quran*.

Without the Sunnah, these texts would have been incomprehensible, stating as known things which were not known. The role of the Sunnah is not limited to clarifying the duties implied in general commandments revealed in the *Quran*. Often the Sunnah establishes new obligations and prohibitions for which no clear reference can be found in the *Quran*. This is not; however, an addition to the legislation of the *Quran*, for a careful study will show that each of these traditions expresses the spirit of a more general teaching in the Book, even though the ties connecting each tradition with its appropriate foundation in the *Quran* are not easily discovered.

For example, the *Quran* made compulsory the alms deducted from gold, silver, and the crops, using also the more general terms "possessions," and "things granted by God"; the Prophet added the requirement that alms should be deducted from the herd. The *Quran* instituted the fast during the month of Ramadan as training in piety and patience and an opportunity to express thankfulness for divine blessings; the Prophet added the requirement that alms be given at the end of the fast of Ramadan as an act which is an additional means of accomplishing those purposes.

The *Quran* forbids usury; the Sunnah forbids those usurious sales in which the increase in price has the same effect. Since such sales, halfway between a legitimate sale and forbidden usury, fell within a doubtful and suspect area of business activity, tradition rightly forbids them under the legislation of the *Quran* which recommends that we abstain from any action when in doubt. Again, the *Quran* prescribes scourging as the punishment for lewdness, while the Sunnah specifies scourging for unmarried persons and calls for death by stoning for adultery - justified by the passage in the *Quran* which says that the punishment for lewdness in women should be confinement to the house up to death, until the time when another punishment should be revealed.

The Sunnah, based on the verified traditions concerning the teachings, actions, and tacit approval of the Prophet, is justifiably binding on all Muslims. Since the *Quran* gave the Prophet full power to enlighten men concerning the meaning of the revelations, he was the best qualified to legislate in matters requiring clarification. The Prophet knew better than any other possible legislator the essence and spirit of the Law. Therefore, it is not surprising that he took new legislative steps, creating the Sunnah, the Traditions binding on all Muslims, through legislation *by* analogy, by precise definition, and by extension of the revelations given in the *Quran*.

We now see how Muslims regard the *Quran* and the Prophet. The *Quran* is a purely divine work, a textual revelation which reached the world through a heavenly Messenger, the Faithful Spirit, and the Archangel Gabriel, who deposited it in the heart of Muhammad. Muhammad's role was limited to receiving the revelation, learning it, writing it down, transmitting, explaining, and applying it. Muhammad could not go beyond or change or modify the *Quran* in any way, nor can any other believer. Any human work can be discussed, controverted, or contradicted by events in the past, present, or future. But the *Quran*, the Word of God, is perfection itself; it is unchallengeably true, infallibly just, and inimitably good and beautiful.

The Prophet Muhammad was but a man, of a purely human nature. He was neither a great god, nor a small god, nor a sub-god, nor even an auxiliary of God. He could not acquire any good or avoid any evil except through God's will. He knew only so much of the past or the future as God revealed to him. He was infallible in his judgments only when sustained by revelation. But he was set apart from the rest of mankind by an excellent inborn morality, by the divine knowledge granted to him, and by the dignity of his apostleship: he is the head of all believers. As the faithful interpreter and living example of the *Quran*, we owe him obedience, respect, and love. The *Quran* urges us to treat him with particular reverence.

The Prophet led us out of the darkness of ignorance into the light of truth. Lost and vicious as we were, he brought us back to the straight path of Islam. But however great our respect for him may be, and however deeply we may love him, in our eyes he is not raised above the level of man. Muhammad never aspired to the rank of divinity; he was God's apostle and servant. In our confession of faith, the Prophet's role as a servant surpasses his role as apostle. For us, he is not an object of worship; we do not pray to him, but pray to God for him, asking God to heap blessings on him.

Islam's monotheistic system is infinitely pure and unmixed.

- There is no God but Allah.
- Muhammad is his servant and apostle.
- All men are brothers.

Such are the three elements of the Muslim creed, as they are stated in three successive Surahs of the *Quran* (XLVII, 19; XLVIII, 29; XLIX, 13). Such is the straight path of Islam, the path of those who submit to the will of God as revealed in the *Quran*, God's Word as given by the Archangel Gabriel to Muhammad, the Messenger of God.

Here are some maxims for dervishes:

"Do not beg unless you are starving. The Caliph Omar flogged a man who begged after having satisfied his hunger. When compelled to beg, do not accept more than you need."

"Be good-natured and uncomplaining and thank God for your poverty."

"Do not flatter the rich for giving, nor blame them for withholding."

"Dread the loss of poverty more than the rich man dreads the loss of wealth."

"Take what is voluntarily offered: it is the daily bread which God sends to you: do not refuse God's gift."

"Let no thought of the morrow enter your mind, else you will incur everlasting perdition."

"Do not make God a spring to catch alms."

The Sufi teachers gradually built up a system of asceticism and moral culture which is founded on the fact that there is in man an element of evil-the lower or appetitive soul. This evil self, the seat of passion and lust, is called *nafs*; it may be considered broadly equivalent to 'the flesh,' and with its allies, the world and the devil, it constitutes the great obstacle to the attainment of union with God. The Prophet said: "Thy worst enemy is thy *nafs*, which is between thy two sides." I do not intend to discuss the various opinions as to its nature, but the proof of its materiality is too curious to be omitted. Mohammed ibn 'Ulyan, an eminent Sufi, relates that one day something like a young fox came forth from his throat, and God caused him to know that it was his *nafs*. He trod on it, but it grew bigger at every kick that he gave it. He said:

"Other things are destroyed by pain and blows: why dost thou increase?" " Because I was created perverse," it replied; "what is pain to other things is pleasure to me, and their pleasure is my pain."

The *nafs* of Hallaj was seen running behind him in the shape of a dog; and other cases are recorded in which it appeared as a snake or a mouse. Mortification of the *nafs* is the chief work of devotion, and leads, directly or indirectly, to the contemplative life. All the Sheykhs are agreed that no disciple who neglects this duty will ever learn the rudiments of Sufism. The principle of mortification is that the *nafs* should be weaned from those things to which it is accustomed, that it should be encouraged to resist its passions, that its pride should be broken, and that it should be brought through suffering and tribulation to recognise the vileness of its original nature and the impurity of its actions. Concerning the outward methods of mortification, such as fasting, silence, and solitude, a great deal might be written, but we must now pass on to the higher ethical discipline which completes the Path.

Self-mortification, as advanced Sufis understand it, is a moral transmutation of the inner man. When they say, "Die before ye die," they do not mean to assert that the lower self can be essentially destroyed, but that it can and should be purged of its attributes, which are wholly evil. These attributes-ignorance, pride, envy, uncharitable ness, etc.-are extinguished, and replaced by the opposite qualities, when the will is surrendered to God and when the mind is concentrated on Him. Therefore 'dying to self' is really 'living in God.' The mystical aspects of the doctrine thus stated will occupy a considerable part of the following chapters; here we are mainly interested in its ethical import.

The Sufi who has eradicated self-will is said, in technical language, to have reached the 'stages' of 'acquiescence' or 'satisfaction' (*rida*) and 'trust in God' (*tawakkul*). A dervish fell into the Tigris. Seeing that he could not swim, a man on the bank cried out, "Shall I tell some one to bring you ashore?" "No," said the dervish. "Then do you wish to be drowned?" "No." "What, then, do you wish?" The dervish replied, "God's will be done! What have I to do with wishing?"

'Trust in God,' in its extreme form, involves the renunciation of every personal initiative and volition; total passivity like that of a corpse in the hands of the washer who prepares it for burial; perfect indifference towards anything that is even remotely connected with one's self. A special class of the ancient Sufis took their name from this 'trust,' which they applied, so far as they were able, to matters of everyday life.

For instance, they would not seek food, work for hire, practice any trade, or allow medicine to be given them when they were ill. Quietly they committed themselves to God's care, never doubting that He, to whom belong the treasures of earth and heaven, would provide for their wants, and that their allotted portion would come to them as surely as it comes to the birds, which neither sow nor reap, and to the fish in the sea, and to the child in the womb.

These principles depend ultimately on the Sufistic theory of the divine unity, as is shown by Shaqiq of Balkh in the following passage:

"There are three things which a man is bound to practise. Whosoever neglects any one of them needs neglect them all, and whosoever cleaves to any one of them must needs cleave to them all. Strive, therefore, to understand, and consider heedfully, "The *first* is this, that with your mind and your tongue and your actions you declare God to be One; and that, having declared Him to be One, and having declared that none benefits you or harms you except Him, you devote all your actions to Him alone. If you act a single jot of your actions for the sake of another, your thought and speech are corrupt, since your motive in acting for another's sake must be hope or fear; and when you act from hope or fear of other than God, who is the lord and sustainer of all things, you have taken to yourself another god to honour and venerate.

"*Secondly,* that while you speak and act in the sincere belief that there is no God except Him, you should trust Him more than the world or money or uncle or father or mother or any one on the face of the earth. "*Thirdly,* when you have established these two things, namely, sincere belief in the unity of God and trust in Him, it behoves you to be satisfied with Him and not to be angry on account of anything that vexes you. Beware of anger! Let your heart be with Him always, let it not be withdrawn from Him for a single moment."

The 'trusting' Sufi has no thought beyond the present hour. On one occasion Shaqiq asked those who sat listening to his discourse:

"If God causes you to die to-day, think ye that He will demand from you the prayers of to-morrow?" They answered: "No; how should He demand from us the prayers of a day on which we are not alive?" Shaqiq said: "Even as He will not demand from you the prayers of to-morrow, so do ye not seek from Him the provender of to-morrow. It may be that ye will not live so long."

In view of the practical consequences of attempting to live 'on trust,' it is not surprising to read the advice given to those who would perfectly fulfill the doctrine: "Let them dig a grave and bury themselves." Later Sufis hold that active exertion for the purpose of obtaining the means of subsistence is quite compatible with 'trust,' according to the saying of the Prophet, "Trust in God and tie the camel's leg." They define *tawakkul* as a habitual state of mind, which is impaired only by self-pleasing thoughts; *e.g.* it was accounted a breach of 'trust' to think Paradise a more desirable place than Hell.

What type of character is such a theory likely to produce? At the worst, a useless drone and hypocrite preying upon his fellow-creatures; at the best, a harmless dervish who remains unmoved in the midst of sorrow, meets praise and blame with equal indifference, and accepts insults, blows, torture, and death as mere incidents in the eternal drama of destiny. This cold morality, however, is not the highest of which Sufism is capable. The highest morality springs from nothing but love, when self-surrender becomes self-devotion. Of that I shall have something to say in due time.

Among the positive elements in the Sufi discipline there is one that Moslem mystics unanimously regard as the keystone of practical religion. I refer to the *dhikr*, an exercise well known to Western readers from the careful description given by Edward Lane in his *Modern Egyptians*, and by Professor D. B. Macdonald in his recently published *Aspects of Islam*. The term *dhikr*-'recollection' seems to me the most appropriate equivalent in English-signifies 'mentioning,' 'remembering,' or simply 'thinking of'; in the Koran the

Faithful are commanded to "remember God often," a plain act of worship without any mystical savour.

But the Sufis made a practice of repeating the name of God or some religious formula, *e.g.* "Glory to Allah" (*subhan Allah*), "There is no god but Allah" (*la ilaha illa 'llah*), accompanying the mechanical intonation with an intense concentration of every faculty upon the single word or phrase; and they attach greater value to this irregular litany, which enables them to enjoy uninterrupted communion with God, than to the five services of prayer performed, at fixed hours of the day and night, by all Moslems. Recollection may be either spoken or silent, but it is best, according to the usual opinion, that tongue and mind should co-operate. Sahl ibn 'Abdallah bade one of his disciples endeavour to say "Allah! Allah!" the whole day without intermission. When he had acquired the habit of doing so, Sahl instructed him to repeat the same words during the night, until they came forth from his lips even while he was asleep. "Now," said he, "be silent and occupy yourself with recollecting them." At last the disciple's whole being was absorbed by the thought of Allah. One day a log fell on his head, and the words "Allah, Allah" were seen written in the blood that trickled from the wound.

Ghazali describes the method and effects of *dhikr* in a passage which Macdonald has summarised as follows:

"Let him reduce his heart to a state in which the existence of anything and its non-existence are the same to him. Then let him sit alone in some corner, limiting his religious duties to what is absolutely necessary, and not occupying himself either with reciting the Koran or considering its meaning or with books of religious traditions or with anything of the sort. And let him see to it that nothing save God most High enters his mind. Then, as he sits in solitude, let him not cease saying continuously with his tongue, 'Allah, Allah,' keeping his thought on it. At last he will reach a state when the motion of his tongue will cease, and it will seem as though the word flowed from it. Let him persevere in this until all trace of motion is removed from his tongue, and he finds his heart persevering in the thought. Let him still persevere until the form of the word, its letters and shape, is removed from his heart, and there remains the idea alone, as though clinging to his heart, inseparable from it. So far, all is dependent on his will and choice; but to bring the mercy of God does not stand in his will or choice. He has now laid himself bare to the breathings of that mercy, and nothing remains but to await what God will open to him, as God has done after this manner to prophets and saints. If he fo11ows the above course, he may be sure that the light of the Real will shine out in his heart. At first unstable, like a flash of lightning, it turns and returns; though sometimes it hangs back. And if it returns, sometimes it abides and sometimes it is momentary. And if it abides, sometimes its abiding is long, and sometimes short."

Another Sufi puts the gist of the matter in a sentence, thus:

"The first stage of *dhikr* is to forget self, and the last stage is the effacement of the worshipper in the act of worship, without consciousness of worship, and such absorption in the object of worship as precludes return to the subject thereof."

Recollection can be aided in various ways. When Shibli was a novice, he went daily into a cellar, taking with him a bundle of sticks. If his attention flagged, he would beat himself until the sticks broke, and sometimes the whole bundle would be finished before evening; then he would dash his hands and feet against the wall. The Indian practice of inhaling and exhaling the breath was known to the Sufis of the ninth century and was much used afterwards. Among the Dervish Orders music, singing, and dancing are favourite means of inducing the state of trance called 'passing-away' (*fana*), which, as appears from the definition quoted above, is the climax and *raison d'être* of the method.

In 'meditation' (*muraqabat*) we recognise a form of self-concentration similar to the Buddhistic *dhyana* and *samadhi*. This is what the Prophet meant when he said, "Worship God as though thou sawest Him, for if thou seest Him not, yet He sees thee." Anyone who feels sure that God is always watching over him will devote himself to meditating on God, and no evil thoughts or diabolic suggestions will find their way into his heart. Nuri used to meditate so intently that not a hair on his body stirred. He declared that he had learned this habit from a cat which was observing a mouse-hole, and that she was far quieter than he. Abu Sa'id ibn Abi 'l-Khayr kept his eyes fixed on his navel. It is said that the Devil is smitten with epilepsy when he approaches a man thus occupied, just as happens to other men when the Devil takes possession of them.

This chapter will have served its purpose if it has brought before my readers a clear view of the main lines on which the preparatory training of the Sufi is conducted. We must now imagine him to have been invested by his Sheykh with the patched frock (*muraqqa'at* or *khirqat*), which is an outward sign that he has successfully emerged from the discipline of the 'Path,' and is now advancing with uncertain steps towards the Light, as when toil-worn travellers, having gained the summit of a deep gorge, suddenly catch glimpses of the sun and cover their eyes.

3

Illumination and Ecstasy

God, who is described in the Koran as "the Light of the heavens and the earth," cannot be seen by the bodily eye. He is visible only to the inward sight of the 'heart.' The 'vision of the heart' (*ru'yat al-qalb*) is defined as "the heart's beholding by the light of certainty that which is hidden in the unseen world." This is what 'Ali meant when he was asked, "Do you see God?" and replied: "How should we worship One whom we do not see?" The light of intuitive certainty (*yaqin*) by which the heart sees God is a beam of God's own light cast therein by Himself; else no vision of Him were possible.

"'Tis the sun's self that lets the sun be seen."

According to a mystical interpretation of the famous passage in the Koran where the light of Allah is compared to a candle burning in a lantern of transparent glass, which is placed in a niche in the wall, the niche is the true believer's heart; therefore his speech is light and his works are light and he moves in light. "He who discourses of eternity," said Bayazid, "must have within him the lamp of eternity."

The light which gleams in the heart of the illuminated mystic endows him with a supernatural power of discernment (*firasat*). Although the Sufis, like all other Moslems, acknowledge Mohammed to be the last of the prophets (as, from a different point of view, he is the Logos or first of created beings), they really claim to possess a minor form of inspiration. When Nuri was questioned concerning the origin of mystical *firasat,* he answered by quoting the Koranic verse in which God says that He breathed His spirit into Adam; but the more orthodox Sufis, who strenuously combat the doctrine that the human spirit is uncreated and eternal, affirm that *firasat* is the result of knowledge and insight, metaphorically called 'light' or 'inspiration,' which God creates and bestows upon His favourites. The Tradition, "Beware of the discernment of the true believer, for he sees by the light of Allah," is exemplified in such anecdotes as these:

Abu 'Abdallah al-Razi said:

"Ibn al-Anbari presented me with a woollen frock, and seeing on the head of Shibli a bonnet that would just match it, I conceived the wish that they were both mine. When Shibli rose to depart, he looked at me, as he was in the habit of doing when he desired me to follow him. So I followed him to his house, and when we had gone in, he bade me put off the frock and took it from me and folded it and threw his bonnet on the top. Then he called for a fire and burnt both frock and bonnet."

Sari al-Saqati frequently urged Junayd to speak in public, but Junayd was unwilling to consent, for he doubted whether he was worthy of such an honour. One Friday night he dreamed that the Prophet appeared and commanded him to speak to the people. He awoke and went to Sari's house before daybreak, and knocked at the door. Sari opened the door and said: "You would not believe me until the Prophet came and told you."

Sahl ibn 'Abdallah was sitting in the congregational mosque when a pigeon, overcome by the intense heat, dropped on the floor. Sahl exclaimed: "Please God, Shah al-Kirmani has just died." They wrote it down, and it was found to be true. When the heart is purged of sin and evil thoughts, the light of certainty strikes upon it and makes it a shining mirror, so that the Devil cannot approach it without being observed. Hence the saying of some gnostic: "If I disobey my heart, I disobey God." It was a man thus illuminated to whom the Prophet said: "Consult thy heart and thou wilt hears the secret ordinance of God proclaimed by the heart's inward knowledge, which is real faith and divinity"-something much better than the learning of divines. I need not anticipate here the question, which will be discussed in the following chapter, how far the claims of an infallible conscience are reconcilable with external religion and morality.

The Prophet, too, prayed that God would put a light into his ear and into his eye; and after mentioning the different members of his body, he concluded, "and makes the whole of me one light." {The reader should be reminded that most, if not all, mystical Traditions ascribed to Mohammed were forged and fathered upon him by the Sufis, who represent themselves as the true interpreters of his esoteric teaching.} From illumination of gradually increasing splendour, the mystic rises to contemplation of the divine attributes, and ultimately, when his consciousness is wholly melted away, he becomes transubstantiated (*tajawhara*) in the radiance of the divine essence. This is the 'station' of well-doing (*ihsan*)-for "God is with the well-doers" (Kor. 29.69), and we have Prophetic authority for the statement that "well-doing consists in worshipping God as though thou wert seeing Him."

I will not waste the time and abuse the patience of my readers by endeavouring to classify and describe these various grades of illumination, which may be depicted symbolically but cannot be explained in scientific language. We must allow the mystics to speak for themselves. Granted that their teaching is often hard to understand, it conveys more of the truth than we can ever hope to obtain from analysis and dissection.

Here are two passages from the oldest Persian treatise on Sufism, the *Kashf al-Mahjub* of Hujwiri:

"It is related that Sari al-Saqati said, 'O God, whatever punishment thou mayst inflict upon me, do not punish me with the humiliation of being veiled from Thee,' because, if I am not veiled from Thee, my torment and affliction will be lightened by the recollection and contemplation of Thee; but if I am veiled from Thee, even Thy bounty will be deadly to me. There is no punishment in Hell more painful and hard to bear than that of being veiled. If God were revealed in Hell to the people of Hell, sinful, believers would never think of Paradise, since the sight of God would so fill them with joy that they would not feel bodily pain. And in Paradise there is no pleasure more perfect than unveiled ness. If the people there enjoyed all the pleasures of that place and other pleasures a hundredfold, but were veiled from God, their hearts would be utterly broken. Therefore it is the way of God to let the hearts of those who love Him have vision of Him always, in order that the delight thereof may enable them to endure every tribulation; and they say in their visions, 'We deem all torments more desirable than to be veiled from Thee. When Thy beauty is revealed to our hearts, we take no thought of affliction.'"

"There are really two kinds of contemplation. The former is the result of perfect faith, the latter of rapturous love, for in the rapture of love a man attains to such a degree that his whole being is absorbed in the thought of his Beloved and he sees nothing else. Muhammad ibn Wasi'said: 'I never saw anything without seeing God therein,' *i.e.* through perfect faith. Shibli said: 'I never saw anything except God,' *i.e.* in the rapture of love and the fervour of contemplation. One mystic sees the act with his bodily eye, and, as he looks, beholds the Agent with his spiritual eye; another is rapt by love of the Agent from all things else, so that he sees only the Agent. The one method is demonstrative, the other is ecstatic. In the former case, a manifest proof is derived from the evidences of God; in the latter case, the seer is enraptured and transported by desire: evidences are a veil to him, because he who knows a thing does not care for aught besides, and he who loves a thing does not regard aught besides, but renounces contention with God and interference with Him in His decrees and acts. When the lover turns his eye away from created things, he will inevitably see the Creator with his heart. God hath said, 'Tell the believers to close their eyes' (Kor. 24.30), *i.e.* to close their bodily eyes to lusts and their spiritual eyes to created things. He who is most sincere in self-mortification is most firmly grounded in contemplation.

Sahl ibn 'Abdallah of Tustar said: 'If any one shuts his eye to God for a single moment, he will never be rightly guided all his life long,' because to regard other than God is to be handed over to other than God, and one who is left at the mercy of other than God is lost. Therefore the life of contemplatives is the time during which they enjoy contemplation; time spent in ocular vision they do not reckon as life, for that to them is really death. Thus, when Bayazid was asked how old he was, he replied, 'Four years.' They said to him, 'How can that be?' He answered, 'I have been veiled from God by this world for seventy years, but I have seen Him during the last four years: the period in which one is veiled does not belong to one's life.'"

I take the following quotation from the *Mawaqif* of Niffari, an author with whom we shall become better acquainted as we proceed:

"God said to me, 'The least of the sciences of nearness is that you should see in everything the effects of beholding Me, and that this vision should prevail over you more than your gnosis of Me.'"

Explanation by the commentator: "He means that the least of the sciences of nearness (proximity to God) is that when you look at anything, sensibly or intellectually or otherwise, you should be conscious of beholding God with a vision clearer than your vision of that thing. There are diverse degrees in this matter. Some mystics say that they never see anything without seeing God before it. Others say, 'without seeing God after it,' or 'with it'; or they say that they see nothing but God. A certain Sufi said, 'I made the pilgrimage and saw the Ka'ba, but not the Lord of the Ka'ba.' This is the perception of one who is veiled. Then he said, 'I made the pilgrimage again, and I saw both the Ka'ba and the Lord of the Ka'ba.' This is contemplation of the Self-subsistence through which everything subsists, *i.e.* he saw the Ka'ba subsisting through the Lord of the Ka'ba. Then he said, 'I made the pilgrimage a third time, and I saw the Lord of the Ka'ba, but not the Ka'ba.' This is the 'station' of *waqfat* (passing-away in the essence). In the present case the author is referring to contemplation of the Self-subsistence."

So much concerning is the theory of illumination. But, as Mephistopheles says, "*grau ist alle Theorie*"; and though to most of us the living experience is denied, we can hear its loudest echoes and feel its warmest afterglow in the poetry which it has created. Let me translate part of a Persian ode by the dervish-poet, Baba Kuhi of Shiriz, who died in 1050 A.D.

"In the market, in the cloister-only God I saw.

In the valley and on the mountain-only God I saw.

Him I have seen beside me oft in tribulation;

In favour and in fortune-only God I saw.

In prayer and fasting, in praise and contemplation,

In the religion of the Prophet-only God I saw.

Neither soul nor body, accident nor substance,

Qualities nor causes-only God I saw.

I oped mine eyes and by the light of His face around me

In all the eye discovered-only God I saw.
Like a candle I was melting in His fire:
Amidst the flames outflashing-only God I saw.
Myself with mine own eyes I saw most clearly,
But when I looked with God's eyes-only God I saw.
I passed away into nothingness, I vanished,
And lo, I was the All-living-only God I saw."

The whole of Sufism rests on the belief that when the individual self is lost, the Universal Self is found, or, in religious language, that ecstasy affords the only means by which the soul can directly communicate and become united with God. Asceticism, purification, love, gnosis, saintship-all the leading ideas of Sufism-are developed from this cardinal principle. Among the metaphorical terms commonly employed by the Sufis as, more or less, equivalent to 'ecstasy' are *fana* (passing-away), *wajd* (feeling), *sama'* (hearing), *dhawq* (taste), *shirb* (drinking), *ghaybat* (absence from self), *jadhbat* (attraction), *sukr* (intoxication), and *hal* (emotion).

It would be tedious and not, I think, especially instructive to examine in detail the definitions of those terms and of many others akin to them which occur in Sufi text-books. We are not brought appreciably nearer to understanding the nature of ecstasy when it is described as "a divine mystery which God communicates to true believers who behold Him with the eye of certainty," or as "a flame which moves in the ground of the soul and is produced by love-desire." The Mohammedan theory of ecstasy, however can hardly be discussed without reference to two of the above-mentioned technical expressions, namely, *fana* and *sama'*.

As I have remarked in the Introduction, the term *fana* includes different stages, aspects, and meanings. These may be summarised as follows:

1. A moral transformation of the soul through the extinction of all its passions and desires.
2. A mental abstraction or passing-away of the mind from all objects of perception, thoughts, actions, and feelings through its concentration upon the thought of God. Here the thought of God signifies contemplation of the divine attributes.
3. The cessation of all conscious thought. The highest stage of *fana* is reached when even the consciousness of having attained fana disappears. This is what the Sufis call 'the passing-away of passing-away' (*fana al-fana*). The mystic is now rapt in contemplation of the divine essence.

The final stage of *fana*, the complete passing-away from self, forms the prelude to *baqa*, 'continuance' or 'abiding' in God, and will be treated with greater fullness in Chapter VI. The first stage closely resembles the Buddhistic Nirvana. It is a 'passing-away' of evil qualities and states of mind, which involves the simultaneous 'continuance' of good qualities and states of mind. This is necessarily an ecstatic process, inasmuch as all the attributes of 'self' are evil in relation to God. No one can make himself perfectly moral, *i.e.* perfectly 'selfless.' This must be done for him, through 'a flash of the divine beauty' in his heart.

While the first stage refers to the moral 'self,' the second refers to the percipient and intellectual 'self.' Using the classification generally adopted by Christian mystics, we may regard the former as the consummation of the Purgative Life, and the latter as the goal of the Illuminative Life. The third and last stage constitutes the highest level of the Contemplative Life.

Often, though not invariably, *fana* is accompanied by loss of sensation. Sari al-Saqati, a famous Sufi of the third century, expressed the opinion that if a man in this state were struck on the face with a sword, he would not feel the blow Abu 'l-Khayr-al-Aqta' had gangrene in his foot.

The physicians declared that his foot must be amputated, but he would not allow this to be done. His disciples said, "Cut it off while he is praying, for he is then unconscious." The physicians acted on their advice, and when Abu 'l-Khayr finished his prayers he found that the amputation had taken place. It is difficult to see how any one far advanced in *fana* could be capable of keeping the religious law-a point on which the orthodox mystics lay great emphasis. Here the doctrine of saintship comes in. God takes care to preserve His elect from disobedience to His commands. We are told that Bayazid, Shibli, and other saints were continually in a state of rapture until the hour of prayer arrived; then they returned to consciousness, and after performing their prayers became enraptured again.

In theory, the ecstatic trance is involuntary, although certain conditions are recognised as being especially favourable to its occurrence. "It comes to a man through vision of the majesty of God and through revelation of the divine omnipotence to his heart." Such, for instance, was the case of Abu Hamza, who, while walking in the streets of Baghdad and meditating on the nearness of God, suddenly fell into an ecstasy and went on his way, neither seeing nor hearing, until he recovered his senses and found himself in the desert. Trances of this kind sometimes lasted many weeks. It is recorded of Sahl ibn 'Abdallah that he used to remain in ecstasy twenty-five days at a time, eating no food; yet he would answer questions put to him by the doctors of theology, and even in winter his shirt would be damp with sweat. But the Sufis soon discovered that ecstasy might be induced artificially, not only by concentration of thought, recollection (*dhikr*), and other innocent methods of autohypnosis, but also by music, singing, and dancing. These are included in the term *sama'*, which properly means nothing more than audition.

That Moslems are extraordinarily susceptible to the sweet influences of sound will not be doubted by any one who remembers how, in the *Arabian Nights,* heroes and heroines alike swoon upon the slightest provocation afforded by a singing-girl touching her lute and trilling a few lines of passionate verse.

The fiction is true to life. When Sufi writers discuss the analogous phenomena of ecstasy, they commonly do so in a chapter entitled 'Concerning the *Sama'*.' Under this heading Hujwiri, in the final chapter of his *Kashf al-Mahjub,* gives us an excellent summary of his own and other Mohammedan theories, together with numerous anecdotes of persons who were thrown into ecstasy on hearing a verse of the Koran or a heavenly voice (*hatif*) or poetry or music. Many are said to have died from the emotion thus aroused. I may add by way of explanation that, according to a well-known mystical belief, God has inspired every created thing to praise Him in its own language, so that all the sounds in the universe form, as it were, one vast choral hymn by which He glorifies Himself.

Consequently those whose hearts He has opened and endowed with spiritual perception hear His voice everywhere, and ecstasy overcomes them as they listen to the rhythmic chant of the muezzin, or the street cry of the saqqa shouldering his water skin, or, perchance, to the noise of wind or the bleating of a sheep or the piping of a bird.

Pythagoras and Plato are responsible for another theory, to which the Sufi poets frequently allude, that music awakens in the soul a memory of celestial harmonies heard in a state of pre-existence, before the soul was separated from God. Thus Jalaluddin Rumi:

"The song of the spheres in their revolutions
Is what men sing with lute and voice?
As we all are members of Adam,
We have heard these melodies in Paradise.
Though earth and water have cast their veil upon us,

We retain faint reminiscences of these heavenly songs;

But while we are thus shrouded by gross earthly veils,

How can the tones of the dancing spheres reach us?"

{E. H. Whinfield, abridged translation of the Masnavi, *p. 182.}*

The formal practice of *sama'* quickly spread amongst the Sufis and produced an acute cleavage of opinion, some holding it to be lawful and praiseworthy, whilst others condemned it as an abominable innovation and incitement to vice. Hujwiri adopts the middle view expressed in a saying of Dhu 'l-Nun the Egyptian:

"Music is a divine influence which stirs the heart to seek God: those who listen to it spiritually attain unto God, and those who listen to it sensually fall into unbelief."

He declares, in effect, that audition is neither good nor bad, and must be judged by its results.

"When an anchorite goes into a tavern, the tavern becomes his cell, but when a wine-bibber goes into a cell, that cell becomes his tavern."

One whose heart is absorbed in the thought of God cannot be corrupted by hearing musical instruments so with dancing.

"When the heart throbs and rapture grows intense, and the agitation of ecstasy is manifested. and conventional forms are gone, this is not dancing nor bodily indulgence, but a dissolution of the soul."

Hujwiri, however, lays down several precautionary rules for those who engage in audition, and he confesses that the public concerts given by dervishes are extremely demoralising. Novices, he thinks, should not be permitted to attend them. In modern times these orgiastic scenes have frequently been described by eye-witnesses. I will now translate from Jami's *Lives of the Saints* the account of a similar performance which took place about seven hundred years ago.

"There was a certain dervish, a negro called Zangi Bashgirdi, who had attained to such a high degree of spirituality that the mystic dance could not be started until he came out and joined in it. One day, in the course of the *sama'*, he was seized with ecstasy, and rising into the air seated himself on a lofty arch which overlooked the dancers. In descending he leaped on to Majduddin of Baghdad, and encircled with his legs the neck of the Sheykh, who nevertheless continued to spin round in the dance, though he was a very frail and slender man, whereas the Negro was tall and heavy. When the dance was finished, Majduddin said, 'I did not know whether it was a Negro or a sparrow on my neck.' On getting off the Sheikh's shoulders, the negro bit his cheek so severely that the scar remained visible ever after. Majduddin often used to say that on the Day of Judgment he would not boast of anything except that he bore the mark of this negro's teeth on his face."

Grotesque and ignoble features-not to speak of grosser deformities-must appear in any faithful delineation of the ecstatic life of Islam. Nothing is gained by concealing their existence or by minimising their importance. If, as Jalaluddin Rumi says:

> *"Men incur the reproach of wine and drugs*
> *That they may escape for a while from self-consciousness,*
> *Since all know this life to be a snare,*
> *Volitional memory and thought to be a hell,".*

4

The Gnosis

The Sufis distinguish three organs of spiritual communication: the heart (*qalb*), which knows God; the spirit (*ruh*), which loves Him; and the inmost ground of the soul (*sirr*), which contemplates Him. It would take us into deep waters if we were to embark upon a discussion of these terms and their relation to each other. A few words concerning the first of the three will suffice.

The *qalb*, though connected in some mysterious way with the physical heart, is not a thing of flesh and blood. Unlike the English 'heart,' its nature is rather intellectual than emotional, but whereas the intellect cannot gain real knowledge of God, the *qalb* is capable of knowing the essences of all things, and when illumined by faith and knowledge reflects the whole content of the divine mind; hence the Prophet said, "My earth and My heaven contain Me not, but the heart of My faithful servant containeth Me." This revelation, however, is a comparatively rare experience.

Normally, the heart is 'veiled,' blackened by sin, tarnished by sensual impressions and images, pulled to and fro between reason and passion: a battlefield on which the armies of God and the Devil contend for victory. Through one gate, the heart receives immediate knowledge of God; through another, it lets in the illusions of sense. "Here a world and there a world," says Jalaluddin Rumi. "I am seated on the threshold." Therefore man is potentially lower than the brutes and higher than the angels.

"Angel and brute man's wondrous leaven compose;
To these inclining, less than these he grows,
But if he means the angel, more than those."

Less than the brutes, because they lack the knowledge that would enable them to rise; more than the angels, because they are not subject to passion and so cannot fall.

How shall a man know God? Not by the senses, for He is immaterial; nor by the intellects, for He is unthinkable. Logic never gets beyond the finite; philosophy sees double; book-learning fosters self-conceit and obscures the idea of the Truth with clouds of empty words. Jalaluddin Rumi, addressing the scholastic theologian, asks scornfully:

"Do you know a name without a thing answering to it?
Have you ever plucked a rose from R, O, S, E?
You name His name; go, seek the reality named by it!
Look for the moon in the sky, not in the water!
If you desire to rise above mere names and letters,
Make yourself free from self at one stroke.
Become pure from all attributes of self,
That you may see your own bright essence,
Yea, see in your own heart the knowledge of the Prophet,
Without book, without tutor, without preceptor."

This knowledge comes by illumination, revelation, inspiration.

"Look in your own heart," says the Sufi, "for the kingdom of God is within you." He who truly knows himself knows God, for the heart is a mirror in which every divine quality is reflected. But just as a steel mirror when coated with rust loses its power of reflex ion, so the inward spiritual sense, which Sufis call the eye of the heart, is blind to the celestial glory until the dark obstruction of the phenomenal self, with all its sensual contaminations, has been wholly cleared away. The clearance, if it is to be done effectively, must be the work of God, though it demands a certain inward co-operation on the part of man. "Whosoever shall strive for our sake, we will guide him into our ways" (Kor. 29.69). Action is false and vain, if it is thought to proceed from one's self, but the enlightened mystic regards God as the real agent in every act, and therefore takes no credit for his good works nor desires to be recompensed for them.

While ordinary knowledge is denoted by the term *'ilm*, the mystic knowledge peculiar to the Sufis is called *ma'rifat* or *'irfan*. As I have indicated in the foregoing paragraphs, *ma'rifat* is fundamentally different from *'irfan*, and a different word must be used to translate it. We need not look far for a suitable equivalent. The *ma'rifat* of the Sufis is the 'gnosis' of Hellenistic theosophy, *i.e.* direct knowledge of God based on revelation or apocalyptic vision. It is not the result of any mental process, but depends entirely on the will and favour of God, who bestows it as a gift from Himself upon those whom He has created with the capacity for receiving it. It is a light of divine grace that flashes into the heart and overwhelms every human faculty in its dazzling beams. "He who knows God is dumb."

The relation of gnosis to positive religion is discussed in a very remarkable treatise on speculative mysticism by Niffari, an unknown wandering dervish who died in Egypt in the latter half of the tenth century. His work, consisting of a series of revelations in which God addresses the writer and instructs him concerning the theory of gnosis is couched in abstruse language and would scarcely be intelligible without the commentary which accompanies it; but its value as an original exposition of advanced Sufism will sufficiently appear from the excerpts given in this chapter.

{I am now engaged in preparing an edition of the Arabic text, together with an English translation and commentary.}

Those who seek God, says Niffari, are of three kinds: *firstly*, the worshippers to whom God makes Himself known by means of bounty, *i.e.* they worship Him in the hope of winning Paradise or some spiritual recompense such as dreams and miracles; *secondly*, the philosophers and scholastic theologians, to whom God makes Himself known by means of glory, *i.e.* they can never find the glorious God whom they seek, wherefore they assert that His essence is unknowable, saying, "We know that we know Him not, and that is our knowledge"; *thirdly*, the gnostics, to whom God makes Himself known by means of ecstasy, *i.e.* they are possessed and controlled by a rapture that deprives them of the consciousness of individual existence.

Niffari bids the gnostic perform only such acts of worship as are in accordance with his vision of God, though in so doing he will necessarily disobey the religious law which was made for the vulgar. His inward feeling must decide how far the external forms of religion are good for him.

"God said to me, Ask Me and say, 'O Lord, how shall I cleave to Thee, so that when my day (of judgment) comes, Thou wilt not punish me nor avert Thy face from me?' Then I will answer thee and say, 'Cleave in thy outward theory and practice to the Sunna (the rule of the Prophet), and cleave in thy inward feeling to the gnosis which I have given thee; and know that when I make Myself known to thee, I will not accept from thee anything of the Sunna but what My gnosis brings to thee, because thou art one of those to whom I speak: thou hearest Me and knowest that thou hearest Me, and thou seest that I am the source of all things.'"

The commentator observes that the Sunna, being general in scope, makes no distinction between individuals, *e.g.* seekers of Paradise and seekers of God, but that in reality it contains exactly what each person requires. The portion especially appropriate in every case is discerned either by means of gnosis, which God communicates to the heart, or by means of guidance imparted by a spiritual director.

"And He said to me, 'My exoteric revelation does not support My esoteric revelation.'"

This means that the gnostic need not be dismayed if his inner experience conflicts with the religious law. The contradiction is only apparent. Religion addresses itself to the common herd of men who are veiled by their minds, by logic, tradition, and so on; whereas gnosis belongs to the elect, whose bodies and spirits are bathed in the eternal Light. Religion sees things from the aspect of plurality, but gnosis regards the all-embracing Unity. Hence the same act is good in religion, but evil in gnosis-a truth which is briefly stated thus:

"The good deeds of the pious are the ill deeds of the favourites of God."

Although works of devotion are not incompatible with gnosis, no one who connects them in the slightest degree with himself is a gnostic. This is the theme of the following allegory. Niffari seldom writes as lucidly as he does here, yet I fancy that few of my readers will find the explanations printed within square brackets altogether superfluous.

THE REVELATION OF THE SEA

"God bade me behold the Sea, and I saw the ships sinking and the planks floating; then the planks too were submerged."

[The Sea denotes the spiritual experiences through which the mystic passes in his journey to God. The point at issue is this: whether he should prefer the religious law or disinterested love. Here he is warned not to rely on his good works, which are no better than sinking ships and will never bring him safely to port. No; if he would attain to God, he must rely on God alone. If he does not rely entirely on God, but let's himself trust ever so little in anything else, he is still clinging to a plank.

Though his trust in God is greater than before, it is not yet complete.]

"And He said to me, 'Those who voyage are not saved.'"

[The voyager uses the ship as a means of crossing the sea: therefore he relies, not on the First Cause, but on secondary causes.]

"And He said to me, 'Those who instead of voyaging cast them into the Sea take a risk.'"

[To abandon all secondary causes is like plunging in the sea. The mystic who makes this venture is in jeopardy, for two reasons: he may regard himself, not God, as initiating and carrying out the action of abandonment,-and one who renounces a thing through 'self' is in worse case than if he had not renounced it,-or he may abandon secondary causes (good works, hope of Paradise, etc.), not for God's sake, but from sheer indifference and lack of spiritual feeling.]

"And He said to me, 'Those who voyage and take no risk shall perish.'"

[Notwithstanding the dangers referred to, he must make God his sole object or fail.]

"And He said to me, 'In taking the risk there is a part of salvation.'"

[Only a part of salvation because perfect selflessness has not yet been attained. The whole of salvation consists in the effacement of all secondary causes, all phenomena, through the rapture which results from vision of God. But this is gnosis, and the present revelation is addressed to mystics of a lower grade. The Gnostic takes no risk, for he has nothing to lose.]

"And the wave came and lifted those beneath it and overran the shore."

[Those beneath the wave are they who voyage in ships and consequently suffer shipwreck. Their reliance on secondary causes casts them ashore, *i.e.* brings them back to the world of phenomena whereby they are veiled from God.]

"And He said to me, 'The surface of the Sea is a gleam that cannot be reached.'"

[Anyone who depends on external rites of worship to lead him to God is following a will-o'-the-wisp.]

"And its bottom is darkness impenetrable."

[To discard positive religion, root and branch, is to wander in a pathless maze.]

"And between the two are fishes which are to be feared."

[He refers to the middle way between pure exotericism and pure esotericism. The 'fishes' are its perils and obstacles.]

"Do not voyage on the Sea, lest I cause thee to be veiled by the vehicle."

[The 'vehicle' signifies the 'ship,' *i.e.* reliance on something other than God.]

"And do not cast thyself into the Sea, lest I cause thee to be veiled by thy casting thyself."

[Whoever regards any act as his own act and attributes it to himself is far from God.]

"And He said to me, 'In the Sea are boundaries: which of them will bear thee on?'"

[The 'boundaries' are the various degrees of spiritual experience. The mystic ought not to rely on any of these, for they are all imperfect.]

"And He said to me, 'If thou givest thyself to the Sea and sinkest therein, thou wilt fall a prey to one of its beasts.'"

[If the mystic either relies on secondary causes or abandons them by his own act, he will go astray.]

"And He said to me, 'I deceive thee if I direct thee to aught save Myself.'"

[If the mystic's inward voice bids him turn to anything except God, it deceives him.]

"And He said to me, 'If thou perishest for the sake of other than Me, thou wilt belong to that for which thou hast perished.'

"And He said to me, 'This world belongs to him whom I have turned away from it and from whom I have turned it away; and the next world belongs to him towards whom have brought it and whom I have brought towards Myself.'"

[He means to say that everlasting joy is the portion of those whose hearts are turned away from this world and who have no worldly possessions. They really enjoy this world, because it cannot separate them from God. Similarly, the true owners of the next world are those who do not seek it, inasmuch as it is not the real object of their desire, but contemplate God alone.]

The Gnostic descries the element of reality in positive religion, but his gnosis is not derived from religion or from any sort of human knowledge: it is properly concerned with the divine attributes, and God Himself reveals the knowledge of these to His saints who contemplate Him.

Dhu 'l-Nun of Egypt, whose mystical speculations mark him out as the father of Moslem theosophy, said that Gnostics are not themselves, and do not subsist through themselves, but so far as they subsist, they subsist through God.

"They move as God causes them to move, and their words are the words of God which roll upon their tongues, and their sight is the sight of God which has entered their eyes."

The Gnostic contemplates the attributes of God, not His essence, for even in gnosis a small trace of duality remains: this disappears only in *fana al-fana*, the total passing-away in the undifferentiated Godhead. The cardinal attribute of God is unity, and the divine unity is the first and last principle of gnosis. {According to some mystics, the gnosis of unity constitutes a higher stage which is called 'the Truth' (*haqiqat*).}

Both Moslem and Sufi declare that God is One, but the statement bears a different meaning in each instance. The Moslem means that God is unique in His essence, qualities, and acts; that He is absolutely unlike all other beings. The Sufi means that God is the One Real Being which underlies all phenomena. This principle is carried to its extreme consequences, as we shall see.

If nothing except God exists, then the whole universe, including man, is essentially one with God, whether it is regarded as an emanation which proceeds from Him, without impairing His unity, like sunbeams from the sun, or whether it is conceived as a mirror in which the divine attributes are reflected. But surely a God who is all in all can have no reason for thus revealing Himself: why should the One pass over into the Many? The Sufis answer-a philosopher would say that they evade the difficulty-by quoting the famous Tradition: "I was a hidden treasure and I desired to be known; therefore I created the creation in order that I might be known." In other words, God is the eternal Beauty, and it lies in the nature of beauty to desire love. The mystic poets have described the self-manifestation of the One with profusion of splendid imagery. Jami says, for example:

- "From all eternity the Beloved unveiled His beauty in

the solitude of the unseen;

- He held up the mirror to His own face, He displayed His loveliness to Himself.
- He was both the spectator and the spectacle; no eye but His had surveyed the Universe.
- All was One, there was no duality, no pretence of 'mine' or 'thine.'
- The vast orb of Heaven, with its myriad incomings and outgoings, was concealed in a single point.
- The Creation lay cradled in the sleep of non-existence, like a child ere it has breathed.
- The eye of the Beloved, seeing what was not, regarded nonentity as existent.
- Although He beheld His attributes and qualities as a perfect whole in His own essence,
- Yet He desired that they should be displayed to Him in another mirror,
- And that each one of His eternal attributes should become manifest accordingly in a diverse form,
- Therefore He created the verdant fields of Time and Space and the life-giving garden of the world,
- That every branch and leaf and fruit might show forth His various perfections,
- The cypress gave a hint of His comely stature; the rose gave tidings of His beauteous countenance.
- Wherever Beauty peeped out, Love appeared beside it; wherever Beauty shone in a rosy cheek, Love lit his torch from that flame.
- Wherever Beauty dwelt in dark tresses, Love came and found a heart entangled in their coils.
- Beauty and Love are as body and soul; Beauty is the mine and Love the precious stone.
- They have always been together from the very first; never have they travelled but in each other's company."

In another work Jami sets forth the relation of God to the world more philosophically, as follows:

"The unique Substance, viewed as absolute and void of all phenomena, all limitations and all multiplicity, is the Real (*al-Haqq*). On the other hand, viewed in His aspect of multiplicity and plurality, under which He displays Himself when clothed with phenomena, He is the whole created universe. Therefore the universe is the outward visible expression of the Real, and the Real is the inner unseen reality of the universe. The universe before it was evolved to outward view was identical with the Real; and the Real after this evolution is identical with the universe."

Phenomena, as such, are not-being and only derive a contingent existence from the qualities of Absolute Being by which they are irradiated. The sensible world resembles the fiery circle made by a single spark whirling round rapidly. Man is the crown and final cause of the universe. Though last in the order of creation he is first in the process of divine thought, for the essential part of him is the primal Intelligence or universal Reason which emanates immediately from the Godhead. This corresponds to the Logos-the animating principle of all things-and is identified with the Prophet Mohammed. An interesting parallel might be drawn here between the Christian and Sufi doctrines.

The same expressions are applied to the founder of Islam which are used by St. John, St. Paul, and later mystical theologians concerning Christ. Thus, Mohammed is called the Light of God, he is said to have existed before the creation of the world, he is adored as the source of all life, actual and possible, he is the Perfect Man in whom all the divine attributes are manifested, and a Sufi tradition ascribes to him the saying, "He that hath seen me hath seen Allah." In the Moslem scheme, however, the Logos doctrine occupies a subordinate place, as it obviously must when the whole duty of man is believed to consist in realising the unity of

God. The most distinctive feature of Oriental as opposed to European mysticism is its profound consciousness of an omnipresent, all-pervading unity in which every vestige of individuality is swallowed up. Not to become *like* God or *personally* to participate in the divine nature is the Sufi's aim, but to escape from the bondage of his unreal selfhood and thereby to be reunited with the One infinite Being.

According to Jami, Unification consists in making the heart single-that is, in purifying and divesting it of attachment to aught except God, both in respect of desire and will and also as regards knowledge and gnosis. The mystic's desire and will should be severed from all things which are desired and willed; all objects of knowledge and understanding should be removed from his intellectual vision. His thoughts should be directed solely towards God, he should not be conscious of anything besides.

So long as he is a captive in the snare of passion and lust, it is hard for him to maintain this relation to God, but when the subtle influence of that attraction becomes manifest in him, expelling preoccupation with objects of sense and cognition from his inward being, delight in that divine communion prevails over bodily pleasures and spiritual joys; the painful task of self-mortification is ended, and the sweetness of contemplation enravishes his soul.

When the sincere aspirant perceives in himself the beginning of this attraction, which is delight in the recollection of God, let him fix his whole mind on fostering and strengthening it, let him keep himself aloof from whatsoever is incompatible with it, and deem that even though he were to devote an eternity to cultivating that communion, he would have done nothing and would not have discharged his duty as he ought.

"Love thrilled the chord of love in my soul's lute,
And changed me all to love from head to foot.
'This was but a moment's touch, yet shall Time ever

To me the debt of thanksgiving imputes."

It is an axiom of the Sufis that what is not *in* a man he cannot know. The Gnostic-Man *par excellence*-could not know God and all the mysteries of the universe, unless he found them in himself. He is the microcosm, 'a copy made in the image of God,' 'the eye of the world whereby God sees His own works.' In knowing himself as he really is, he knows God, and he knows himself through God, who is nearer to everything than its knowledge of itself. Knowledge of God proceeds, and is the cause of, self-knowledge.

Gnosis, then, is unification, realisation of the fact that the appearance of 'otherness' beside Oneness is a false and deluding dream. Gnosis lays this spectre, which haunts unenlightened men all their lives; which rises, like a wall of utter darkness, between them and God. Gnosis proclaims that 'I' is a figure of speech, and that one cannot truly refer any will, feeling, thought, or action to one's self.

Niffari heard the divine voice saying to him:

"When thou regardest thyself as existent and dost not regard Me as the Cause of thy existence, I veil My face and thine own face appears to thee. Therefore consider what is displayed to thee, and what is hidden from thee!"

[If a man regards himself as existing through God, that which is of God in him predominates over the phenomenal element and makes it pass away, so that he sees nothing but God. If, on the contrary, he regards himself as having an independent existence, his unreal egoism is displayed to him and the reality of God becomes hidden from him.]

"Regard neither My displaying nor that which is displayed, else thou wilt laugh and weep; and when thou laughest and weepest, thou art thine, not Mine."

[He who regards the act of divine revelation is guilty of polytheism, since revelation involves both a revealing subject and a revealed object; and he who regards the revealed object which is part of the created universe, regards something other than God. Laughter signifies joy for what you have gained, and weeping denotes grief for what you have lost. Both are selfish actions. The Gnostic neither laughs nor weeps.]

"If thou dost not put behind thee all that I have displayed and am displaying, thou wilt not prosper; and unless thou prosper, thou wilt not become concentrated upon Me."

[Prosperity is true belief in God, which requires complete abstraction from created things.]

Logically, these doctrines annul every moral and religious law. In the Gnostic's vision there are no divine rewards and punishments, no human standards of right and wrong. For him, the written word of God has been abrogated by a direct and intimate revelation.

"I do not say," exclaimed Abu 'l-Hasan Khurqani, "that Paradise and Hell are non-existent, but I say that they are nothing to me, because God created them both, and there is no room for any created object in the place where I am."

From this standpoint all types of religion are equal, and Islam is no better than idolatry. It does not matter what creed a man professes or what rites he performs.

"The true mosque in a pure and holy heart
Is builded: there let all men worship God;
For there He dwells, not in a mosque of stone."

Amidst all the variety of creeds and worshippers the Gnostic sees but one real object of worship.

"Those who adore God in the sun" (says Ibn al-'Arabi) "behold the sun, and those who adore Him in living things see a living thing, and those who adore Him in lifeless things see a lifeless thing, and those who adore Him as a being unique and unparalleled see that which has no like. Do not attach yourself" (he continues) "to any particular creed exclusively, so that you disbelieve in all the rest; otherwise, you will lose much good, nay; you will fail to recognise the real truth of the matter. God, the omnipresent and omnipotent, is not limited by any one creed, for He says (Kor. 2.109), 'Wheresoever ye turn, there is the face of Allah.' Every one praises what he believes; his god is his own creature, and in praising it he praises himself. Consequently he blames the beliefs of others, which he would not do if he was just, but his dislike is based on ignorance. If he knew Junayd's saying, 'The water takes its colour from the vessel containing it,' he would not interfere with other men's beliefs, but would perceive God in every form of belief."

And Hafiz sings, more in the spirit of the freethinker, perhaps, than of the mystic:

"Love is where the glory falls
Of Thy face-on convent walls
Or on tavern floors, the same
Unextinguishable flame.
Where the turbaned anchorite
Chanteth Allah day and night,
Church bells ring the call to prayer
And the Cross of Christ is there."

Sufism may join hands with freethought-it has often done so-but hardly ever with sectarianism. This explains why the vast majority of Sufis have been, at least nominally, attached to the catholic body of the Moslem community. 'Abdallah Ansari declared that of two thousand Sufi Sheykhs with whom he was acquainted only two were Shi'ites. A certain man who was a descendant of the Caliph 'Ali, and a fanatical Shi'ite, tells the following story:

"For five years," he said, "my father sent me daily to a spiritual director. I learned one useful lesson from him: he told me that I should never know anything at all about Sufism until I got completely rid of the pride which I felt on account of my lineage."

Superficial observers have described Babism as an offshoot of Sufism, but the dogmatism of the one is naturally opposed to the broad eclecticism of the other. In proportion as the Sufi gains more knowledge of God, his religious prejudices are diminished. Sheykh 'Abd al-Rahim ibn al-Sabbagh, who at first disliked living in Upper Egypt, with its large Jewish and Christian population, said in his old age that he would as readily embrace a Jew or Christian as one of his own faith.

While the innumerable forms of creed and ritual may be regarded as having a certain relative value in so far as the inward feeling which inspires them is ever one and the same, from another aspect they seem to be veils of the Truth, barriers which the zealous

Unitarian must strive to abolish and destroy.

"This world and that world are the egg and the bird within it. Is in darkness and broken-winged and scorned and despised.

Regard unbelief and faith as the white and the yolk in this egg,

Between them, joining and dividing, a barrier which they shall not pass.

When He hath graciously fostered the egg under His wing, Infidelity and religion disappear: the bird of Unity spreads its pinions."

The great Persian mystic, Abu Sa'id ibn Abi 'l-Khayr, speaking in the name of the Calendars or wandering dervishes, expresses their iconoclastic principles with astonishing boldness:

"Not until every mosque beneath the sun
Lies ruined, will our holy work be done;
And never will true Musalman appear
Till faith and infidelity are one."

Such open declarations of war against the Mohammedan religion are exceptional. Notwithstanding the breadth and depth of the gulf between full-blown Sufism and orthodox Islam, many, if not most, Sufis have paid homage to the Prophet and have observed the outward forms of devotion which are incumbent on all Moslems. They have invested these rites and ceremonies with a new meaning; they have allegorised them, but they have not abandoned them.

Take the pilgrimage, for example. In the eyes of the genuine Sufi it is null and void unless each of the successive religious acts which it involves is accompanied by corresponding 'movements of the heart.'

A man who had just returned from the pilgrimage came to Junayd. Junayd said:

"From the hour when you first journeyed from your home have you also been journeying away from all sins?" He said "No." "Then," said Junayd, "You have made no journey. At every stage where you halted for the night did you traverse a station on the way to God?" "No," he replied. "Then," said Junayd, "you have not trodden the road stage by stage. When you put on the pilgrim's garb at the proper place, did you discard the qualities of human nature as you cast off your clothes?" "No." "Then you have not put on the pilgrim's garb. When you stood at 'Arafat, did you stand one moment in contemplation of God?" "No." "Then you have not stood at 'Arafat. When you went to Muzdalifa and achieved your desire, did you renounce all sensual desires?" "No." "Then you have not gone to Muzdalifa.

When you circumambulated the Ka'ba, did you behold the immaterial beauty of God in the abode of purification?" "No." "Then you have not circumambulated the Ka'ba. When you ran between Safa and Marwa, did you attain to purity (*safa*) and virtue (*muruwwat*)?" "No." "Then you have not run. When you came to Mina, did all your wishes (*muna*) cease?" "No." "Then you have not yet visited Mina. When you reached the slaughter-place and offered sacrifice, did you sacrifice the objects of worldly desire?" "No." "Then you have not sacrificed. When you threw the pebbles, did you throw away whatever sensual thoughts were accompanying you?" "No." "Then you have not yet thrown the pebbles, and you have not yet performed the pilgrimage."

This anecdote contrasts the outer religious law of theology with the inner spiritual truth of mysticism, and shows that they should not be divorced from each other.

"The Law without the Truth," says Hujwiri, "is ostentation, and the Truth without the Law is hypocrisy. Their mutual relation may be compared to that of body and spirit: when the spirit departs from the body, the living body becomes a corpse, and the spirit vanishes like wind. The Moslem profession of faith includes both: the words, 'There is no god but Allah,' are the Truth, and the words, 'Mohammed is the apostle of Allah,' are the Law; any one who denies the Truth is an infidel, and any one who rejects the Law is a heretic."

Middle ways, though proverbially safe, are difficult to walk in; and only by a *tour de force* can the Koran be brought into line with the esoteric doctrine which the Sufis derive from it. Undoubtedly they have done a great work for Islam. They have deepened and enriched the lives of millions by ruthlessly stripping off the husk of religion and insisting that its kernel must be sought, not in any formal act, but in cultivation of spiritual feelings and in purification of the inward man. This was a legitimate and most fruitful development of the Prophet's teaching. But the Prophet was a strict monotheist, while the Sufis, whatever they may pretend or imagine, are theosophists, pantheists, or monists. When they speak and write as believers in the dogmas of positive religion, they use language which cannot be reconciled with such a theory of unity as we are now examining. 'Afifuddin al-Tilimsani, from whose commentary on Niffari I have given some extracts in this chapter, said roundly that the whole Koran is polytheism-a perfectly just statement from the monistic point of view, though few Sufis have dared to be so explicit.

The mystic Unitarians admit the appearance of contradiction, but deny its reality. "The Law and the Truth" (they might say) "is the same thing in different aspects. The Law is for you, the Truth for us. In addressing you we speak according to the measure of your understanding, since what is meat for Gnostics is poison to the uninitiated, and the highest mysteries ought to be jealously guarded from profane ears. It is only human reason that sees the single as double, and balances the Law against the Truth. Pass away from the world of opposites and become one with God, who has no opposite."

The Gnostic recognises that the Law is valid and necessary in the moral sphere. While good and evil remain, the Law stands over both, commanding and forbidding, rewarding and punishing. He knows, on the other hand, that only God really exists and acts: therefore, if evil really exists, it must be divine, and if evil things are really done, God must be the doer of them. The conclusion is false because the hypothesis is false. Evil has no real existence; it is not-being, which is the privation and absence of being, just as darkness is the absence of light. "Once," said Nuri, "I beheld the Light, and I fixed my gaze upon it until I became the Light." No wonder that such illuminated souls, supremely indifferent to the shadow-shows of religion and morality in a phantom world, are ready to cry with Jalaluddin:

"The man of God is made wise by the Truth,
The man of God is not learned from book.
The man of God is beyond infidelity and faith,
To the man of God right and wrong are alike."

It must be borne in mind that this is a theory of perfection, and that those whom it exalts above the Law are saints, spiritual guides, and profound theosophists who enjoy the special favour of God and presumably do not need to be restrained, coerced, or punished. In practice, of course, it leads in many instances to antinomianism and libertinism, as among the Bektashis and other orders of the so-called 'lawless' dervishes. The same theories produced the same results in Europe during the middle Ages, and the impartial historian cannot ignore the corruptions to which a purely subjective mysticism is liable; but on the present occasion we are concerned with the rose itself, not with its cankers.

Not all Sufis are gnostics; and, as I have mentioned before, those who are not yet ripe for the gnosis receive from their gnostic teachers the ethical instruction suitable to their needs. Jalaluddin Rumi, in his collection of lyrical poems entitled *The Divan of Shamsi Tabriz,* gives free rein to a pantheistic enthusiasm which sees all things under the form of eternity.

"I have put duality away, I have seen that the two worlds are one;

One I seek, One I know, One I see, One I call.

I am intoxicated with Love's cup, the two worlds have passed out of my ken;

I have no business save carouse and revelry."

But in his *Masnavi*-a work so famous and venerated that it has been styled 'The Koran of Persia'-we find him in a more sober mood expounding the Sufi doctrines and justifying the ways of God to man. Here, though he is a convinced optimist and agrees with Ghazali that this is the best of all possible worlds, he does not airily dismiss the problem of evil as something outside reality, but endeavours to show that evil, or what seems evil to us, is part of the divine order and harmony, I will quote some passages of his argument and leave my readers to judge how far it is successful or, at any rate, suggestive.

The Sufis, it will be remembered, conceive the universe as a projected and reflected image of God. The divine light, streaming forth in a series of emanations, falls at last upon the darkness of not-being, every atom of which reflects some attribute of Deity. For instance, the beautiful attributes of love and mercy are reflected in the form of heaven and the angels, while the terrible attributes of wrath and vengeance are reflected in the form of hell and the devils. Man reflects all the attributes, the terrible as well as the beautiful: he is an epitome of heaven and hell. Omar Khayyam alludes to this theory when he says:

"Hell is a spark from our fruitless pain,

Heaven a breath from our time of joy"

-a couplet which Fitz Gerald moulded into the magnificent stanza:

"Heav'n but the Vision of fulfilled Desire,

And Hell the Shadow from a Soul on fire,

Cast on the Darkness into which Ourselves So late emerged from, shall so soon expire."

Jalaluddin, therefore, does in a sense make God the author of evil, but at the same time he makes evil intrinsically good in relation to God-for it is the reflexion of certain divine attributes which in themselves are absolutely good. So far as evil is really evil, it springs from not-being. The poet assigns a different value to this term in its relation to God and in its relation to man. In respect of God not-being is nothing, for God is real being, but in man it is the principle of evil which constitutes half of human nature. In the one case it is a pure negation, in the other it is positively and actively pernicious. We need not quarrel with the poet for coming to grief in his logic. There are some occasions when intense moral feeling is worth any amount of accurate thinking.

It is evident that the doctrine of divine unity implies predestination. Where God is and naught beside Him, there can be an Other agent than He, no act but His. "Thou didst not throw, when thou threwest, but God threw". Compulsion is felt only by those who do not love. To know God is to love Him; and the gnostic may answer, like the dervish who was asked how he fared:

"I fare as one by whose majestic will
The world revolves, floods rise and rivers flow,
Stars in their courses move; yea, death and life
Hang on his nod and fly to the ends of earth,
His ministers of mourning or of joy."

This is the Truth; but for the benefit of such as cannot bear it, Jalaluddin vindicates the justice of God by asserting that men have the power to choose how they will act, although their freedom is subordinate to the divine will. Approaching the question, "Why does God ordain and create evil?" he points out that things are known through their opposites, and that the existence of evil is necessary for the manifestation of good.

"Not-being and defect, wherever seen,
Are mirrors of the beauty of all that is.
The bone-setter, where should he try his skill
But on the patient lying with broken leg?
Were no base copper in the crucible,
How could the alchemist his craft display?"

Moreover, the divine omnipotence would not be completely realised if evil had remained uncreated.

"He is the source of evil, as thou sayest,
Yet evil hurts Him not. To make that evil
Denotes in Him perfection. Hear from me
A parable. The heavenly Artist paints

Beautiful shapes and ugly: in one picture
The loveliest women in the land of Egypt
Gazing on youthful Joseph amorously;
And lo, another scene by the same hand,
Hell-fire and Iblis with his hideous crew:
Both master-works, created for good ends,
To show His perfect wisdom and confound
The skeptics who deny His mastery.
Could He not evil make, He would lack skill;
Therefore He fashions infidel alike
And Moslem true, that both may witness bear
To Him, and worship One Almighty Lord."

In reply to the objection that a God who creates evil must Himself be evil, Jalaluddin, pursuing the analogy drawn from Art, remarks that ugliness in the picture is no evidence of ugliness in the painter. Again, without evil it would be impossible to win the proved virtue which is the reward of self-conquest. Bread must be broken before it can serve as food, and grapes will not yield wine till they are crushed. Many men are led through tribulation to happiness. As evil ebbs, good flows. Finally, much evil is only apparent.

What seems a curse to one may be a blessing to another; nay, evil itself is turned to good for the righteous. Jalaluddin will not admit that anything is absolutely bad.

"Fools buy false coins because they are like the true.
If in the world no genuine minted coin
Were current, how would forgers pass the false?
Falsehood were nothing unless truth were there,
To make it specious. 'Tis the love of right
Lures men to wrong. Let poison but be mixed
With sugar, they will cram it into their mouths.

Oh, cry not that all creeds are vain! Some scent
Of truth they have, else they would not beguile.
Say not, 'How utterly fantastical!'
No fancy in the world is all untrue.
Amongst the crowd of dervishes hides one,
One true fakir. Search well and thou wilt find!"

Surely this is a noteworthy doctrine. Jalaluddin died only a few years after the birth of Dante, but the Christian poet falls far below the level of charity and tolerance reached by his Moslem contemporary. How is it possible to discern the soul of goodness in things evil? By means of love, says Jalaluddin, and the knowledge which love alone can give, according to the word of God in the holy Tradition:

"My servant draws nigh unto Me, and I love him; and when I love him, I am his ear, so that he hears by Me, and his eye, so that he sees by Me, and his tongue, so that he speaks by Me, and his hand, so that he takes by Me."

Although it will be convenient to treat of mystical love in a separate chapter, the reader must not fancy that a new subject is opening before him. Gnosis and love are spiritually identical; they teach the same truths in different language.

5

Divine Love

Any one acquainted, however slightly, with the mystical poetry of Islam must have remarked that the aspiration of the soul towards God is expressed, as a rule, in almost the same terms which might be used by an Oriental Anacreon or Herrick. The resemblance, indeed, is often so close that, unless we have some clue to the poet's intention, we are left in doubt as to his meaning. In some cases, perhaps, the ambiguity serves an artistic purpose, as in the odes of Hafiz, but even when the poet is not deliberately keeping his readers suspended between earth and heaven; it is quite easy to mistake a mystical hymn for a drinking-song or a serenade. Ibn al-'Arabi, the greatest theosophist whom the Arabs have produced, found himself obliged to write a commentary on some of his poems in order to refute the scandalous charge that they were designed to celebrate the charms of his mistress. Here are a few lines:

- "Oh, her beauty-the tender maid! Its brilliance gives light like lamps to one traveling in the dark.
- She is a pearl hidden in a shell of hair as black as jet,
- A pearl for which Thought dives and remains unceasingly in the deeps of that ocean.
- He who looks upon her deems her to be a gazelle of the sand-hills, because of her shapely neck and the loveliness of her gestures."

It has been said that the Sufis invented this figurative style as a mask for mysteries which they desired to keep secret. That desire was natural in those who proudly claimed to possess an esoteric doctrine known only to them; moreover, a plain statement of what they believed might have endangered their liberties, if not their lives. But, apart from any such motives, the Sufis adopt the symbolic style because there is no other possible way of interpreting mystical experience. So little does knowledge of the infinite revealed in ecstatic vision need an artificial disguise that it cannot be communicated at all except through types and emblems drawn from the sensible world, which, imperfect as they are, may suggest and shadow forth a deeper meaning than appears on the surface.

"Gnostics," says Ibn al-'Arabi, "cannot impart their feelings to other men; they can only indicate them symbolically to those who have begun to experience the like." What kind of symbolism each mystic will prefer depends on his temperament and character. If he be a religious artist, a spiritual poet, his ideas of reality are likely to clothe themselves instinctively in forms of beauty and glowing images of human love. To him the rosy cheek of the beloved represents the divine essence manifested through its attributes; her dark curls signify the One veiled by the Many; when he says, "Drink wine that it may set you free from yourself," he means, "Lose your phenomenal self in the rapture of divine contemplation." I might fill pages with further examples.

This erotic and bacchanalian symbolism is not, of course, peculiar to the mystical poetry of Islam, but nowhere else is it displayed so opulently and in such perfection. It has often been misunderstood by European critics, one of whom even now can describe the ecstasies of the Sufis as "inspired partly by wine and strongly tinged with sensuality." As regards the whole body of Sufis, the charge is altogether false. No intelligent and unprejudiced student of their writings could have made it, and we ought to have been informed on what sort of evidence it is based. There are black sheep in every flock, and amongst the Sufis we find many hypocrites, debauchees, and drunkards who bring discredit on the pure brethren. But it is just as unfair to judge Sufism in general by the excesses of these impostors as it would be to condemn all Christian mysticism on the ground that certain sects and individuals are immoral.

"God is the Saqi {Cupbearer} and the Wine:

He knows what manner of love is mine,"

Said, Jalaluddin. Ibn al-'Arabi declares that no religion is more sublime than a religion of love and longing for God. Love is the essence of all creeds: the true mystic welcomes it whatever guise it may assume.

"My heart has become capable of every form: it is a pasture for gazelles and a convent for Christian monks,

And a temple for idols, and the pilgrim's Ka'ba, and the tables of the Tora and the book of the Koran.

I follow the religion of Love, whichever way his camels take.

My religion and my faith is the true religion.

We have a pattern in Bishr, the lover of Hind and her sister,and in Qays and Lubna, and in Mayya and Ghaylan."

Commenting on the last verse, the poet writes:

"Love, *quâ* love, is one and the same reality to those Arab lovers and to me; but the object of our love is different, for they loved a phenomenon, whereas I love the Real. They are a pattern to us, because God only afflicted them with love for human beings in order that He might show, by means of them, the falseness of those who pretend to love Him, and yet feel no such transport and rapture in loving Him as deprived those enamoured men of their reason, and made them unconscious of themselves."

Most of the great medieval Sufis lived saintly lives, dreaming of God, intoxicated with God. When they tried to tell their dreams, being men, they used the language of men. If they were also literary artists, they naturally wrote in the style of their own day and generation. In mystical poetry the Arabs yield the palm to the Persians. Any one who would read the secret of Sufism, no longer encumbered with theological articles nor obscured by metaphysical subtleties-let him turn to 'Attar, Jalaluddin Rumi, and Jami, whose works are partially accessible in English and other European languages. To translate these wonderful hymns is to break their melody and bring their soaring passion down to earth, but not even a prose translation can quite conceal the love of Truth and the vision of Beauty which inspired them. Listen again to Jalaluddin:

"He comes, a moon whose like the sky ne'er saw, awake or dreaming,

Crowned with eternal flame no flood can lay.

Lo, from the flagon of Thy love, O Lord, my soul is swimming,

And ruined all my body's house of clay.

When first the Giver of the grape my lonely heart befriended,

Wine fired my bosom and my veins filled up,

But when His image all mine eye possessed, a voice descended,

'Well done, O sovereign Wine and peerless Cup!'"

The love thus symbolised is the emotional element in religion, the rapture of the seer, the courage of the martyr, the faith of the saint, the only basis of moral perfection and spiritual knowledge. Practically, it is self-renunciation and self-sacrifice, the giving up of all possessions-wealth, honour, will, life, and whatever else men value-for the

Beloved's sake without any thought of reward. I have already referred to love as the supreme principle in Sufi ethics, and now let me give some illustrations.

"Love," says Jalaluddin, "is the remedy of our pride and self-conceit, the physician of all our infirmities. Only he whose garment is rent by love becomes entirely unselfish."

Nuri, Raqqam, and other Sufis were accused of heresy and sentenced to death. "When the executioner approached Raqqam, Nuri rose and offered himself in his friend's place with the utmost cheerfulness and submission. All the spectators were astounded. The executioner said, 'Young man, the sword is not a thing that people are so eager to meet; and your turn has not yet arrived.' Nuri answered, 'My religion is founded on unselfishness. Life is the most precious thing in the world: I wish to sacrifice for my brethren's sake the few moments which remain.'"

On another occasion Nuri was overheard praying as follows:

"O Lord, in Thy eternal knowledge and power and will Thou dost punish the people of Hell whom Thou hast created; and if it be Thy inexorable will to make Hell full of mankind, Thou art able to fill it with me alone, and to send them to Paradise."

In proportion as the Sufi loves God, he sees God in all His creatures, and goes forth to them in acts of charity. Pious works are naught without love.

"Cheer one sad heart: thy loving deed will be
More than a thousand temples raised by thee.
One freeman whom thy kindness hath enslaved
Outweighs by far a thousand slaves set free."

The Moslem *Legend of the Saints* abounds in tales of pity shown to animals (including the despised dog), birds, and even insects. It is related that Bayazid purchased some cardamom seed at Hamadhan, and before departing put into his gabardine a small quantity which was left over. On reaching Bistam and recollecting what he had done, he took out the seed and found that it contained a number of ants. Saying, "I have carried the poor creatures away from their home," he immediately set off and journeyed back to Hamadhan-a distance of several hundred miles.

This universal charity is one of the fruits of pantheism. The ascetic view of the world which prevailed amongst the early Sufis, and their vivid consciousness of God as a transcendent Personality rather than as an immanent Spirit, caused them to crush their human affections relentlessly. Here is a short story from the life of Fudayl ibn 'Iyad. It would be touching if it were not so edifying.

"One day he had in his lap a child four years old, and chanced to give it a kiss, as is the way of fathers. The child said, 'Father, do you love me?' 'Yes,' said Fudayl. 'Do you love God?' 'Yes.' 'How many hearts have you?' 'One.' 'Then,' asked the child, 'how can you love two with one heart?' Fudayl perceived that the child's words were a divine admonition. In his zeal for God he began to beat his head and repented of his love for the child, and gave his heart wholly to God."

The higher Sufi mysticism, as represented by Jalaluddin Rumi, teaches that the phenomenal is a bridge to the Real.

"Whether it be of this world or of that,
Thy love will lead thee yonder at the last."

And Jami says, in a passage which has been translated by Professor Browne:

"Even from earthly love thy face avert not,
Since to the Real it may serve to raise thee.
Ere A, B, C are rightly apprehended,
How canst thou con the pages of thy Koran?

A sage (so heard I), unto whom a student
Came craving counsel on the course before him,
Said, 'If thy steps be strangers to love's pathways,
Depart, learn love, and then return before me!
For, shouldst thou fear to drink wine from Form's flagon,
Thou canst not drain the draught of the Ideal.
But yet beware! Be not by Form belated:
Strive rather with all speed the bridge to traverse.
If to the bourne thou fain wouldst bear thy baggage,
Upon the bridge let not thy footsteps linger.'"

Emerson sums up the meaning of this where he says:

"Beholding in many souls the traits of the divine beauty, and separating in each soul that is divine from the taint which it has contracted in the world, the lover ascends to the highest beauty, to the love and knowledge of the Divinity, by steps on this ladder of created souls."

"Man's love of God," says Hujwiri, "is a quality which manifests itself, in the heart of the pious believer, in the form of veneration and magnification, so that he seeks to satisfy his Beloved and becomes impatient and restless in his desire for vision of Him, and cannot rest with any one except Him, and grows familiar with the recollection of Him, and abjures the recollection of everything besides. Repose becomes unlawful to him, and rest flees from him. He is cut off from all habits and associations, and renounces sensual passion, and turns towards the court of love, and submits to the law of love and knows God by His attributes of perfection."

Inevitably such a man will love his fellow-men. Whatever cruelty they inflict upon him, he will perceive only the chastening hand of God, "whose bitters are very sweets to the soul." Bayazid said that when God loves a man, He endows him with three qualities in token thereof: a bounty like that of the sea, a sympathy like that of the sun, and a humility like that of the earth. No suffering can be too great, no devotion too high, for the piercing insight and burning faith of a true lover. Ibn al-'Arabi claims that Islam is peculiarly the religion of love, inasmuch as the Prophet Mohammed is called God's beloved (*Habib*), but though some traces of this doctrine occur in the Koran, its main impulse was unquestionably derived from Christianity.

While the oldest Sufi literature, which is written in Arabic and unfortunately has come down to us in a fragmentary state, is still dominated by the Koranic insistence on fear of Allah, it also bears conspicuous marks of the opposing Christian tradition.

As in Christianity, through Dionysius and other writers of the Neoplatonic school, so in Islam, and probably under the same influence, the devotional and mystical love of God soon developed into ecstasy and enthusiasm which finds in the sensuous imagery of human love the most suggestive medium for its expression. Dr. Inge observes that the Sufis "appear, like true Asiatics, to have attempted to give a sacramental and symbolic character to the indulgence of their passions." I need not again point out that such a view of genuine Sufism is both superficial and incorrect.

Love, like gnosis, is in its essence a divine gift, not anything that can be acquired. "If the whole world wished to attract love, they could not; and if they made the utmost efforts to repel it, they could not." Those who love God are those whom God loves. "I fancied that I loved Him," said Bayazid, "but on consideration I saw that His love preceded mine." Junayd defined love as the substitution of the qualities of the Beloved for the qualities of the lover. In other words, love signifies the passing-away of the individual self; it is an uncontrollable rapture, a God-sent grace which must be sought by ardent prayer and aspiration.

"O Thou in whose bat well-curved my heart likes a ball is laid,

Nor ever a hairbreadth swerved from Thy bidding nor disobeyed,

I have washed mine outward clean, the water I drew and poured;

Mine inward is Thy demesne-do Thou keep it stainless, Lord!"

Jalaluddin teaches that man's love is really the effect of God's love by means of an apologue. One night a certain devotee was praying aloud, when Satan appeared to him and said:

"How long wilt thou cry, 'O Allah'? Be quiet, for thou wilt get no answer." The devotee hung his head in silence. After a little while he had a vision of the prophet Khadir, who said to him, "Ah, why hast thou ceased to call on God?" "Because the answer 'Here am I' came not," he replied. Khadir said, "God hath ordered me to go to thee and say this:

"'Was it not I that summoned thee to service?
Did not I make thee busy with My name?
Thy calling "Allah!" was *My "Here am I,"*
Thy yearning pains My messenger to thee.
Of all those tears and cries and supplications
I was the magnet, and I gave them wings.'"

Divine love is beyond description, yet its signs are manifest. Sari al-Saqati questioned Junayd concerning the nature of love. "Some say," he answered, "that it is a state of concord, and some say that it is altruism, and some say that it is so-and-so." Sari took hold of the skin on his forearm and pulled it, but it would not stretch; then he said, "I swear by the glory of God, were I to say that this skin hath shrivelled on this bone for love of Him, I should be telling the truth." Thereupon he fainted away, and his face became like a shining moon.

Love, 'the astrolabe of heavenly mysteries,' inspires all religion worthy of the name, and brings with it, not reasoned belief, but the intense conviction arising from immediate intuition. This inner light is its own evidence; he who sees it has real knowledge, and nothing can increase or diminish his certainty.

Hence the Sufis never weary of exposing the futility of a faith which supports itself on intellectual proofs, external authority, self-interest, or self-regard of any kind. The barren dialectic of the theologian; the canting righteousness of the Pharisee rooted in forms and ceremonies; the less crude but equally undisinterested worship of which the motive is desire to gain everlasting happiness in the life hereafter; the relatively pure devotion of the mystic who, although he loves God, yet thinks of himself as loving, and whose heart is not wholly emptied of 'otherness'-all these are 'veils' to be removed.

A few sayings by those who know will be more instructive than further explanation. "O God! Whatever share of this world Thou hast allotted to me, bestow it on Thine enemies; and whatever share of the next world Thou hast allotted to me, bestow it on Thy friends. Thou art enough for me." (Rabi'a)

"O God! If I worship Thee in fear of Hell, burn me in Hell; and if I worship Thee in hope of Paradise, exclude me from Paradise; but if I worship Thee for Thine own sake, withhold not Thine everlasting beauty!" (Rabi'a.)

"Notwithstanding that the lovers of God are separated from Him by their love, they have the essential thing, for whether they sleep or wake, they seek and are sought, and are not occupied with their own seeking and loving, but are enraptured in contemplation of the Beloved. It is a crime in the lover to regard his love, and an outrage in love to look at one's own seeking while one is face to face with the Sought." (Bayazid.)

"His love entered and removed all besides Him and left no trace of anything else, so that it remained single even as He is single." (Bayazid.)

"To feel at one with God for a moment is better than all men's acts of worship from the beginning to the end of the world." (Shibli.)

"Fear of the Fire, in comparison with fear of being parted from the Beloved, is like a drop of water cast into the mightiest ocean." (Dhu 'L Lun.)

"Unless I have the face of my heart towards Thee,
I deem prayer unworthy to be reckoned as prayer.
If I turn my face to the Ka'ba, 'tis for love of Thine;
Otherwise I am quit both of prayer and Ka'ba."
(Jalaluddin Rumi.)

Love, again, is the divine instinct of the soul impelling it to realise its nature and destiny. The soul is the first-born of God: before the creation of the universe it lived and moved and had its being in Him, and during its earthly manifestation it is a stranger in exile, ever pining to return to its home.

"This is Love: to fly heavenward,
To rend, every instant, a hundred veils;
The first moment, to renounce life;
The last step, to fare without feet;
To regard this world as invisible,
Not to see what appears to one's self."

All the love-romances and allegories of Sufi poetry-the tales of Layla and Majnun, Yusuf (Joseph) and Zulaykha, Salaman and Absal, the Moth and the Candle, the Nightingale and the Rose-are shadow-pictures of the soul's passionate longing to be reunited with God. It is impossible, in the brief space at my command, to give the reader more than a passing glimpse of the treasures which the exuberant fancy of the East has heaped together in every room of this enchanted palace. The soul is likened to a moaning dove that has lost her mate; to a reed torn from its bed and made into a flute whose plaintive music fills the eye with tears; to a falcon summoned by the fowler's whistle to perch again upon his wrist; to snow melting in the sun and mounting as vapour to the sky; to a frenzied camel swiftly plunging through the desert by night; to a caged parrot, a fish on dry land, a pawn that seeks to become a king.

These figures imply that God is conceived as transcendent, and that the soul cannot reach Him without taking what Plotinus in a splendid phrase calls "the flight of the Alone to the Alone." Jalaluddin says:

"The motion of every atom is towards its origin;

A man comes to be the thing on which he is bent.

By the attraction of fondness and yearning, the soul and the heart

Assume the qualities of the Beloved, who is the Soul of souls."

'A man comes to be the thing on which he is bent': what, then does the Sufi become? Eckhart in one of his sermons quotes the saying of St. Augustine that Man *is* what he loves, and adds this comment:

"If he loves a stone, he is a stone; if he loves a man, he is a man; if he loves God-I dare not say more, for if I said that he would then be God, ye might stone me."

The Moslem mystics enjoyed greater freedom of speech than their Christian brethren who owed allegiance to the medieval Catholic Church, and if they went too far the plea of ecstasy was generally accepted as a sufficient excuse. Whether they emphasise the outward or the inward aspect of unification, the transcendence or the immanence of God, their expressions are bold and uncompromising. Thus Abu Sa'id:

"In my heart Thou dwellest-else with blood I'll drench it;
In mine eye Thou glowest-else with tears I'll quench it.
Only to be one with Thee my soul desireth-
Else from out my body, by hook or crook, I'll wrench it!"

Jalaluddin Rumi proclaims that the soul's love of God is God's love of the soul, and that in loving the soul God loves Himself, for He draws home to Himself that which in its essence is divine.

"Our copper," says the poet, "has been transmuted by this rare alchemy," meaning that the base alloy of self has been purified and spiritualised. In another ode he says:

"O my soul, I searched from end to end: I saw in thee naught save the Beloved;

Call me not infidel, O my soul, if I say that thou thyself art He."

And yet more plainly:

"Ye who in search of God, of God, pursue,
Ye need not search for God is you, is you!
Why seek ye something that was missing ne'er?
Save you none is, but you are-where, oh, where?"

Where is the lover when the Beloved has displayed Himself? Nowhere and everywhere: his individuality has passed away from him. In the bridal chamber of Unity God celebrates the mystical marriage of the soul.

6

Saints and Miracles

No account of Islam is complete if it does not take into consideration the extraordinary efforts which the various Muslim sects have made to understand Islam, and the results which they have achieved. Islam is not merely a body of doctrines expressed in the *Quran* and the prophetic Traditions; neither is it best represented by the orthodox school at any particular time. It is a living religion which has received and is still receiving its vitality from the people who confess it; it is a great movement which has passed through various stages of development over its long and complicated history, influencing and being influenced by the religious and cultural forces in its environment. Through the interaction between Islam in its original form and those external forces some of the fundamental concepts of Muslim dogmas and practices were reinterpreted and reshaped. Some of these interpretations are not orthodox, it is true, but they are nevertheless Islamic, at least insofar as they are based on Islamic texts, even though the texts are examined under a different light.

It is the purpose of this chapter to discuss the interpretations gleaned from the writings of the old schools of Muslims - mystics and rationalists, including both the theologians and the philosophers - who are not usually regarded by the orthodox school as strict Muslims, but whose influence on Muslim thought and practical religious life is felt even today. The earliest rationalists were known as Mu'tazilites, and the mystics of Islam are the Sufis. The discussion in this chapter will be limited to the theological, philosophical, and mystical attitudes toward certain of the fundamental problems of dogmatic beliefs and religious practices in Islam.

THE THEOLOGICAL ATTITUDE

Islam, like all other great religions, has a theology of its own which aims at the establishment of its fundamental articles of faith and the refutation of heresy and innovation. The Prophet Muhammad was no theologian - nor was any prophet before him. In fact, the revelations that prophets have brought into the world defy any serious attempt at a systematic theology. The systematization of religious dogmas in Islam was a task undertaken by the followers of Muhammad when the need for the establishment of a Muslim theology was felt. The criterion for the early theology was taken by writers such as Ibn Khaldun and Adud al-Din al-Iji to be the teachings of the early Muslims and the orthodox party. In the opinion of these writers the Mu'tazilites (rationalists) and the Shi'as and many other theological schools are heretical.

This is too narrow a view to be adopted, and in dealing with Muslim theology here the term "theology" is used in a wider sense to include the speculative thinking of orthodox and non-orthodox theological schools. The fundamental principle which Muslim theology has always endeavored to establish is the principle of the unity of God.

On this principle Muslim theologians know no compromise. It is the keynote of Muslim faith and the root from which all other dogmas of Islam are derived. Hence Muslim theology is also called the science of unification (of God), because its object is to determine the nature of God and His attributes, and to explain the relation between Him and His creation, all of which follow as corollaries from a definite concept of Allah as the Absolute One.

The *Quran*, though not itself a book on theology, contains the rudiments of almost all theological problems. It speaks of God as the only one to be served, the Supreme Master and Ruler of the world. It asserts His absolute transcendence in these words, "Say: He is God alone. God the eternal: He begetteth not, nor is begotten; and there is nothing like unto Him" (Surah CXLI).

The *Quran* contains a long list of the attributes of God over which there has been much discussion and disputation among the Muslim theologians. It condemns polytheism, atheism, and deism; and it emphatically denies the eternity of the world. Although on the whole it is sympathetic to Christianity, it rejects the Christian Trinity and all its implications. In discussing these theological problems the style of the *Quran* varies considerably. Sometimes it takes the form of a logical argument - a syllogistic proof or an argument based on analogy - but more often it adopts the rhetorical style, calling on man to reflect upon himself and the wonderful world around him so that by means of such reflection he might know his Lord.

When dealing with moral precepts the *Quran* appeals to man's own conscience and bids him reflect upon his actions and the actions of his fellow men. Such were the seeds from which, under favorable conditions, an elaborate theology developed in the Muslim world. There was no science of theology during the lifetime of the Prophet and the first four Caliphs. The early Muslims accepted the word of the *Quran* literally. They raised no metaphysical or theological questions. When they were in doubt about a Quranic verse dealing with God or any of His attributes they were told to accept it as it was stated in the *Quran* with no further explanation or interpretation. The idea was to have faith in Islam, to propagate it, and to defend it, rather than to inquire into its nature. The orthodox party represented by Ahmad Ibn Hanbal (died 241; AD. 855) adhered strictly to tradition and opposed any form of independent thinking. Later on they even rejected the theological investigations made on strict Quranic lines, and looked with suspicion upon the teaching of the ascetics of their time.

They would only allow discussion of questions related to the law (shari'a) and the practical affairs of everyday life. But soon after the death of Muhammad political questions relating to his rightful successor were raised, and with them arose certain theological questions concerning the nature of the true Imam (Muslim head of state), the meaning of faith, sin, infidelity, punishment in the Future World, and so on. The interest was primarily political, but the contending parties gave their views a religious coloring, and there was much persecution and bloodshed in the name of religion. Political, or rather political-theological, parties appeared on the scene - the Kharijites, the Qadarites, the Shi'ites, the Murjites, and the Umayyads, who were the state party and the bitterest opponents of Ali and his followers.

This was a period of strife and dissension within the Muslim community during which the whole future of Islam was at stake. What interests us here is their discussion of faith, sin, and retribution. The Murjites - literally those who postpone; here, those who postpone judgment until it is pronounced by God on the Day of Judgment - were more tolerant than the others in their political views and more liberal-minded on theological questions. They believed that faith alone is sufficient for man salvation. The sinful believer who professes the unity of God and acknowledges His Prophet thus will not suffer everlasting punishment in Hell, a. view which was diametrically opposite to that of the Kharijites.

They even went so far as to say that a believer need not be a professed Muslim, for faith is a confession of the heart while Islam is an outward or public confession of the tongue. The question was taken up more seriously later when it lost its political significance and became a theological problem of academic interest. What is the real nature of faith, and what is its relation to religious practice? Does faith admit any degrees? That is, can one man be more faithful than another, or can one and the same person ascend higher and higher in the scale of faith? The Murjites denied the quantitative evaluation of faith, while the rest of the theologians held the view that faith admits increase and decrease. Faith is more nearly perfect when it is accompanied by actions, or better still, when it is so deeply rooted in the heart that it becomes the principle from which righteous actions necessarily follow.

Faith which is not accompanied by good works is like a tree which bears no fruit, but true faith becomes a "faculty of the heart" - as Ibn Khaldun calls it - which urges the faithful to perform their religious obligations and to abstain from sin. "A true believer," the Prophet says, "commits no adultery and no theft." In other words, to have real faith and to sin is a contradiction in terms. The theory that faith increases and decreases has its roots in the *Quran* in such passages as this, "The believers are they whose hearts thrill with fear when God's name is mentioned, and whose faith increases at each recital of His words, and who put trust in their Lord" (Surah VIII, 2). Such were the beginnings of the era in which Muslim theology was being formed. But these rudimentary and altogether primitive speculations on certain religious problems soon assumed larger proportions when Muslim scholars who were skilled in the art of dialectic and tolerably conversant with Greek philosophy appeared on the scene. There were now two important factors which helped the development of the new theology, one internal and the other external.

The internal factor is the nature of the *Quran* itself. As has been pointed out in previous chapters, the *Quran* contains two different types of verses, those which form the main substance of the Book and are clear and definite in their meaning, and the comparatively few verses which are dubious or less definite. This is admitted in one of the Medina revelations which run as follows, "He (God) it is who hath sent down to thee the Book. Some of its verses are of themselves perspicuous; they are the basis of the Book; and others are dubious. Those whose hearts are inclined to error follow the dubious verses, thereby seeking discord and seeking interpretation. But none knoweth its interpretation save God. Those who are firm in knowledge say: We believe therein- it is all from our Lord. But none will bear this in mind save men endued with understanding" (Surah III, 7).

The reason for the presence of these dubious verses in the *Quran* has been discussed by theologians. The majority incline to believe that they are purposely given as a trial in order to test the strength and validity of man's faith. Those whose faith is firm accept them unquestionably, while others whose hearts are inclined to error - as the *Quran* says - reject them or interpret them in such a way as to cause discord in the Muslim community. Whatever the real reason may be, the fact remains that these dubious verses played an important role in stirring up dispute among Muhammad's followers of the second generation. Out of these disputes emerged different parties, each supporting a different point of view. It is worth while quoting Ibn Khaldun on the subject. He says, in his *Prolegomena:*

In the *Quran* there are passages which describe God as an absolutely transcendent Being. Their meaning is clear and admits of no interpretation. They are all negative statements; and, on account of their clarity, are accepted by all believers.... The other passages which are comparatively few are suggestive of anthropomorphism [these are the dubious passages]. They were accepted [by the early Muslims] without any enquiry into their meaning.

But the innovators of their time resorted to a different method, by subjecting the dubious passages to critical examination. Some exaggerated their anthropomorphic side and attributed to God hands, face, feet, and so on, thus falling into gross corporealism and violating the absolute transcendence of God which is explicitly mentioned in numerous other passages and with such undoubted clarity. Others admitted anthropomorphism with regard to the attributes of God such as occupying a place, sitting on the Throne, coming and going and speaking in words, and so on. They, like the others, also drifted into corporealism.

The disputes centering around such passages had a far-reaching effect on the course of the development of many theological doctrines which occupied the minds of Muslims for generations. We can even find some traces of these theological disputes in modern times. The second, or external, factor in the development of Muslim theology is the cultural influences which were brought to bear upon Islam from without. Up to the second half of the second century we meet only the individual men who expressed their opinions on some religious problems. There was no general or recognized system of religious thought; there were no real theological schools, although there was what we might call semi-theological parties. The course of development changed when foreign influence came into play. Some ethical problems were raised, particularly the problem of determinism and free will.

Such metaphysical problems as were inspired by the *Quran* also came to the fore - the problem of the attributes of God, the divine attribute of speech and the *Quran* as the eternal word of God, the problem of beholding the vision of God in the next world, and so on. It is significant that most of the major issues in religion were discussed in Syria, which was an important center of Christian theology. We know that John of Damascus the great doctor of the Greek Church was a Vizier (Minister) under the Umayyads, and that he and his pupil Theodorus Abucara wrote polemic treatises on Islam summarizing discussions between Christians and Muslims. Some of these treatises were written in a catechetical form: If a Muslim asks you such and such a question, answer so and so. This is taken as evidence that direct contact between Muslim and Christian scholars must have taken place at an early stage. But while the possibility of such contact is admitted, there is no justification for the exaggerated view put forward by such scholars as De Boer, Von Kremer, and D. B. Macdonald that the development of Muslim theology was largely influenced by Christian thought.

The other foreign factor which influenced Muslim theology, particularly in its mature form, is Greek philosophy. We can see traces of it in almost all the leading theological theories - either in the bearing of some Greek concepts on such theories, or in the way they were presented and discussed. Yet, here again, Greek ideas never remained unaltered; they were given such a turn as to harmonize with the fundamental concepts of Islam. A consideration of the two major issues in Muslim theology - God and the problem of divine attributes, and man and the problem of free will - will illustrate the significant trends in the development of Islamic theological thought.

THE THEOLOGICAL CONCEPTION OF GOD

A variety of concepts of God, ranging from crude anthropomorphism to absolute transcendentalism, have their roots in the *Quran*. V/hen the Muslim theologians began to reflect on the nature of God, they found themselves faced with two types of Quranic verses: those which describe God in relation to His creation, and those which describe Him in Himself. According to the former, God sees, hears, speaks to His people, creates with His hands, sits on His Throne, comes with His Angels, and will be seen on the Day of Judgment. They also ascribe to God typically human qualities such as pleasure and displeasure, love and hatred, and the like. These attributes are some of the ingredients, so to speak, of the personality of the one God who speaks to His servants and hears their call, loves the righteous, and hates the wicked. The Prophet says, "Pray to God as if thou seest Him, for if thou seest Him not, He seeth thee." That is, picture God as a person, for you cannot address yourself in prayer to the Absolute.

The second set of Quranic verses, those which describe God in Himself, refer to the divine attributes of transcendence by which God is distinguished from created beings. The question is: Can we predicate attributes of God at all? The *Quran* certainly does. God is described as omnipotent, as omniscient, as knowing and willing, as eternal, infinite, everlasting, and unlike all created beings. Some of these attributes are positive, others are negative. Can they all be predicated of God in the same way? The orthodox party maintains that they can, but they do not go into what such predication logically implies. The Mu'tazilites examine the implications of such predication. The negative attributes present no difficulty and are therefore admitted by them. The positive ones are either reduced to negations or denied as separate entities distinct from or added to the divine Essence. They do not deny that God knows, wills, and does things, but deny that His knowledge or will or action is different from and coeternal with His Essence. They are all identical with the Essence.

To assert the separate existence of the divine attributes which are eternal because they belong to God is to assert a plurality of eternal beings, which is contrary to the oneness of God. Some Mu'tazilites went so far as to deny all positive attributes. To say that God knows such and such a thing, they say, means that He is not ignorant thereof, and the same with the rest of the attributes. It is interesting to notice that the first Muslim thinker to deny the divine attributes in the above sense was Wasil Ibn Ata (died 131; AD. 748) in his refutation of the Christian doctrine of the Trinity, which he considered a plurality of eternal attributes in one Essence. His view received more elaboration in the later circles of the Mu'tazilites who gave it a more philosophical turn. God was reduced by them to a simple monad stripped of all attributes and qualities. Hence they were called by their opponents *Mu'attila,* that is, those who render the divine attributes useless or functionless. The opposite view was held by the orthodox party and later by the Ash'arite school. Their argument on the whole is not very convincing, and most of it is quibbling with words.

God, they say, has attributes, but they are neither identical with His Essence nor different from it. They are "states" which though distinguishable from the Essence are yet inherent in it. The whole trouble, it seems, rested on one fundamental misconception: they personified the attributes but went on thinking they were dealing with the ordinary simple attributes of God. To talk about an eternal attribute which is different from the divine Essence but coexistent with it is to personify it and give it the status of a substance - a position very similar to that of the Christian Trinity. Had these theologians said that the attributes were mere intelligible relations qualifying the Essence, or mere names with which God has described Himself, the question as to their identity or nonidentity with the divine Essence and the other question as to their eternity or temporality would not have arisen? The failure to realize the significance of describing the attributes of God from two different aspects is responsible for most of the disputes and futile arguments with which Muslim books on theology abound.

The two contending parties - the traditionalists and rationalists - concentrated on one set of attributes to the comparative neglect of the other. The result was two extreme views, with corporealism or moderate anthropo-morphism on the one side and absolute trans-cendentalism on the other. The Mu'tazilites, who were the champions of transcendentalism, resorted to a method of interpretation which explained away all the anthropomorphic passages in the *Quran*, and they discarded the anth-ropomorphic Prophetic Traditions as invalid or not authentic. This was necessary to preserve their conception of the absolute unity and transcendence of God. The traditionalists wavered between immanence and transcendence but were more inclined toward immanence. The rational interpretation of the Mu'tazilites had its advantages as well as its disadvantages. In one respect it helped to liberate Islam from the materialistic and mythological concepts of God by insisting on the more spiritual and abstract attributes. But it was carried to an extreme by some of the rationalists who reduced the Godhead to an abstraction void of all content.

The enquiry into the nature of the divine attributes naturally led to a discussion on the nature of the *Quran* as the revealed word of God or the external manifestation of the attribute of divine speech. The orthodox, who held the doctrine of the eternity of the attributes, said the *Quran* was eternal. The rationalists said it was created, or there would be something eternal other than God, and this would be a violation of His oneness. The Prophet to whom the *Quran* was revealed did not hear the words of God, but heard a voice which God created in a material medium and which conveyed to him the content of the divine mind. The *Quran* as we know it is therefore created. This was the doctrine of the Mu'tazilites which was championed by the Abbasid Caliph al-Ma'mun. When the triumphant days of the Mu'tazilites were ended, the orthodox party saw their opportunity once again and declared that all was uncreated, even the very Word written in the Book and recited in man's prayer.

The Ash'arite school took up the problem later and discussed it on a higher level. They were influenced by older speculations on a similar subject, particularly the Christian and Jewish theories of the Logos, which in their turn were influenced by ancient Greek theories. The Ash'arites held that God's speech was eternal. The *Quran*, the divine command, and the creative Word *Be*, were all forms of the eternal attribute of speech. "The command of God," says the *Quran*, "is such that when God wills a thing, He says to it: Be; and it is" (Surah XXXVI, 81). The creative command and the creative Word *Be* are therefore prior to all phenomenal existence. The *Quran* also says, "One of His signs is that the heavens and the earth are sustained by His command" (Surah XXX, 25). Thus the divine command is not only the instrument of creation, it is also the sustaining principle of the created world. Such verses were originally meant to emphasize the absolute sovereignty of God as the supreme Creator and Maintainer of the universe, but a new meaning was read into them by the Ash'arites in support of a Logos theory comparable in many respects to the Christian and Stoic theories.

The divine command and creative Word were personified and given power to create and sustain that which they create. Moreover, the Word, or Logos, is in one respect identical with God, in another different from Him and coeternal with Him. Thus the Word of God gradually took a place similar to that of the Memra in Jewish theology, and the Second Person in the Christian doctrine of the Trinity. The Ash'arites went a step further.

They distinguished between two kinds of speech, the external and the internal. The external, which consists of words and sounds and can be put down in writing, is created. The internal, which is expressed by such words and sounds, is identical with the divine consciousness and is therefore eternal. This distinction is certainly borrowed from the philosophy of the Stoics who spoke of potential and actual, or internal and external Logoi. It is also in line with the Christian theory of the Logos which distinguishes the Word which was from eternity with God and was God from the Word which appeared in a temporal manifestation in the form of Christ.

Perhaps the earlier Ash'arites did not express themselves in such plain words. They did not work out the metaphysical implications of their theory. They were more concerned with the problems of the eternity of the *Quran* which they thought they had proved. What they actually proved is the eternity of the divine mind or the divine knowledge, and the temporal manifestation of this knowledge when revealed to the Prophet. This position was taken up by al-Ghazali and later Ash'arites.

DETERMINISM AND FREE WILL

The ethical problem of determinism and free will has its roots in the much wider metaphysical problem of the conception of God in His relation to the world in general and mankind in particular. The pessimistic attitude of the Semitic mind toward the world as a fleeting shadow, the notion that it has value only as a place in which man prepares himself for a more permanent life, led to the conception that God is the absolute sovereign power which rules all things, including man and his actions. We have a definite trace of this conception in the *Quran*. God is the supreme King of Heaven and earth whose authority is not to be challenged. The following examples are typical of a large number of similar texts in the *Quran*. "He should not be asked concerning what He does" (Surah XXI, 23). "He createth what He will" (Surah XXX, 54) "He it is Who created you from dust" (Surah XL, 67). "He alone misguides whomever He pleases and guides whomever He pleases" (Surah XXXV, 8).

And in talking to his people, Noah says, "Nor shall my counsel profit you if God wills to misguide you, though I fain would counsel you aright. God is your Lord, and unto Him shall ye return" (Surah XI, 34). This is one side of the picture; in its theological aspect it emphasizes the absolute authority of God over His creation and in its ethical aspect suggests a deterministic theory of man's actions. The other side of the picture shows the same two aspects closely related to one another. God, who is described as supreme power and will, is also described as just. The following typical passage from thc *Quran* illustrates the justice of God. "We will not burden a soul beyond its power; with us is a Book which speaks the truth, and they shall not be unjustly treated" (Surah XXIII, 62). "These are the signs of God: we recite them to thee in truth and God wills not injustice to mankind" (Surah III, 108). "God does them no injustice; it is they who are unjust to themselves" (Surah III, 117). "In truth has God created the heavens and the earth that each soul shall be rewarded for what he has earned, and that they shall not be wronged" (Surah XLV, 22). Thus, according to the *Quran,* justice is an essential attribute of God, and it is inconceivable that God can be the absolute despot who wills and acts as He pleases even if His actions are contrary to justice.

It is obvious that the two opposite theories, determinism and free will, can be traced back to a conflict between two conceptions of the nature of God - God as absolute power and God as just. The early Muslims who were the true sons of the desert preferred to think of God after the pattern of a tribal God with unlimited authority, a conception from which they derived their ethical theory of determinism. Their God can do everything, even that which is unjust or unreasonable. On the ethical side they taught that man was nothing but an instrument in the hands of his Lord, subjected to the strictest laws of determinism. This theory, known as oriental fatalism, has caused Islam to be stigmatized as a fatalistic religion, but nothing could be farther from the truth, for Islam attaches the greatest importance to the role which man plays in the sphere of his actions.

The Mu'tazilites, on the other hand, emphasized man s responsibility for his own actions. They argued against the despotism of God as well as against determinism and fatalism and put their whole trust in human reason, which to them was sacred. They taught that appeal should be made to reason first, rather than to the religious law. Reason tells us that we are the authors of our own actions and that some of them are right and others are wrong. Perception of right and wrong is an innate power of the human mind not due to knowledge taught by religion. Man therefore is a free agent and the maker of his own destiny. He is also the maker of his own moral law which must coincide with the religious law because the religious law is rational. There can be no religious injunction which is contrary to reason.

Man, however, is not purely rational, according to the Mu'tazilites. There is an irrational element in man to which he sometimes yields. This is why he sometimes goes astray and falls into error and sin, and this is why religion is needed as a reminder to the forgetful and to those whose rational will is thwarted by carnal desires. The Muslim rationalists were certainly on the road to Kant.

The good will is the only thing that has intrinsic value in moral life, and it is man's own without freedom of the will and personal responsibility, retribution, punishment and reward, and the Future Life with its. Heaven and Hell are all empty words void of meaning. Rationality is not only the guiding principle in man's actions and beliefs, according to the Muslim rationalists; it is also the ruling principle in the cosmos. This world is the best of all possible worlds because it is the work of a supreme Mini The so-called evil in the world is an integral part of the goodness of the whole.

The root of the doctrine of free will is to be found in the *Quran* itself and there is no justification for seeking an external source for it. In fact, the Quranic passages in favor of free will by far outnumber those which are suggestive of determinism. "And say: The truth is from your Lord: let him then who will, believe, and let him who will be an infidel" (Surah XVIII, 30). "This truly is a reminder: and who so wills, takes the road to his Lord" (Surah LXXVI, 29). "Say: Everyone acts after his manner; but your Lord knows who is best guided in his path" (Surah XVII, 84). "He who does evil or acts unjustly against himself, then asks pardon of God, will find God forgiving, merciful. And he who commits a crime, commits it to his own hurt" (Surah IV, 111-12).

According to the *Quran* man is free to choose his actions and beliefs, and he merits punishment or reward according to whether his choice is right or wrong. It is for God to show the right path, and for man to follow it or not follow it. Everything is predestined in the sense that it is predetermined by man's nature and known as such to God from eternity. The eternal knowledge of God does not interfere one iota with man's choice. Only in this sense can any meaning be attached to moral and religious obligations. Man alone works out his salvation and this by faith and good deeds. Faith is rarely mentioned alone in the *Quran;* it is usually coupled with good deeds as the necessary prerequisites for entering paradise. "Bring good tidings to those who believe and do the good things that are right, that for them are gardens 'neath which rivers flow" (Surah II, 25). "Those who have believed and done the good things that are right; they shall be the inmates of Paradise" (Surah II, 82).

THE PHILOSOPHICAL ATTITUDE

The attitude of the Muslim philosophers toward Islam is somewhat different from that of the theologians. The main object of the theologians was to defend, in their own way, Islamic dogmas. The philosophers sought to reconcile Islamic dogmas with philosophic ideas, to arrive at a conception of God which would satisfy the requirements of free thought as well as those of religious beliefs. The conception of God as the ultimate ground of all phenomenal existence had somehow or other to be brought into harmony with the conception of the personal God of Islam.

To what extent the attempt was successful we shall see later. The first Muslims to philosophize about the simple ideas of Islam were the Mu'tazilites. They were followed by the philosophers al-Kindi, al-Farabi, and Ibn Sina (Avicenna). The philosophers were on the whole contemptuous of their predecessors. Even al-Ghazali could not conceal his disappointment with the method of the theologians. "Their method," he says, "is right only insofar as it accomplishes their own objective; but it is of no avail to anyone who admits nothing but self-evident truths."

Generally speaking one can say that the theological method had no philosophic basis, though this applies more to the school of the Ash'arites than the Mu'taziites. The Ash'arites were skeptical in their attitude toward sense data. They denied causality and causal necessity and even refused to call God the First Cause. They taught that natural phenomena appear to be uniform not because they are subject to necessary laws but because the human mind reads sequence into them. At any moment God may interrupt such uniformities and cause miraculous things to happen. Nothing takes place as a result of interrelations between natural phenomena. Everything is fresh creation. Their whole conception of God and the natural world was different from, and directed against, the Aristotelian philosophy which forms the basis of the thinking of the Muslim philosophers.

It is impossible to give an account of the individual systems of all the philosophers of Islam here. In this general treatment of the subject the aim will be to set forth the attitude of the school of al-Farabi and Ibn Sina, who represent Muslim philosophy in its strict and more limited sense. Ibn Sina in particular represents this philosophy in its mature and final form in a clear and well-reasoned manner. His object, like that of all Muslim philosophers before and after him, was to find a formula by which religious dogmas and philosophic principles can be reconciled. In this he was the faithful follower of al-Farabi. For both of them Greek philosophy was almost infallible, yet they acknowledged, in their own way, the basic theological principles of Islam. Their philosophy therefore is a mixture of ideas often irreconcilable except with the help of the drastic method of explaining away the opposite concepts.

It is also highly eclectic in character, but eclecticism was not entirely the work of the Muslim mind as some scholars maintain. Two of the most important sources from which the Muslim thinkers drew considerable material reached them in an already eclectic form - Neo-platonism and Hermetic philosophy. Plato and Aristotle had already been brought into some harmony and their ideas interpreted in the light of the ancient wisdom of the Orient with its characteristic religious sentiment. This made them all the more appealing to the Muslim philosophers whose aim was to philosophize Islam. When Greek thought found its way into the Muslim world, the philosophers found them faced with a problem which they attempted to solve. On the one hand Islam called them to a simple faith in God who is the sole creator and sustainer of the world. It offered them no philosophy or even a basis for one.

On the other hand, Greek philosophy in the form in which it came to them represented the final achievements reached by the Greek mind in its search for a solution of the problem of existence. It was impossible for Muslims to accept without alteration any religious teaching which, outwardly at least, contradicted their philosophic ideas. But it was equally impossible to go the full length with Greek philosophical theories and accept their necessary consequences. Therefore, the only way left open to them was to reconcile the two. The question was - which of the Greek philosophical theories should they accept? Aristotle's theory of a Prime Mover who set the whole world in motion, then left it to its own fate? Or Plato's theory of God as the supreme Idea of Good - whose relation to the existing world he left unexplained? Or the Stoic's theory of pantheism or the Neo-platonic theory of emanation?

Those were the chief Greek theories of the nature of God known to the Muslims, and none of them could possibly be accepted by them without serious modification. The pantheistic view of reality never appeared in the Muslim philosophy of the type we are discussing here, but a full-fledged theory of pantheism was put forward later by the greatest of all Muslim mystics, Muhy al-Din Ibn Arabi. We shall say more about him later. The Muslim philosophers made use of Platonic, Aristotelian, and Neo-platonic ideas in constructing their own metaphysics, in which Islamic ideas also play an important part. But even the Islamic concepts were interpreted in such a way as to make them more philosophical, thus narrowing the gulf between Islamic and pagan thought.

The problem with which Muslim philosophers were faced was that of the relation between the external world, with its multiplicity of spatio-temporal and changeable phenomena, and an ultimate, immutable, and unchangeable First Principle. In philosophical language, the problem was that of the relation between the one and the many, or the noumenon and the phenomena; in theological language it was the problem of God and the universe. The Greek thinkers were far from the idea of the Godhead as explained in revealed religions. Aristotle's philosophy is one of strict determinism in which both the material world and God are subject to a supreme law of self-necessity. The metaphysical-poetical conception of Plato reduces God to a mere abstraction. It was the Neoplatonists who, though in the main adhering to their pagan tradition, put forward some sort of a philosophy of religion.

It is no wonder therefore that they paved the way for establishing Christian and Muslim philosophy of religion, and that their influence in Muslim religious thought in particular was predominant. The attempt to reconcile Islam with Greek philosophy in general and Neo-platonism in particular was an honest but a very daring one. Whether the Muslim philosophers succeeded or failed is another matter, but the fact remains that through making the effort they made their genuine contribution to the history of human thought. They also exposed themselves to the severest criticism of their adversaries. Ghazali's vehement attacks on their views will be referred to later. Ibn Sina is generally regarded as a true representative of the philosophy which sought to reconcile Islamic and Neoplatonic thought. His metaphysical views are regarded by no less an authority than Ghazali as being the most typical of his school, and when Ghazali launches his attacks against the philosophers he has Ibn Sina in mind all the time.

Al-Farabi is also an excellent type, but he lacks the clarity and comprehensiveness of his successor. Al-Kindi is more of a logician, natural philosopher, and theologian. Ibn Rushd's (Averroes) greatness is to be found more in his commentaries on Aristotle than in independent philosophical thought. The rest of the Muslim philosophers of the West are mere satellites moving around al-Farabi and Ibn Sina.

GOD AND THE WORLD

Ibn Sina prefers to call God the Necessary Being, or the Self-Subsistent Being, rather than Allah. His intention is to bridge the gulf between the religious and philosophical concepts of the Deity, and thus to be able to follow up his analysis of being and necessity, or self-subsistence, to their logical conclusions. The name Allah has some Muslim associations which make it unphilosophical. Ibn Sina starts his analysis of the relation between God and the world with a consideration of the notion of being - a purely ontological procedure - which he divides into necessary and contingent being. The necessary being is that being whose existence is self-necessitated; it exists *per se*; its essence and existence are identical; the supposition of its nonexistence involves contradiction. The contingent being is that which has no essential or necessary reason for its existence; its being or nonbeing are equally possible; its essence is different from its existence.

This is the phenomenal world; it is all that is "other than God." Ibn Sina says that the mere fact that we have a notion of the Necessary Being proves that He exists. Existence is a positive quality of perfection, and if we have an idea of the Perfect Being, that Perfect Being must exist, or our idea would be self-contradictory. This is the ontological argument used in modern philosophy by Descartes and Leibnitz, though the consequences which Ibn Sina draws are different. Ibn Sina also makes use of the Aristotelian distinction between necessity and contingency, but goes far beyond what Aristotle has said in the subject, both in his proof of the existence of God and in his explanation of the relation between God and the universe. He criticizes the cosmological argument of the theologians by which they infer the existence of an eternal Creator from the existence of the phenomenal world. Contingency, he says, not origination in time, is the cause of the dependence of the world upon God.

To say that it is origination in time - that is, creation - leads to these absurdities: that God's will and creative power were idle for an infinite time before the creation of the world; that to choose the creation of the world at a certain time, and not before or after that time, must have been due to circumstances outside God's nature, which means that some sort of change must have taken place in Him; and that the world after it has been created could very well be independent of its Creator, since its need of Him is only for creation and not for preservation after creation. A contingent universe, on the other hand, has no temporal beginning and is dependent for its existence and the continuity of its existence on God. It is an eternal being which derives its existence every moment from God. There is only logical - not temporal - priority between them, the priority of cause to effect.

The cause has never existed in time before its effect in this case. We can also call it priority of rank since the cause is usually regarded as superior to the effect. Here Ibn Sina is in complete agreement with Aristotle and in complete disagreement with the theologians who insist on the idea of creation, which is one of the principle dogmas of Islam. The world, they hold, was created out of nothing by the will of God and at the time He appointed. No question should be asked as to why it was not created before or after, because such relations as before and after have no application within the domain of the eternal Will. This is the argument adduced by Ghazali in his refutation of the philosophers' doctrine of the eternity of the world.

In spite of his theory of the eternity of the world, Ibn Sina describes God as the Maker, the Fashioner, and sometimes the Creator of the world. These epithets occur in the *Quran* and have one definite sense in common - bringing the world into existence from nothing. Ibn Sina, who believed in the impossibility of creation out of nothing, explains these terms in such a way as to deprive them of their temporal significance. That which comes into being need not always have a temporal beginning, nor need it be the result of an act of will. It can be the result of a spontaneous and necessary overflowing of being from an original source, like the overflowing of the rays from the sun. This is the case with regard to the world in its relation to God. If eternity and necessity are essential attributes of God as the Primary Cause, so must they be attributes of His actions, which are His effects. Thus we see how far Ibn Sina went in his deterministic philosophy. Necessity is the fundamental law to which both the phenomenal world and God Himself are subjected.

THE ATTRIBUTES OF GOD

The conception of God in Muslim philosophy, in spite of all that has been said, is not quite the same as the Aristotelian conception. God, according to al-Farabi and Ibn Sina, is not a mere principle of action within the material world but is an independent and transcendent Being over and above the material world, forever producing it and preserving it.

Their conception of the Godhead is both theological and philosophical. God has two different kinds of attributes: metaphysical attributes, which can be inferred directly or indirectly from the definition of God as the Necessary Being; and theological attributes with which God describes Himself in the *Quran*. Even the metaphysical attributes are often tinged with a religious color and explained in a way which makes them partly ethical and partly theological. This is because these philosophers are forever oscillating between philosophy and religion, although their loyalty on the whole is to philosophy.

According to Ibn Sina the divine attributes are simplicity, oneness, absolute perfection, pure goodness; God is the contemplator and the contemplated; God has neither equal nor opposite. Simplicity logically follows from the definition of God as the Necessary Being; for complexity, whether material, quantitative, or even intelligible, is contrary to necessity and self-subsistence. The complex, whatever it is, is dependent on its constituent parts and on something else to make it a whole.

It follows, therefore, that God is not a material substance, is not divisible, is not a compound of two or more substances, and is not definable. Oneness is an attribute of God; for God is one m every He has no partner who participates either in His or in His attributes. This is the first article of the faith. Plurality of gods contradicts the notion of self-necessity.

Absolute perfection is an attribute of God. God is perfect and complete. In Aristotle's language, God is pure actuality; there is nothing that is possible in Him which is actually not realized - His will, His knowledge, and His action, the whole of His nature. Everything else is in the process of becoming. The perfection of everything other than God is a potentiality which God brings into an actuality. Pure goodness is an attribute inferred from God's being free from matter and potentiality. Goodness here is equivalent to positive being, the opposite of evil or not-being. All other things possess the two aspects of being and not-being, because in one respect they are actual and in another they are potential. God is not only the pure good. He is also the fountainhead from which good - positive being - is forever flowing into everything in the world. The whole realm of existence turns toward Him in love-like fashion for the good it receives from Him, for the qualities of being through which the world advances along the road to perfection.

The world in fact does love God, because it loves the good, and good is the only thing that is loved for its own sake. Through love, therefore, God sets the whole world in motion, and whatever takes place in existence is the fruit of this love. Ibn Sina, who is not so successful in his theory about God as the Active Cause, admirably succeeds in portraying Him as the Final Cause. His argument here is potent, clear, and free from verbal quibbling. In fact, it is the most beautiful part of his metaphysics; it is here that his philosophy and mysticism meet. The relation between God and the external world is here expressed in terms of love and revelation - love on the part of the world, and revelation on the part of the Beloved. The divine act of bestowing being on things is the very act of self-revelation. God reveals Himself to His creatures in a manner suitable to the requirements of their inner nature, which is fixed and immutable, or in proportion to the degree of perfection which they aspire to achieve.

The divine Providence is the work of a mind which comprehends an orderly system gradually unfolding itself. The self-unfolding of the phenomenal world is paralleled in the eternal self-revelation of God, and the two processes are inseparable.

Ibn Sina's theodicy, aesthetics, and optimistic theory of the nature of the world branch off from this mystical philosophy. It is here that he seems to be more under the influence of Plato and Plotinus than Aristotle. For Ibn Sina, God is essentially an intellect whose sole activity is to contemplate Himself. He is the contemplator and the contemplated, the subject and the object in one. There is no duality in Him as there is in other minds. Duality of any kind is contrary to His absolute unity and simplicity.

There is a great deal of discussion about the knowledge of the Divine Mind. The theologians, following the *Quran,* hold that God knows everything past, present, and future, seen and unseen. They say that He is omniscient, that nothing takes place in the world which is not in accordance with His prior knowledge. The philosophers, on the other hand, maintain that God's knowledge is primarily of Himself and that, knowing Him; He knows the world in a general way. He is the Ultimate Cause of things, as we have explained, and knowledge of the cause entails knowledge of the effect. They argue that knowledge of individual happenings in the world depends on a temporal relation between the knower and the known and therefore involves change in the knower, but God's knowledge is above time and change.

Ibn Sina also maintains that God has neither an equal nor an opposite. He has no equal because it is impossible for two necessary beings (gods) to be. He has no opposite because two opposites must be similar in one respect and dissimilar in another respect, in which they are said to be opposites - and God has no similar in any respect whatsoever. Therefore He has no opposite.

The Muslim philosophers do not omit the Quranic attributes of God such as omnipotence, omniscience, justice, generosity, and the like, but they interpret them philosophically or explain them away. We have already given the attributes of knowledge and will as examples. So it is quite evident that their concept of God is neither the pagan conception of the Greek philosophers nor the strictly orthodox Islamic conception.

The denial of creation in its ordinary sense and the doctrine of the eternity of the world are definitely non-Islamic. In their view, however, they have shifted the problem to a higher plane by maintaining that the world is the outcome of God's inner necessity and the eternal urge within Him to give an outward manifestation of His bounty and generosity.

Although on the theoretical side the Muslim philosophers certainly seemed to be anti-Islamic, at least in some of their views, on the practical side they were true Muslims, insofar as we can gather from their biographies. Al-Farabi is said to have led a saintly life of religious devotion and contemplation. Ibn Sina, though allowing himself some bodily indulgences, is not reported to have neglected his religious duties. It is true that his conceptions of Heaven and Hell and the Resurrection are somewhat unorthodox, but he does not completely deny the orthodox concepts. We will conclude this section with his own words, taken from his *Nine Epistles:*

> The ultimate object of man wherein lies his greatest happiness in future life is to gain knowledge of the realities of things so far as his nature allows, and do what is incumbent upon him. Only in this way does man's soul become more honorable and perfect, an intelligible microcosm comparable to the existing Macrocosm, and become ready to enjoy the greatest happiness in the world to come.

THE MYSTICAL ATTITUDE

The mysticism of Islam is known as Sufism, a name said to be derived from the Arabic word *suf* which means wool, referring to the woollen mantles worn by the Sufis. With Muslim mysticism we see the climax of the development of religious life and teaching in Islam. Neither the philosophers nor the theologians nor the canon lawyers have contributed so much as the mystics toward deepening the meaning of their religion and enriching its teachings. It is due to them that Islam, in the way they understand it, can be compared with other great religions of the world, for mysticism is the only ground on which the great religions meet.

Muslim mysticism has, from the time of its inception, been a spiritual revolution against a variety of forms and systems, both social and religious. After a long period of hard struggle, Sufism established itself in two quite different ways: as a religious philosophy and as the popular religion of Islam. During some of its flourishing periods, the Sufis were counted by the millions all over the Muslim Empire and in some countries their influence was so great that the heads of their orders were the practical rulers, with supreme authority in every major problem concerning the religious or secular institutions. Such influence can be found even now in some Muslim communities.

As an ideal mode of spiritual life, Sufism has passed through various stages. At some times it was thoroughly orthodox, at others so far removed from orthodoxy as to become a mere system of religious philosophy. It has also undergone some periods of stagnation and corruption during which its followers completely lost sight of the noble and lofty ideals of the original founders, preserving an outward appearance of ritual with nothing to correspond to it in the heart. But these remarks belong more to the history of Sufism. Our immediate object here is to try to set forth the mystical attitude toward Islam so far as it can be gleaned from the lives and teachings of the great Sufi masters, leaving everything else out of our account.

The special attitude of the Muslim mystics toward Islam was quite clear from the time their movement started. Until the end of the second century (eighth century AD.) religious laws were based on the literal texts of the *Quran* and Prophetic Traditions, and scrupulously carried out. They were thoroughly studied and strictly adhered to in practice. Knowledge of the canon law - jurisprudence - was the most venerated of all knowledge, and adherence to its rules was the ultimate aim as well as the true mark of every pious Muslim. When the Sufis appeared on the scene, they came with another religious ideal. To them the examination of the esoteric meaning of the law was a more worthy objective than the study of the law in its esoteric sense. Hence arose the distinction between the outward expression of the law and its inward significance, and with it the distinction between the study of jurisprudence on the one hand and Sufism on the other. The jurists became known as the externalists and the Sufis as the internalists. Gradually the opposition between the two camps grew more and more intense as they realized that they stood for two different conceptions of Islam and its teachings.

The differences between the legalists and the Sufis were apparent in their interpretations of the meaning of religious law and the ways in which it should be derived and justified. They differed as to the nature of worship and the way it should be performed. They did not agree as to which actions are lawful or unlawful or what parts of the law are basic to Islam. Nor did they agree as to the object and value of obligatory and supererogatory religious devotions. Is God the object of formal worship or of love? They differed on many points of Islamic dogma, especially concerning the conception of God in His relation to man, and the meaning of the unity of God.

It is obvious that such disputes touch the very core of Islam, and it is no wonder that the Muslim theologians and jurists became the bitterest enemies of the Sufis and fought them on all fronts for centuries. The first opposition to their movement came from the traditionalist Ahmad Ibn Hanbal (died 241; AD. 855). He could not conceal his admiration for a Sufi like al-Harith al-Muhasibi (died 243; AD. 857), but admitted that al-Muhasibi spoke in his sermons a language unknown to him, the language of the Sufis. He did not doubt his sincerity but was full of suspicion and apprehension. Relentless persecution of the Sufis was carried on by Ibn Hanbal's party and other theological sects in order to put an end to their growing influence.

Gradually the new mysticism of Sufism - or rather, the new religious spirit - gained ground. It was realized that Islam as understood by the jurists was ultimately reduced to formal ritual which consisted in the performance of certain bodily movements. Prayer, fasting, and pilgrimage were well-defined and measured physical movements, almost void of genuine feeling. Such an attitude toward Islam was sure to satisfy the externalists whose main concern was to give precise definitions to religious terms, lay down general laws, and see that they were strictly observed. It did not satisfy the religious sentiment of the Sufis, who looked for a deeper meaning behind the outward forms. Qushayri tells us that Ruwaym of Baghdad (died 303; AD. 915) said, "All people hold fast to external appearances [of religion], but this community [the Sufis] holds fast to realities. All people consider it their duty to observe the external aspect of the religious law; the Sufis consider it their duty to strive after piety and unremitting sincerity." In these few words Ruwaym sums up the whole situation by pointing out the real difference between the Sufis and the rest of the Muslims in their respective attitudes toward Islam. For the Sufis, Islam is *haqiqa,* a reality hidden behind words and forms, while for the rest of the Muslims it is principally words and forms.

Such a distinction was practically unknown to the early Muslims. The idea started with the Shi'a who taught that the *Quran*, like everything else, had two aspects, one external and the other internal. The latter is what the Sufis call the esoteric meaning of the *Quran*, which is only revealed to the chosen people of God. They extended the idea to everything in Islam. A real contrast was made between the shari'a (religious law) aspect of a religious principle or usage and its haqiqa aspect, that is, between the religious law as such and its real meaning.

It is true that the great teachers of Sufism agree that shari'a should be strictly observed, and that the abandonment of shari'a on the pretext that haqiqa, the reality or spirit of the law, has been obtained is not only impiety but infidelity. Haqiqa without shari'a, they say, is baseless, and shari'a without haqiqa is meaningless. A reasonable balance between the two is essential for a truly religious life. Such a balance is described by Ghazali in these words, He who says that haqiqa is contrary to shari'a, and the internal [side of religion] is contrary to the external is nearer to infidelity. Every haqiqa that has no root in shari'a should be rejected. Shari'a is the law enjoined upon people; haqiqa is seeing the work of Divine Providence. Shari'a is worship of God; haqiqa is to behold him. Shari'a is to obey the Divine Command; haqiqa is to know by mystic vision what God has predestined, what He has revealed and what He has concealed.

So, according to Ghazali, haqiqa is the spiritual justification and proof of religion. The true meaning of religious teachings is seen by the mystic in his heart. Its real nature is revealed to him. When, for instance, the mystic is called upon to worship God, the meaning of the Godhead and of worship is freshly perceived by the inner light. This is the general attitude adopted by the majority of orthodox Sufis and ardently defended by such men as Tustari (died 273; AD. 886), Kharraz (died 277; AD. 890), Junayd (died 297; AD. 909), and Ghazali (died 505; AD. 1111). But some

Sufis went too far in emphasizing haqiqa and minimizing the importance of shari'a and were eventually led into various degrees of the erroneous belief that the awareness of inner reality frees one from the moral obligations of the law. They represent the other extreme of Sufism which is condemned by the genuinely pious Muslims. Others among the Sufis held fast to shari'a, but understood it in ways which were much wider and more liberal than the interpretation of the orthodox, looking upon the law as either a system of self-discipline or as a set of symbols representing hidden religious meanings.

Those Sufis who regarded the law as essentially a system of self-discipline rejected the claim that the shari'a is a collection of norms and codes divided and subdivided into more norms and codes. For them it must not be understood within the narrow limits and strict definitions of the lawyers and theologians. The value of any religious work should not be judged on the basis of its compliance with the law; its value should be determined by the degree to which it fulfills the ideal of the lawgiver. Voluntary acts of devotion are considered superior to obligatory acts because they fulfill a higher ideal - the love of God - while obligatory acts of devotion only show submissive obedience to God's commands. The Sufis quote the following Tradition in which God says, "In no way does My servant so draw nigh unto Me as when he performs those duties which I have imposed on him; and My servant continues to draw near to Me through works of supererogation, until I love him. And when I love him, I am his eye, so that he sees by Me, and his ear, so that he hears by Me, and his tongue, so that he speaks by Me, and his hand, so that he takes by Me."

This means that in the act of devotion he becomes completely absorbed in God and loses every vestige of his individual being and feels himself to be one with his Beloved. Such a state is not attained by the ordinary performance of religious duties. The Sufi seeks the attainment of the spiritual benefits which he gains through his acts of devotion, not the mere performance of outward acts as such. Thus the real essence of religion is that which resides in the heart, not that which is performed by the body. The religious command should be addressed to the heart, not to the bodily organs.

This attitude, noble as it is, seems to have paved the way to antinomianism in some Sufi circles. Religious duties, they argued, are a means to an end, and if the end is reached we can very well dispense with the means. Haqiqa, religious truth, is for them the end and shari'a, religious law, is the means. That there were such men even in the golden age of Sufism who allowed themselves all sorts of license and indulgences under the pretext that they had reached their goal is evident from the scathing remarks which we read in the opening chapters of the treatise on Sufism by Qushayri (died 465; AD. 1072). He attacks most mercilessly the men of his time who believed that haqiqa frees one from the moral obligations of the law, and appeals for a revision of Sufism in the light of the teachings of the old masters, calling upon the Sufis to lead a true religious life in accordance with the *Quran* and the example of the founders of the Sufi path.

Qushayri's warning was not in vain, for fifty years later it found a remarkable response in the writings of Ghazali who took upon himself the task of reconciling Sufism with Islam. He interpreted the principles of Sufism in the light of Islam and showed their interdependence. It is true that Ghazali was primarily concerned with the solution of his own spiritual problem when he was in search of the truth, but in solving his own problem he solved the problem for thousands of others who were and still are searching for the same truth. This truth he found in the Sufi way of life lived according to strict Muslim law. Religious truth is the inner meaning of the law revealed in the heart of the Sufi by the Divine Light.

In addition to the Sufis who looked upon the law as a means of self-discipline there were those who looked upon the shari'a as a set of symbols standing for hidden religious meanings. Those symbols are of value only as a reminder or an occasion in which the hidden meanings are realized. The pious Muslim should perform the acts of worship prescribed by the shari'a with his heart set on their spiritual meanings, otherwise his worship is merely an empty mechanical action.

This attitude takes into account the external, physical acts of worship as well as the internal acts of the heart. The danger is that it might lead to discarding the external acts altogether on the ground that they are superfluous. The Sufis who insisted on the observation of both the external and internal acts of worship read into the external teachings of Islam meanings undreamed of by canon lawyers.

Prayer, for instance, is not regarded as a set of words to be uttered and movements to be performed but is looked upon as essentially a spiritual discourse between man and his Creator. All movements and words are symbols whose meanings form a part of that inner discourse. Similarly, pilgrimage is not a mere trip to the Holy Shrine of Mecca; it is the spiritual journey of the human soul to God. Each step of the journey, each of the rites of the pilgrimage - such as circumambulation of the Ka'ba, the kissing of the Black Stone, the standing on Mount Arafat - is a symbol of great spiritual significance. Each bodily movement of the pilgrimage has a corresponding movement of the heart.

The mention of God, known as *dhikr*, is another example of the symbolic interpretation of Islamic worship. It is not a mere repetition of the name Allah, but is the silent recollection and contemplation of God, done in such a way that the heart of the contemplator becomes occupied with nothing but Him and the lover becomes completely absorbed in his Beloved.

The Sufis go through the rest of the forms of worship in the same way. The man who performs religious rites without observing their hidden meanings is, according to them, like a child who reads the words of a book without understanding them. His religious life is void because his heart is void. In the case of prayer and dhikr, such a man's heart is occupied merely with the name of God, not with God Himself.

The Sufi conception of God

Just as the attitude of the Sufis toward the religious teachings of Islam was a revolt against the jurists who stifled the true spirit of religion in order to preserve its form, their attitude toward God was also a revolt directed against the theologians and the philosophers. The barren speculations of the Muslim rationalists deprived the Godhead of its positive content, and God was reduced to a logical abstraction. The orthodox theologians made of Him a despot whose absolute power could do everything, even the impossible and the irrational. The philosophers, in their attempt to reconcile Islamic dogmas with Greek philosophy, were obliged to abandon many of the theological attributes of God, or explain them away, and put an active or final cause in place of a creator of the world. To the majority of the Sufis, God is essentially a personal being endowed with attributes which determine His relations with the world in general and man in particular. The outline of their picture of God is taken from the *Quran*, but the details which bring out the main features of the pictures are supplied by them, each in his own way.

God, they say, is the Creator of the world, the Maintainer, the sole Doer of everything, the Light of heaven and earth, the Merciful, the Compassionate, but above all He is the God who abides in the hearts of men. "Neither My heaven nor My earth contains Me," He says in a Tradition often quoted by the Sufis, "but I am contained in the heart of My servant who is a believer." So the Sufi does not look afar for his God, for the kingdom of God is in his heart if he can only see it.

The ultimate goal of the Muslim mystics is to bring this state into full realization, to feel the presence of God in the heart in such a way that nothing else is allowed to occupy it. Their aim is the complete absorption of the individual self in the contemplation of God.

If we pass in review over the long and complicated history of Sufism, we find that three different conceptions of God - ethical, aesthetic, and pantheistic - appear in successive stages of its development. They all had their roots directly or indirectly in the *Quran* and Prophetic Traditions, or were brought into relation with such texts by means of interpretation.

The ethical conception of God was predominant in the earliest period of Muslim asceticism. The essence of God was regarded as absolute power and will. God was the supreme author of all things, including men's actions.

The present life was essentially evil and therefore should be abandoned if the everlasting happiness of the Future World was to be attained. The early Sufis had an exaggerated sense of guilt and of the terrible torments that awaited the sinners in Hell. Consequently an overwhelming fear of God and His wrath seized their hearts, and their pious devotions were regarded as a means of escape from the judgment to come. They had almost forgotten the words of God in which He says, "My mercy embraces all things," and, "God pardons everything except associating other gods with Him." This fear colored the moral and religious life of the early ascetics, and determined their attitude toward God, the world, and their fellowmen.

The aesthetic conception of God in Sufi metaphysics was based on the idea of reciprocal love between God and man. The root of this doctrine is to be found in the *Quran*, but further elaborations of it were due to foreign influences coming from Manichaeanism and Neo-platonism. The first note in this direction was struck by the woman saint of Basra, Rabi'a (died 185; AD. 801). From the third century onward, the doctrine of divine love became the dominant feature of Sufism. God was the Beloved of the Sufis, and loving Him for His own sake was the end of their entire endeavor. It was no longer the fear of Hell or the hope of Paradise, but the hope of obtaining a glimpse of the everlasting beauty of God which motivated the Sufis. Rabi'a says in one of her prayers, "0 God! If I worship Thee in fear of Hell, burn me in Hell, and if I worship Thee in hope of Paradise, exclude me from Paradise. But if I worship Thee for Thine own sake, withhold not Thine everlasting beauty." Also attributed to her is the following verse:

Two ways I love Thee: selfishly,
And next, as worthy is of Thee.
'Tis selfish love that I do naught
Save think on Thee with every thought.
'Tis purest love when Thou dost raise
The veil to my adoring gaze.
Not mine the praise in that or this
Thine is the praise in both I wis.

(Translated by R. A. Nicholson in Legacy of Islam, *pp. 213-14)*

As time went on, the idea of divine love went deeper and deeper into the life and thought of the Muslim mystics. On the practical side it became the sole motive of their actions. Moral ideas centered around it, just as they centered around the fear of God in the earlier period. Altruism or selflessness became the highest virtue. This meant the abandonment of worldly pleasures and the absolute denial of selfishness for the sake of God. "The essence of love is self-denial," says Ghazali. "It is the ultimate end of all mystic stations. Every state that comes after it is a fruit thereof; and every station that precedes it is a step toward it." Jalal al-Din Rumi, the great Sufi mystic, says, "Love is the remedy of our pride and self-conceit, the physician of all our infirmities."

The Sufis devoted their lives to the worship of God because they loved Him and were anxious to win His love. On the theoretical side, divine love was regarded as the sole reason for the creation of the world. Creation is an expression of God's love, it is His eternal Beauty reflected in an external form. The Sufis quote the following Tradition in which God says, "I was a hidden treasure and I loved to be known, so I created the creation that they might know Me." Moreover they maintain that love is the key to all Heavenly mysteries, and the essence of all true religion. It brings with it, not reasoned convictions, but convictions based on the infallible proof of immediate intuition. It is the celestial light that guides the traveler on his way to God.

Pantheism did not appear in Muslim mysticism - or at least not in a systematic form - before Muḥy al-Din Ibn Arabi (died 638; AD. 1240), the greatest of all Arabic-speaking myṣtics of Islạm. Pantheistic tendencies were seen as early as the third century, for instance in some of the utterances of Bayazid of Bistam (died 261; AD. 875), but they were not worked out into a consistent pantheistic doctrine. Ibn Arabi, on the other hand, was the first to produce a full-fledged pantheistic philosophy which left its indelible marks on the whole of Sufism ever since his time. The fundamental principle of this philosophy is the principle of the unity of all Being. His understanding of this principle is best summed up in his own words: "Glory to God who created all things, being Himself their very essence." In his *Fusus* he says,

O Thou who created all things in Thyself,
Thou unitest that which Thou createst.

Thou createst what existeth infinitely
In Thee, for Thou art the narrow and the All-embracing.

In Islamic pantheism the phenomenal world is reduced to a mere shadow of reality, and God is regarded as the only real Being who is the ultimate ground of all that was, is, and will be. There is no actual duality of God and the phenomenal world, but there is an apparent duality asserted by the unaided intellect, which is incapable of comprehending the essential unity of the whole. It is at most a duality of aspects of One Being - not of two independent beings. Looking at the two aspects within one whole, reality is God and the universe, the One and the many, the transcendent and the immanent, the internal and the external. If we think - as we usually do - in terms of duality, we predicate of Reality all pairs of opposite attributes. But mystic intuition asserts that God is the only Real Being who is above all description and qualifying attributes, and the world is a mere illusion.

There is therefore a definite place for God in this philosophy, although in some respects He is far removed from the God of Islam. Ibn Arabi makes a distinction which is the dividing line between his metaphysical theory and his theology; it is a distinction between God as the unknowable and incommunicable Reality, and God as the object of belief, worship, and love. His conception of God as the object of belief comes very close to that of the ordinary monotheist, but the gap between pantheism and strict Muslim monotheism was too great for him to bridge. God is the object of worship not in the sense that He is exclusively the God of the Muslims, the Christians, or the adherents of any other religion, but in the sense that He is the Essence of everything that is worshiped. He is not to be confined to any particular form of belief or creed. Everything that is worshiped is one of the infinite numbers of forms in which He reveals Himself. To confine Him to one particular form to the exclusion of all other forms is infidelity, and to acknowledge Him in all forms of worship is the true spirit of religion.

This is the universal religion which the pantheistic Ibn Arabi preaches, a religion which comprises all religions and unites all beliefs. In his *Tarjumanu al-Ashwaq* he expresses this conviction,

My heart has become a receptacle of every form;

It is a pasture for gazelles and a convent for Christian monks,

And a temple for idols, and pilgrims' Ka'ba,

And the Tablets of the Torah and the Book of the Quran.

I follow the religion of love whichever way its camels take;

For this is my religion and my faith.

The religion of love, according to Ibn Arabi, is religion in its widest and most universal sense. All worshipers do in fact worship God, although they appear to worship their particular gods. And since love is the essence of worship - for to worship is to love to the extreme - and since the objects of worship are nothing but the external manifestations of God, it follows that God is both the supremely beloved and the supremely worshiped One.

This brief discussion shows some of the ways in which the interpretations of Muslim theologians, philosophers, and mystics have contributed to the vitality of Islam throughout its long history, making their varied contributions to the development of Muslim thought and influencing Islamic practices. Although they have often been considered as unorthodox by the leaders of Islam, their attempts to provide a rational basis for Islamic beliefs and a mystical basis for Islamic worship have for centuries enriched and stimulated the Muslim community.

Let us suppose that the average Moslem could read English, and that we placed in his hands one of those admirable volumes published by the Society for Psychical

Research. In order to sympathise with his feelings on such an occasion, we have only to imagine what our own would be if a scientific friend invited us to study a treatise setting forth the evidence in favour of telegraphy and recording well-attested instances of telegraphic communication. The Moslem would probably see in the telegraph some kind of spirit-an *afreet* or *jinni*. Telepathy and similar occult phenomena he takes for granted as self-evident facts. It would never occur to him to investigate them. There is something in the constitution of his mind that makes it impervious to the idea that the supernatural may be subject to law. He believes, because he cannot help believing, in the reality of an unseen world which 'lies about us,' not in our infancy alone, but always and everywhere; a world from which we are in no wise excluded, accessible and in some measure revealed to all, though free and open intercourse with it is a privilege enjoyed by few. Many are called but few chosen.

"Spirits every night from the body's snare
Thou freest, and makest the tablets clean.
{By erasing all the sensuous impressions which form a veil between
the soul and the world of reality.}
Spirits are set free every night from this cage,
Independent, neither ruled nor ruling.
At night prisoners forget their prison,
At night kings forget their power:
No sorrow, no brooding over gain and loss,
No thought of this person or that person.
This is the state of the gnostic, even when he is awake;
God hath said, 'Thou wouldst deem them awake while they slept.'
He is asleep, day and night, to the affairs of the world,
Like a pen in the controlling hand of the Lord."

The Sufis have always declared and believed themselves to be God's chosen people. The Koran refers in several places to His elect. According to the author of the *Kitab al-Luma'*, this title belongs, firstly, to the prophets, elect in virtue of their sinlessness, their inspiration, and their apostolic mission; and secondly, to certain Moslems, elect in virtue of their sincere devotion and self-mortification and firm attachment to the eternal realities: in a word, the saints. While the Sufis are the elect of the Moslem community, the saints are the elect of the Sufis.

The Mohammedan saint is commonly known as a *wali* (plural, *awliya*). This word is used in various senses derived from its root-meaning of 'nearness'; *e.g.* next of kin, patron, protector, friend. It is applied in the Koran to God as the protector of the Faithful, to angels or idols who are supposed to protect their worshippers, and to men who are regarded as being especially under divine protection.

Mohammed twits the Jews with professing to be *protégés* of God (*awliya lillah*). Notwithstanding its somewhat equivocal associations, the term was taken over by the Sufis and became the ordinary designation of persons whose holiness brings them near to God, and who receive from Him, as tokens of His peculiar favour, miraculous gifts (*karamat, charísmata*); they are His friends, on whom "no fear shall come and they shall not grieve" {Kor. 10.63}; any injury done to them is an act of hostility against Him.

The inspiration of the Islamic saints, though verbally distinguished from that of the prophets and inferior in degree, is of the same kind. In consequence of their intimate relation to God, the veil shrouding the supernatural, or, as a Moslem would say, the unseen world, from their perceptions is withdrawn at intervals, and in their fits of ecstasy they rise to the prophetic level.

Neither deep learning in divinity, nor devotion to good works, nor asceticism, nor moral purity makes the

Mohammedan a saint; he may have all or none of these things, but the only indispensable qualification is that ecstasy and rapture which is the outward sign of 'passing-away' from the phenomenal self. Anyone thus enraptured (*majdhub*) is a *wali* {*Waliyyat,* if the saint is a woman.}, and when such persons are recognised through their power of working miracles, they are venerated as saints not only after death but also during their lives. Often, however, they live and die in obscurity. Hujwiri tells us that amongst the saints "there are four thousand who are concealed and do not know one another and are not aware of the excellence of their state, being in all circumstances hidden from themselves and from mankind."

The saints form an invisible hierarchy, on which the order of the world is thought to depend. Its supreme head is entitled the *Qutb* (Axis). He is the most eminent Sufi of his age, and presides over the meetings regularly held by this august parliament, whose members are not hampered in their attendance by the inconvenient fictions of time and space, but come together from all parts of the earth in the twinkling of an eye, traversing seas and mountains and deserts as easily as common mortals step across a road. Below the *Qutb* stand various classes and grades of sanctity. Hujwiri enumerates them, in ascending series, as follows: three hundred *Akhyar* (Good), forty *Abdal* (Substitutes), seven *Abrar* (Pious), four *Awtad* (Supports), and three *Nuqaba* (Overseers).

"All these know one another and cannot act save by mutual consent. It is the task of the *Awtad* to go round the whole world every night, and if there should be any place on which their eyes have not fallen, next day some flaw will appear in that place, and they must then inform the *Qutb* in order that he may direct his attention to the weak spot and that by his blessing the imperfection may be remedied."

We are studying in this book the mystical life of the individual Moslem, and it is necessary to keep the subject within the narrowest bounds. Otherwise, I should have liked to dwell on the external and historical organisation of Sufism as a school for saints, and to describe the process of evolution through which the *wali* privately conversing with a small circle of friends became, first, a teacher and spiritual guide gathering disciples around him during his lifetime, and finally the head of a perpetual religious order which bore his name. The earliest of these great fraternities date from the twelfth century. In addition to their own members-the so-called 'dervishes'-each order has a large number of lay brethren attached to it, so that their influence pervades all ranks of Moslem society. They are "independent and self-developing.

There is rivalry between them; but no one rules over the other. In faith and practice each goes its own way, limited only by the universal conscience of Islam. Thus strange doctrines and grave moral defects easily develop unheeded, but freedom is saved." {D. B. Macdonald, *The Religious Life and Attitude in Islam*.} Of course, the typical *wali* is incapable of founding an order, but Islam has produced no less frequently than Christendom men who combine intense spiritual illumination with creative energy and aptitude for affairs on a grand scale. The Mohammedan notion of the saint as a person possessed by God allows a very wide application of the term: in popular usage it extends from the greatest Sufi theosophists, like Jalaluddin Rumi and Ibn al-'Arabi, down to those who have gained sanctity only by losing sanity-victims of epilepsy and hysteria, half-witted idiots and harmless lunatics.

Both Qushayri {author of a famous work designed to close the breach between Sufism and Islam died in 1074 A.D.} and Hujwiri discuss the question whether a saint can be conscious of his saint ship, and answer it in the affirmative. Their opponents argue that consciousness of saint ship involves assurance of salvation, which is impossible, since no one can know with certainty that he shall be among the saved on the Day of Judgment. In reply it was urged that God may miraculously assure the saint of his predestined salvation, while maintaining him in a state of spiritual soundness and preserving him from disobedience. The saint is not immaculate, as the prophets are, but the divine protection which he enjoys is a guarantee that he will not persevere in evil courses, though he may temporarily be led astray. According to the view generally held, saint ship depends on faith, not on conduct, so that no sin except infidelity can cause it to be forfeited. This perilous theory, which opens the door to antinomianism, was mitigated by the emphasis laid on fulfillment of the religious law. The following anecdote of Bayazid al-Bistami shows the official attitude of all the leading Sufis who are cited as authorities in the Moslem text-books.

"I was told (he said) that a saint of God was living in such-and-such a town, and I set out to visit him. When I entered the mosque, he came forth from his chamber and spat on the floor. I turned back without saluting him, saying to myself, 'A saint must keep the religious law in order that God may keep him in his spiritual state. Had this man been a saint, his respect for the law would have prevented him from spitting on the floor, or God would have saved him from marring the grace vouchsafed to him."

Many *walis*, however, regard the law as a curb that is indeed necessary so long as one remains in the disciplinary stage, but may be discarded by the saint. Such a person, they declare, stands on a higher plane than ordinary men, and is not to be condemned for actions which outwardly seem irreligious. While the older Sufis insist that a *wali* who breaks the law is thereby shown to be an impostor, the popular belief in the saints and the rapid growth of saint-worship tended to aggrandise the *wali* at the expense of the law, and to foster the conviction that a divinely gifted man can do no wrong, or at least that his actions must not be judged by appearances. The classical instance of this *jus divinum* vested in the friends of God is the story of Moses and Khadir, which is related in the Koran (18.64-80). Khadir or Khizr-the Koran does not mention him by name-is a mysterious sage endowed with immortality, which is said to enter into conversation with wandering Sufis and impart to them his God-given knowledge. Moses desired to accompany him on a journey that he might profit by his teaching, and Khadir consented, only stipulating that Moses should ask no questions of him.

"So they both went on, till they embarked in a boat and he (Khadir) staved it in. 'What!' cried Moses, 'hast thou staved it in that thou mayst drown its crew? Verily, a strange thing hast thou done.'

"He said, 'Did not I tell thee that thou couldst no way have patience with me?'

"Then they went on until they met a youth, and he slew him. Said Moses, 'Hast thou slain him who is free from guilt of blood? Surely now thou hast wrought an unheard-of thing!'"

After Moses had broken his promise of silence for the third time, Khadir resolved to leave him.

"But first," he said, "I will tell thee the meaning of that with which thou couldst not have patience. As to the boat, it belonged to poor men, toilers on the sea, and I was minded to damage it, for in their rear was a king who seized on every boat by force. And as to the youth, his parents were believers, and I feared lest he should trouble them by error and unbelief."

The Sufis are fond of quoting this unimpeachable testimony that the *wali* is above human criticism, and that his hand, as Jalaluddin asserts, is even as the hand of God. Most Moslems admit the claim to be valid in so far as they shrink from applying conventional standards of morality to holy men. I have explained its metaphysical justification in an earlier chapter.

A miracle performed by a saint is termed *karamat, i.e.* a 'favour' which God bestows upon him, whereas a miracle performed by a prophet is called *mu'jizat, i.e.* an act which cannot be imitated by any one. The distinction originated in controversy, and was used to answer those who held the miraculous powers of the saints to be a grave encroachment on the prerogative of the Prophet. Sufi apologists, while confessing that both kinds of miracle are substantially the same, take pains to differentiate the characteristics of each; they declare, moreover, that the saints are the Prophet's witnesses, and that all their miracles (like 'a drop trickling from a full skin of honey') are in reality derived from him.

This is the orthodox view and is supported by those Mohammedan mystics who acknowledge the Law as well as the Truth, though in some cases it may have amounted to little more than a pious opinion. We have often noticed the difficulty in which the Sufis find themselves when they try to make a logical compromise with Islam. But the word 'logic' is very misleading in this connexion. The beginning of wisdom, for European students of Oriental religion, lies in the discovery that incongruous beliefs-I mean, of course, beliefs which our minds cannot harmonise-dwell peacefully together in the Oriental brain; that their owner is quite unconscious of their incongruity; and that, as a rule, he is absolutely sincere. Contradictions which seem glaring to us do not trouble him at all.

The thaumaturgic element in ancient Sufism was not so important as it afterwards became in the fully developed saint-worship associated with the Dervish Orders. "A saint would be none the less a saint," says Qushayri, "if no miracles were wrought by him in this world." In early Mohammedan *Vitæ Sanctorum* it is not uncommon to meet with sayings to the effect that miraculous powers are comparatively of small account.

It was finely said by Sahl ibn 'Abdallah that the greatest

miracle is the substitution of a good quality for a bad one; and the *Kitab al-Luma'* gives many examples of holy men who disliked miracles and regarded them as a temptation. "During my novitiate," said Bayazid, "God used to bring before me wonders and miracles, but I paid no heed to them; and when He saw that I did so, He gave me the means of attaining to knowledge of Him." Junayd observed that reliance on miracles is one of the 'veils' which hinder the elect from penetrating to the inmost shrine of the Truth. This was too high doctrine for the great mass of Moslems, and in the end the vulgar idea of saint ship triumphed over the mystical and theosophical conception.

All such warnings and scruples were swept aside by the same irresistible instinct which rendered vain the solemn asseverations of Mohammed that there was nothing supernatural about him, and which transformed the human Prophet of history into an omnipotent hierophant and magician. The popular demand for miracles far exceeded the supply, but where the *walis* failed, a vivid and credulous imagination came to their rescue and represented them, not as they were, but as they ought to be.

Year by year the *Legend of the Saints* grew more glorious and wonderful as it continued to draw fresh tribute from the unfathomable ocean of Oriental romance. The pretensions made by the *walis*, or on their behalf, steadily increased, and the stories told of them were ever becoming more fantastic and extravagant. I will devote the remainder of this chapter to a sketch of the *wali* as he appears in the vast medieval literature on the subject.

The Moslem saint does not say that he has wrought a miracle; he says, "a miracle was granted or manifested to me." According to one view, he may be fully conscious at the time, but many Sufis hold that such 'manifestation' cannot take place except in ecstasy, when the saint is entirely under divine control.

His own personality is then in abeyance, and those who interfere with him oppose the Almighty Power which speaks with his lips and smites with his hand. Jalaluddin (who uses incidentally the rather double-edged analogy of a man possessed by a peri {One of the spirits called collectively Jinn.}) relates the following anecdote concerning Bayazid of Bistam, a celebrated Persian saint who several times declared in ecstatic frenzy that he was no other than God.

After coming to himself on one of these occasions and learning what blasphemous language he had uttered, Bayazid ordered his disciples to stab him with their knives if he should offend again. Let me quote the sequel, from Mr. Whinfield's abridged translation of the *Masnavi*:

"The torrent of madness bore away his reason
And he spoke more impiously than before:
'Within my vesture is naught but God,
Whether you seek Him on earth or in heaven.'
His disciples all became mad with horror,
And struck with their knives at his holy body.
Each one who aimed at the body of the Sheykh-
His stroke was reversed and wounded the striker.
No stroke took effect on that man of spiritual gifts,
But the disciples were wounded and drowned in blood."

Here is the poet's conclusion:

"Ah! you who smite with your sword him beside himself,
You smite yourself therewith. Beware!
For he that is beside himself is annihilated and safe;
Yea, he dwells in security for ever.
His form is vanished; he is a mere mirror;
Nothing is seen in him but the reflexion of another.
If you spit at it, you spit at your own face,

And if you hit that mirror, you hit yourself.
If you see an ugly face in it, 'tis your own,
And if you see a Jesus there, you are its mother Mary.
He is neither this nor that-he is void of form;
'Tis your own form which is reflected back to you."

The life of Abu 'l-Hasan Khurqani, another Persian Sufi who died in 1033 A.D., gives us a complete picture of the Oriental pantheist, and exhibits the mingled arrogance and sublimity of the character as clearly as could be desired. Since the original text covers fifty pages, I can translate only a small portion of it here. "Once the Sheykh said, 'this night a great many persons (he mentioned the exact number) have been wounded by brigands in such-and-such a desert.' On making inquiry, they found that his statement was perfectly true. Strange to relate, on the same night his son's head was cut off and laid upon the threshold of his house, yet he knew nothing of it.

His wife, who disbelieved in him, cried, 'What think you of a man who can tell things which happen many leagues away, but does not know that his own son's head has been cut off and is lying at his very door?' 'Yes,' the Sheykh answered, 'when I saw that, the veil had been lifted, but when my son was killed, it had been let down again.'" "One day Abu 'l-Hasan Khurqani clenched his fist and extended the little finger and said, 'Here is the *qibla* {the *qibla* is the point to which Moslems turn their faces when praying, *i.e.* the Ka'ba.}, if any one desires to become a Sufi.' These words were reported to the Grand Sheykh, who, deeming the co-existence of two *qiblas* an insult to the divine Unity, exclaimed, 'Since a second *qibla* has appeared, I will cancel the former one.'

After that, no pilgrims were able to reach Mecca. Some perished on the way; others fell into the hands of robbers, or were prevented by various causes from accomplishing their journey. Next year a certain dervish said to the Grand

Sheykh, 'What sense is there in keeping the folk away from the House of God?' Thereupon the Grand Sheykh made a sign, and the road became open once more. The dervish asked, 'Whose fault is it that all these people have perished?' The Grand Sheykh replied, 'When elephants jostle each other, who care if a few wretched birds are crushed to death?'"

"Some persons who were setting forth on a journey begged Khurqani to teach them a prayer that would keep them safe from the perils of the road. He said, 'If any misfortune should befall you, mention my name.' This answer was not agreeable to them; they set off, however, and while travelling were attacked by brigands. One of the parties mentioned the saint's name and immediately became invisible, to the great astonishment of the brigands, who could not find either his camel or his bales of merchandise; the others lost all their clothes and goods. On returning home, they asked the Sheykh to explain the mystery. 'We all invoked God,' they said, 'and without success; but the one man who invoked you vanished from before the eyes of the robbers.' 'You invoke God formally,' said the Sheykh, 'whereas I invoke Him really. Hence, if you invoke me and I then invoke God on your behalf, your prayers are granted; but it is useless for you to invoke God formally and by rote.'"

"One night, while he was praying, he heard a voice cry, 'Ha! Abu 'l-Hasan! Dost thou wish Me to tell the people what I know of thee, that they may stone thee to death?' 'O Lord God,' he replied, 'dost Thou wish me to tell the people what I know of Thy mercy and what I perceive of Thy grace, that none of them may ever again bow to Thee in prayer?' The voice answered, 'Keep thy secret, and I will keep Mine.'"

"He said, 'O God, do not send to me the Angel of Death, for I will not give up my soul to him. How should I restore it to him, from whom I did not receive it? I received my soul from Thee, and I will not give it up to any one but Thee.'"

"He said, 'After I shall have passed away, the Angel of Death will come to one of my descendants and set about taking his soul, and will deal hardly with him. Then will I raise my hands from the tomb and shed the grace of God upon his lips.'"

"He said, 'If I bade the empyrean move, it would obey, and if I told the sun to stop, it would cease from rolling on its course.'"

"He said, 'I am not a devotee nor an ascetic nor a theologian nor a Sufi. O God, Thou art One, and through Thy Oneness I am One.'"

"He said, 'The skull of my head is the empyrean, and my feet are under the earth, and my two hands are East and West.'"

"He said, 'If any one does not believe that I shall stand up at the Resurrection and that he shall not enter Paradise until I lead him forward, let him not come here to salute me.'"

"He said, 'Since God brought me forth from myself, Paradise is in quest of me and Hell is in fear of me; and if Paradise and Hell were to pass by this place where I am, both would become annihilated in me, together with all the people whom they contain.'"

"He said, 'I was lying on my back, asleep. From a corner of the Throne of God something trickled into my mouth, and I felt sweetness in my inward being.'"

"He said, 'If a few drops of that which is under the skin of a saint should come forth between his lips, all the creatures of heaven and earth would fall into panic.'"

"He said, 'Through prayer the saints are able to stop the fish from swimming in the sea and to make the earth tremble, so that people think it is an earthquake.'"

"He said, 'If the love of God in the hearts of His friends were made manifest, it would fill the world with flood and fire.'"

"He said, 'He that lives with God hath seen all things visible, and heard all things audible, and done all that is to be done, and known all that is to be known.'"

"He said, 'All things are contained in me, but there is no room for myself in me.'"

"He said, 'Miracles are only the first of the thousand stages of the Way to God.'"

"He said, 'Do not seek until thou art sought, for when thou findest that which thou seekest, it will resemble thee.'"

"He said, 'Thou must daily die a thousand deaths and come to life again, that thou mayst win the life immortal.'"

"He said, 'When thou givest to God thy nothingness, He gives to thee His All.'"

It would be an almost endless task to enumerate and exemplify the different classes of miracles which are related in the lives of the Mohammedan saints-for instance, walking on water, flying in the air (with or without a passenger), rain-making, appearing in various places at the same time, healing by the breath, bringing the dead to life, knowledge and prediction of future events, thought-reading, telekinesis, paralysing or beheading an obnoxious person by a word or gesture, conversing with animals or plants, turning earth into gold or precious stones, producing food and drink, etc. To the Moslem, who has no sense of natural law, all these 'violations of custom,' as he calls them, seem equally credible. We, on the other hand, feel ourselves obliged to distinguish phenomena which we regard as irrational and impossible from those for which we can find some sort of 'natural' explanation.

Modern theories of psychical influence, faith-healing, telepathy, veridical hallucination, hypnotic suggestion and the like, have thrown open to us a wide avenue of approach to this dark continent in the Eastern mind. I will not, however, pursue the subject far at present, full of interest as it is. In the higher Sufi teaching the miraculous powers of the saints play a more or less insignificant part and the excessive importance which they assume in the organized mysticism of the Dervish Orders is one of the clearest marks of its degeneracy.

The following passage, which I have slightly modified, gives a fair summary of the hypnotic process through which a dervish attains to union with God:

"The disciple must, mystically, always bear his Murshid (spiritual director) in mind, and become mentally absorbed in him through a constant meditation and contemplation of him. The teacher must be his shield against all evil thoughts. The spirit of the teacher follows him in all his efforts, and accompanies him wherever he may be, quite as a guardian spirit.

To such a degree is this carried that he sees the master in all men and in all things, just as a willing subject is under the influence of the magnetiser. This condition is called 'self-annihilation' in the Murshid or Sheykh. The latter finds in his own visionary dreams, the degree which the disciple has reached, and whether or not his spirit has become bound to his own.

"At this stage the Sheykh passes him over to the spiritual influence of the long-deceased Pir or original founder of the Order, and he sees the latter only by the spiritual aid of the Sheykh. This is called 'self-annihilation' in the Pir. He now becomes so much a part of the Pir as to possess all his spiritual powers.

"The third grade leads him, also through the spiritual aid of the Sheykh, up to the Prophet himself, whom he now sees in all things. This state is called 'self-annihilation' in the Prophet.

"The fourth degree leads him even to God. He becomes united with the Deity and sees Him in all things."

An excellent concrete illustration of the process here described will be found in the well-known case of Tawakkul Beg, who passed through all these experiences under the control of Molla-Shah. His account is too long to quote in full; moreover, it has recently been translated by Professor D. B. Macdonald in his *Religious Life and Attitude in Islam*. I copy from this version one paragraph describing the first of the four stages mentioned above.

"Thereupon he made me sit before him, my senses being as though intoxicated, and ordered me to reproduce my own image within myself; and, after having bandaged my eyes, he asked me to concentrate all my mental faculties on my heart. I obeyed, and in an instant, by the divine favour and by the spiritual assistance of the Sheykh, my heart opened. I saw, then, that there was something like an overturned cup within me. This having been set upright, a sensation of unbounded happiness filled my being. I said to the master, 'This cell where I am seated before you-I see a faithful reproduction of it within me, and it appears to me as though another Tawakkul Beg were seated before another Molla-Shah.' He replied, 'Very good! The first apparition which appears to thee is the image of the master.' He then ordered me to uncover my eyes; and I saw him, with the physical organ of vision, seated before me. He then made me bind my eyes again, and I perceived him with my spiritual sight, seated similarly before me. Full of astonishment, I cried out, 'O Master! Whether I look with my physical organs or with my spiritual sight, always it is you that I see!'"

Here is a case of autohypnotism, witnessed and recorded by the poet Jami:

"Mawlana Sa'duddin of Kashghar, after a little concentration of thought (*tawajjuh*), used to exhibit signs of unconsciousness. Anyone ignorant of this circumstance would have fancied that he was falling asleep. When I first entered into companionship with him, I happened one day to be seated before him in the congregational mosque. According to his custom, he fell into a trance. I supposed that he was going to sleep, and I said to him, 'If you desire to rest for a short time, you will not seem to me to be far off.' He smiled and said, 'Apparently you do not believe that this is something different from sleep.'"

The following anecdote presents greater difficulties:

"Mawlana Nizamuddin Khamush relates that one day his master, 'Ala'uddin 'Attar, started to visit the tomb of the celebrated saint Mohammed ibn 'Ali Hakim, at Tirmidh.'I did not accompany him,' said Nizamuddin, 'but stayed at home, and by concentrating my mind (*tawajjuh*) I succeeded in bringing the spirituality of the saint before me, so that when the master arrived at the tomb he found it empty. He must have known the cause, for on his return he set to work in order to bring me under his control. I, too, concentrated my mind, but I found myself like a dove and the master like a hawk flying in chase of me. Wherever I turned, he was always close behind. At last, despairing of escape, I took refuge with the spirituality of the Prophet (on whom be peace) and became effaced in its infinite radiance. The master could not exercise any further control. He fell ill in consequence of his chagrin, and no one except me knew the reason.'"

'Ala'uddin's son, Khwaja Hasan 'Attar, possessed such powers of 'control' that he could at will throw any one into the state of trance and cause them to experience the 'passing-away' (*fana*) to which some mystics attain only on rare occasions and after prolonged self-mortification. It is related that the disciples and visitors who were admitted to the honour of kissing his hand always fell unconscious to the ground.

Certain saints are believed to have the power of assuming whatever shape they please. One of the most famous was Abd 'Abdallah of Mosul, better known by the name of Qadib al-Ban. One day the Cadi of Mosul, who regarded him as a detestable heretic, saw him in a street of the town, approaching from the opposite direction. He resolved to seize him and lay a charge against him before the governor, in order that he might be punished. All at once he perceived that Qadib al-Ban had taken the form of a Kurd; and as the saint advanced towards him, his appearance changed again, this time into an Arab of the desert. Finally, on coming still nearer, he assumed the guise and dress of a doctor of theology, and cried, "O Cadi! Which Qadib al-Ban will you hale before the governor and punish?" The Cadi repented of his hostility and became one of the saint's disciples.

In conclusion, let me give two alleged instances of 'the obedience of inanimate objects,' *i.e.* telekinesis:

"Whilst Dhu 'l-Nun was conversing on this topic with some friends, he said, 'Here is a sofa. It will move round the room, if I tell it to do so.' No sooner had he uttered the word 'move' than the sofa made a circuit of the room and returned to its place. One of the spectators, a young man, burst into tears and gave up the ghost. They laid him on that sofa and washed him for burial."

"Avicenna paid a visit to Abu 'l-Hasan Khurqani and immediately plunged into a long and abstruse discussion. After a time the saint, who was an illiterate person, felt tired, so he got up and said, 'Excuse me; I must go and mend the garden wall'; and off he went, taking a hatchet with him. As soon as he had climbed on to the top of the wall, the hatchet dropped from his hand. Avicenna ran to pick it up, but before he reached it the hatchet rose of itself and came back into the saint's hand. Avicenna lost all his self-command, and the enthusiastic belief in Sufism which then took possession of him continued until, at a later period of his life, he abandoned mysticism for philosophy."

I am well aware that in this chapter scanty justice has been done to a great subject. The historian of Sufism must acknowledge, however deeply he may deplore, the fundamental position occupied by the doctrine of saint ship and the tremendous influence which it has exerted in its practical results-grovelling submission to the authority of an ecstatic class of men, dependence on their favour, pilgrimage to their shrines, adoration of their relics, devotion of every mental and spiritual faculty to their service. It may be dangerous to worship God by one's own inner light, but it is far more deadly to seek Him by the inner light of another. Vicarious holiness has no compensations. This truth is expressed by the mystical writers in many an eloquent passage, but I will content myself with quoting a few lines from the life of 'Ala'uddin 'Attar, the same saint who, as we have seen, vainly tried to hypnotise his pupil in revenge for a disrespectful trick which the latter had played on him. His biographer relates that he said, "It is more right and worthy to dwell beside God than to dwell beside God's creatures," and that the following verse was often on his blessed tongue:

"How long will you worship at the tombs of holy men?

Busy yourself with the *works* of holy men, and you are saved!"(*"tu ta kay gur-i mardan-ra parasti bi-gird-i kar-i mardan gard u rasti."*)

7

The Unitive State

No one can claim to speak with final authority concerning the diversity found among the more than five hundred million Muslims who seek to follow the straight path of Islam. One can only record some observations concerning the variations in practices among the Muslims from Morocco and the Balkans to China and Indonesia. It is possible, however, to be much more explicit about the basic unity of Islam, for throughout the Muslim world there is general agreement concerning the sources of Islam, the fundamentals of the faith, and the particular requirements which are the obligations of all believers.

THE SOURCES OF ISLAM

There is general agreement that the sources of Islam are the *Quran*, the Sunnah, and reasoning about them. Of these, the primary source is the *Quran*. Concerning matters not explicitly clear in the *Quran*, the Sunnah is the secondary, supplementary source; and when the answer to questions needs further clarification the third source for Muslims is reasoning about the intent of the *Quran* and Sunnah by those men who are recognized as having the training and experience which qualifies them to reason properly. It is the final revelation, the Word of God given through His Prophet as a guide to all men everywhere, regardless of race, or color, or nationality. Within two years of the death of the Prophet it was compiled in book form and has been the primary source of Islam for almost fourteen centuries, without question and without variant versions. Since it was revealed in Arabic it has necessitated knowledge of Arabic, and this has been a unifying cultural factor throughout the Muslim world.

It was recognized, however, that the people in the various countries often read the *Quran* in Arabic without understanding its meaning. The uneducated people even thought that it was sufficient to pronounce the words correctly, and that such repetition - even without understanding the meaning - would bring them blessings from God and save their souls. Some even used verses of the *Quran* as amulets against dangers and diseases! Half a century ago the orthodox Muslims believed that it was forbidden to translate the *Quran,* fearing that translations would supplant the original Arabic version and that versions in different languages would cause disagreements and misinterpretations of the revelation of God. While it is true that because of its very high literary style it is difficult, if not impossible, to translate the *Quran* into any other language without losing the beauty and vigor of the original, translations in the languages of the people are necessary in order that they may understand the meaning of this book which is the source of Islam.

Today the *Quran* is available in translation in most of the languages of the world. Sometimes people ask why the *Quran* was revealed in Arabic if it is intended to be the Holy Book for all human beings. This question cannot be answered definitely, for if the *Quran* had been revealed in any other language - for example, in English - the question would still remain as to why that one language was chosen. Thus we have to content ourselves with the fact that, regardless of any possible reasons, the *Quran* was revealed in Arabic. The second source for Islam is the Sunnah.

During Muhammad's lifetime, Muslims could ask him to guide them in solving any problem when they did not find a clear answer in the *Quran*. For instance, once a man asked him if it would be proper to perform a pilgrimage on behalf of his deceased mother.

The Prophet replied that it would be proper since such an act could be compared to a debt which she owed and the son was obligated to pay. When the Prophet was dying, and knew that he would not be present to give such advice, he told the people that they would not go astray so long as they held to the two guides he was leaving for them - the *Quran*, the Book of God, and the example of his own way of life, the Sunnah. The *Quran*, in Surah XXXIII, verse 21, establishes the Sunnah as the second source of Islam:

"There is a good example in the Apostle of Allah for those who wish to meet God and the Day of Judgment, and to remember God much."

The Sunnah is made up of the deeds, speech, and approbation of the Prophet. His deeds include the way he prayed, or washed his hands, or took a bath, and the like. His words have been preserved for us, as for example when he said, "I am sent to perfect high morality." By approbation is meant that when Muhammad saw something done, or heard words uttered in his presence and did not object, such actions or words are approved.

Approbation was applied chiefly to customs of the Arab society which were not in contradiction to the spirit of Islam. For example, when Muhammad saw a man dancing with a sword he smiled and showed his pleasure, so later jurists concluded that dancing with the sword is permitted. Such approval has been applied to customary practices and laws in all Islamic countries where such customs do not contradict the spirit of Islamic laws - for example, in the marriage ceremonies. The codification of the Sunnah, the Traditions, began a century and a half after the Prophet when Malik Ibn Anas wrote a compilation of the Traditions concerning Islamic laws.

The compilation of the Traditions took final form at the hands of Bukhari and Muslim in the third century (ninth century A.D.), and today most Muslims recognize their work as the two correct books on Traditions. Those two compilers established conditions for determining which Traditions would be accepted as authentic, conditions which related only to the persons who narrated the Traditions. Such persons must be of good moral character, pious, honest, of sound discretion, and blessed with a good memory; and the series of such transmitters must be continuous from generation to generation. The first generation was called the Companions, the second was known as the followers, and the third as the followers of the followers. Thus a tradition narrated by the followers only would not be accepted by Bukhari because there would be a gap of a generation from the time of the Prophet.

It must be explained, however, that those conditions for the correctness of a Tradition did not touch the subject matter, for internal criticism was unknown at the time. Consequently we find in the two compilations some Traditions, such as those about the signs of the approaching of the Day of Judgment, which we do not understand even yet. The lapse of two and a half centuries between the death of the Prophet and the compilation of the Sunnah has resulted in many differences between Muslims which continue in our time. In the civil war and struggle for power in the time of Uthman, the third Caliph, irreligious elements among the Muslim people did not refrain from fabricating traditions concerning the merits of some political figures. Accurate judgments concerning the narrators of Traditions became difficult because the political feuds sometimes made the judgments far from objective. Knowledge of the way in which the Traditions were compiled and transmitted facilitates an understanding of the various attitudes toward the Traditions which are found in Muslim countries today.

The *Quran*, which was revealed almost fourteen centuries ago, and the Traditions concerning the Prophet who lived that long ago exclusively in a desert society cannot serve as explicit guides for every situation which might arise centuries later, and especially in the complex societies of the present day. This was recognized by the Prophet himself. Once when he was sending one of his Companions to Yemen to serve as governor, he tested the man by asking him what principles he would follow in his new position. He answered that he would hold to the teachings of the *Quran*. The Prophet asked, "And if you do not find a particular guide in the *Quran*?" He replied, "I shall look for it in the Sunnah." Then the Prophet asked, "Well, what *if* you do not find it in the Sunnah either?" He replied, "In such a case, I shall make use of my own opinion." The Prophet was very pleased with that answer and said, "Thanks to God who has guided the messenger of the Messenger of Allah."

Thus a third basis for Islam became established, the basis of reasoning. We find in the *Quran* many verses which mention reasoning, or thinking, or knowing - verses which exhort us to make use of our brains instead of following blindly the traditions which our ancestors followed. Concerning the Unbelievers of old, the *Quran* says, "Nay, for they say only: Lo we found our fathers following a religion, and we are guided by their footprints" (Surah XLIII, 22). While exhorting us to contemplate nature, the *Quran* says, "In the creation of skies and the earth, the difference between night and day, the ships which run at sea carrying that which is useful for mankind, the rain water which Allah sends down from the sky to revive the earth after its death, and to spread animals on it, and the arrangement of winds and clouds between sky and earth, in all those things there are evidences (for the existence of God) for those who make use of their brains" (Surah II, 164). There is even a verse which says that once upon a time the people of Hell said to one another, "If we had made use of our ears or our brains we would not have been the inhabitants of this Hell" (Surah LXVII, 10).

Originally the word used for reasoning, *qiyas*, meant measure, used in the sense of thinking by comparing one thing with another - reasoning by analogy. As the third source of Islamic law it means determining the proper course of action by reasoning from the *Quran* and the Sunnah. Some men, however, speak of a fourth source of the law of Islam - consensus of opinion, or the agreement of capable men in their judgment on a specific question. This concept was introduced by al Shafi'i, the founder of one of the schools of law. Some people have misunderstood consensus to mean simply public opinion, and have asserted that if public opinion approves an action it is therefore acceptable to Islam. For Muslim legislators, consensus is the agreement reached among qualified religious leaders in one place at one time.

There has never been a means by which such agreement might be found for all Muslims everywhere. True consensus, ijma, was possible only during the time of the first two Caliphs and part of the rule of the third Caliph. Ijma now only means that some agreement has been found in some places concerning the interpretation of certain verses of the *Quran*. As a basic source for Islam, it is reasoning, not consensus which is the third source. The *Quran*, the Sunnah, and reasoning are the generally accepted sources of Islam.

There are, as has been seen, some exceptions to the position that these are the three sources of Islam, for some people hold that only the *Quran* and Sunnah can give us a solid foundation for Islam. Their attitude, however, is easily refuted for it must be admitted that the problems of the world today are very different from those of the time of

Muhammad, and their attitude would make Islam a dead religion.

Actually, Islam is a dynamic religion, based on the *Quran*, the Sunnah, and reasoning. Some people confuse ijtihad with reasoning, but if used in the sense of a personal preference it is obviously not the same thing. In the sense of careful reasoning as to the implications of the *Quran* and the Sunnah, it is the same as reasoning. Unchecked, ijtihad might even lead to disagreement concerning such basic ideas as right and wrong, good and bad! To understand the unity and diversity in Islam it is necessary to understand these three sources of Islamic law: the *Quran*, the Sunnah, and the proper use of reason.

THE CREED OF ISLAM

The unity in Islam is shown in the acceptance of the six articles of belief, the fundamentals of Islam - belief in God, Angels, revealed scriptures, prophets, the Day of Judgment, and the destiny of man for good or evil. These beliefs are held by all Muslims.

The proof for the existence of God is found in the *Quran* through meditation on the beauty and order of nature. The harmony of the natural world shows that there is one benevolent Allah who created the universe and all human beings. The oneness of God is His most distinctive characteristic, as is shown in Surah CXII of the *Quran*, "He is One. He it is to whom we address our demands. He never gives birth and He was never born, nothing is similar to Him."

In addition, all good qualities can be ascribed to God; He is the Merciful, the Generous, the Lover, the Great, and the High. Some traditions mention ninety-nine names of God, but it is probable that the number is to be understood, not literally, but only as a very great number. Thus a Muslim may choose among those names of God the one which is psychologically relevant in the circumstances, a practice which is common throughout the Muslim world. Theological treatises mention that there are twenty attributes of God, usually listed in four divisions. The first division includes only the essential attribute of existence. The second division is made up of the five negative attributes - no beginning, no end (eternity), difference from contingent things, independence of existence, unity (uniqueness). The third division includes the seven abstract attributes of power, will, knowledge, life, and the ability to hear, see, and speak. The fourth division, which is called the correlative of the abstract attributes, is made up of present participles of the abstract attributes of the third division - powerful (overpowering), willing, knowing, living, hearing, seeing, speaking.

The theologians stressed that the attributes of God are not separate from the essence of God. This division of attributes is arbitrary and not clear, but most of the people consider it to be an essential element of belief. The series of attributes is clearly an artificial reflection of a reaction to Greek philosophy; it is not found in this form in the *Quran* or the Hadith, and has made people think in an unhealthy way. It is more appropriate to understand the existence of God through contemplating nature, as is revealed in the *Quran*. The differences of opinion among Muslims as to whether or not God resembles human beings, and the opinion of some common people that God resembles a medieval absolute king, arise only from different patterns of education; they are not fundamental to Islam.

Angels are creatures who serve as liaison between God the Almighty and His apostles, bringing the Godly messages and revelations to them. Some Traditions speak of Angels who guard Hell, some who guard Paradise, some who ask dead people about their beliefs, and some who record all of man s actions; there is also an Angel who will blow the trumpet to awaken all human beings on the Day of Judgment. Common people tend to understand such

Traditions literally, while educated people prefer to understand them figuratively with an interpretation more or less acceptable to reason. The *Quran*, the holy revealed Book of Islam, mentions three former revealed books - the Book of David, the Book of Moses, and the Book of Jesus. This does not necessarily mean that there were no other revealed books, but only that we do not know whether or not any other books were revealed. Most people believe that there were no other revealed books than those three and the *Quran*.

The names of twenty-five apostles are found in the *Quran*, beginning with Adam. Muslims depend entirely on the text of the *Quran* for information concerning those prophets since the *Quran* is the only source about which there is not the slightest doubt. It is fortunate that the career of Muhammad is well-known, that there is nothing vague in the records of his life. The Traditions picture him in a very human way. - dealing in commerce, getting married, having children, losing his wife and his sons, sharing all common experiences - in no sense a supernatural being. The only difference between Muhammad and the rest of mankind is that he received the revelations of God.

All Muslims recognize Muhammad as a Prophet, and the last of the prophets. They see that the proof of his revelation lies not in external miracles but in the nature of the revelation itself. When the question is asked as to whether or not the teachers of other religions, such as the Buddha or Confucius, were prophets, no clear answer can be given. The *Quran* is not explicit on that point, for it says, "I have sent many apostles before you (Muhammad). I have told you about some of them, and I have not told you about some others" (Surah XL, 78). Some people conclude that the teachers of other religions are included in the "some others" that God has not told about, but other people say that only by studying the spirit and fundamentals of those religions can one determine whether or not they are of the same spirit as Islam, and their founders might be considered to have been prophets.

The Day of Judgment is mentioned in many verses in the *Quran*. When the sky is split, when the stars collide, when the mountains are like cotton, when the earth quakes - that is the Day of Judgment. On that day all people are awakened and their deeds are weighed; those having a heavy weight of good records will live happily in Paradise and those who have light weights will go to a Hell full of fire. The descriptions of Paradise are in such beautiful language that they make a deep impression on anyone who listens to the recital of the parts of the *Quran* which refer to it. On the other hand, Hell is described in a horrible way in many passages in the *Quran*. Although the common people are inclined to understand the descriptive passages in a literal sense, educated people recognize them as figurative. When the passages which describe Paradise and Hell are meditated upon it is easy to understand what great power they have to motivate people toward good actions.

The sixth fundamental belief of Islam is the belief in destiny for good or for evil. There has been much misunderstanding of the meaning of the word destiny. Many people have thought that a belief in destiny implies that everything will happen by itself, whether we wish it or not, and that such a belief will make people apathetic and indifferent toward all progress. The real meaning of belief in destiny, however, is that one believes that God created an orderly world and one should act according to the nature of that world. Thus a man with a sense of destiny will be active in doing anything which he judges to be good, knowing that if anything bad happens in spite of all precautionary measures, then there will be no reason for regret or for blaming oneself. Then he would say that it was the destiny of Allah.

This meaning was illustrated by the Caliph Umar Ibn al-Khattab when he decided not to visit Palestine while there was an epidemic there. A companion asked him, "Are you evading the destiny of God?" He answered, "Yes. I run from the destiny of God to another destiny of God."

There is no difference among Muslims concerning these six fundamental beliefs of Islam. Every Muslim believes in God, in Angels, in revealed scriptures, in apostles, in the Day of Judgment, and in destiny. The differences are only in the interpretations, as mentioned above, and these differences result primarily from the differences in standards of education.

THE PILLARS OF ISLAM

The fundamental beliefs of Islam have their practical consequences in everyday life. Tradition says that the worship obligations, or requirements, of Islam are known as the Pillars of Islam; and the guide for dealings, for the responsibilities of human beings in society, are covered by fiqh, Islamic law.

According to Tradition, Islam is based on five foundations: the confession that there is no God but Allah and that Muhammad is the Apostle of Allah; prayer; almsgiving; fasting during Ramadan; and pilgrimage to Mecca by those who are able to go.

Of these five pillars, concerning the first one there is no variation anywhere in the Islamic world. All Muslims know the Word of Witness, the confession of faith in Allah and the recognition of Muhammad as His Messenger, and all Muslims repeat it as their confession of faith. The prayers are of two kinds, obligatory and optional. The five daily prayers are obligatory, including the obligation to attend the congregational prayer on Friday in the mosque. It is impossible to estimate what proportion of the people perform the five daily prayers regularly, since women usually say their prayers in the home and men may perform the salat at the mosque, at work, or at home.

There is no religious superior who checks on the performance of the prayers. It is possible, however, to observe the attendance at the Friday noon prayers in the mosque. Large number of people will be seen at the mosque on Friday in Indonesia, in Turkey, Egypt, and parts of the Maghrib, and in the Shi'a mosques of Iran, to mention only the most obvious places. The smallest attendance at the Friday service would be found in China, and in the Soviet Union. The optional, or facultative, prayers are of many kinds, such as the additional prayers before and after the obligatory prayers, prayers on the holiday after the month of fasting, prayers at the festival which marks the end of the pilgrimage, and prayers in times of need - which are offered by anyone at any time or place when the help of God is sought. Prayer for a person who died is necessary, since the spirit of such a person continues to live. Optional prayers can be performed at any time because a Muslim is in constant relation with God.

There are minor differences from country to country in the manner of praying, differences of no importance which have grown up through varying interpretations in the schools of jurisprudence. Some people emphasize the performance of optional prayers after the Friday prayers, while others do not. There are slight differences in posture; for example, in some countries, while standing, the people put their hands one upon the other in front of the lower part of the chest, while others who follow the school of Malik or of the Shi'as bend their hands down. Such differences are of no importance, and the unity is shown by the complete harmony among Muslims as to the times of prayer, the ablutions which must be performed before prayer, and the facing toward the Ka'ba in Mecca.

The mosques are the centers for prayer, teaching, and service in the Muslim world and are recognized as the distinctive symbol of Islam even though they differ considerably from country to country. Originally the mosque was very simple, for any ground can be made a place for prayer. The first mosque built by Muhammad in Medina was a simple plot of ground with clay walls on all sides and a roof of palm branches. As Islam spread to other countries the mosques adopted the architecture of those countries. In China, for example, we find mosques which resemble pagodas in many ways; in Indonesia most mosques are built near streams which the people can use for ablutions; in Arab countries the big mosques have one section roofed for winter use and an open area for use in summer. In recent years the greatest activity in building new mosques has been in Turkey and Indonesia.

There is great variety in the minarets which are used for the call to prayer. They may be simple square or round towers, as in the Levant; or elaborate architectural designs as in Egypt; or the slender, pencil-shaped minarets of Turkey; in Iraq and Iran the minarets in Shi'a mosques are often beautifully decorated with colorful ceramic tiles; in Indonesia they stand as separate towers, or in the villages may even be a chair in a high tree; and in China the government did not permit the building of minarets. Indonesia is unique in using drums for the call to prayer.

It is generally agreed that a Muslim should give alms which amount to a tenth of the agricultural yield immediately after harvest, and a fortieth part of his wealth of goods, or of gold after a lapse of one year if it reaches the quantity of thirty.-eight grams - and about the same proportion of wealth in animals. The *Quran* specifies that such alms are to be given to the poor, the needy, the collectors of zakat, and whose hearts are to be appeased, slaves, travelers, debtors, and those who are on the path of God. While the source and the recipients of zakat are generally agreed upon, there are variations in the practice of distribution, largely because most Islamic countries do not have official collectors or an official organization for administering almsgiving. Turkey has a ministry of waqfs, as a part of the government; some of the Arab countries have governmental departments which are concerned with the administration of religious endowments; but in most countries almsgiving in goods or money is a voluntary gift either to individuals or to pious foundations. In Arabia they still give animals as alms since they have official collectors, but there is no almsgiving of goods or gold. In Indonesia people pay zakat on agricultural products to the religious men in the Islamic country reaches the proportion imposed by religion.

Pilgrimage remains a very important force making for unity in the Muslim world. Each year Muslims from all over the world, Muslims of every color and race, gather in the Holy Land to fulfill their obligation to make the pilgrimage. After almost fourteen centuries the pilgrimage retains its importance for Islam in spite of the development of new means of communication, for there Muslims from all over the world, religious leaders and common folk, meet and exchange views. Such personal contact is necessary to keep the spirit of universal brotherhood alive. The minor details in practices associated with the pilgrimage are only variations which developed in the different schools of law and are not significant.

In modern times the improvement in travel facilities has made it possible for large numbers of people to make the pilgrimage even from distant lands, an important factor in bringing the Muslims of the Far East into closer relations with their brothers of the Turkish and Arab areas of Islam. In recent years the major obstacles to the pilgrimage, other than the ever-present difficulty of being able to afford the expense, have been currency restrictions and the limitations imposed by the governments of the Soviet Union and China. Pilgrimage remains one of the vital pillars of Islam, wisely instituted by the *Quran* and Sunnah as a form of worship which brings Muslims closer to God and to each other.

ISLAMIC LAW

As we have seen, the practical consequences of the six fundamentals of Islam include both worship, as outlined under the five Pillars of Islam, and dealings, or the responsibilities of Muslims in their everyday life. These practical consequences, the particular requirements of religion, have been codified in the four schools of law which exist amicably side by side in the Muslim world.

The Maliki school which was founded during the second century after Muhammad shows preference for the Traditions and practices of Medina where the Prophet lived for thirteen years; it is found today chiefly in North Africa, some parts of Egypt, and in the Sudan. Also in the second century there lived in Baghdad a silk merchant named Abu Hanifah, a rationalist who based his teachings concerning the consequences of religion on the *Quran* and the Traditions. He wrote no book himself, but his disciples spread his liberal teachings and founded the Hanaifi School of jurisprudence which is found in Turkey, Afghanistan, Central Asia, Pakistan, India, and Egypt.

Another of Abu Hanifah's disciples, Muhammad Ibn Idris al-Shafi'i, founded the Shafi'i school in the third century; he was a great systematic jurist who took an Intermediate position between extreme legalism and traditionalism. The school of Shafi'i interpretation is predominant in South Arabia, South India, Thailand, Malaya, Indonesia, and the Philippines. The fourth school of law was also founded in the third century after the Prophet by Ahmad Hanbal, a resident in Baghdad; he stressed the Traditions and distrusted the use of reason. The Hanbalis arc found in Central Arabia, Syria, and some parts of Africa.

These four schools of law - covering the four divisions of rites, contracts, matrimonial law, the penal codes - were worked out so completely by their founders over a thousand years ago that those who came after them found fully adequate systems of law which met all the requirements of their times. A Muslim was free to choose any one of the four systems for his personal guidance, but the prevailing practice was to choose the school of law which was followed in the place of a man's birth. Thus a man born in Indonesia is usually a follower of Shafi'i law, while a man born in Turkey will be a Hanafite.

The influence of birth was so great that many Muslims later became convinced that one did not need to look back to the original sources of the *Quran* and the Sunnah, for they believed wrongly that no one in these later days has a capacity for reasoning equal to that of the founders of the schools of law. They became imitators of their predecessors on the basis of a belief that every period since the time of the Prophet has been inferior to the earlier days. While it might be true that those who lived in the time of the Prophet could understand religion better than the people of today who must study Islam by means of documents only, we cannot ignore the considerable change in the social situation and world conditions during the past fourteen centuries. The insistence on imitating the predecessors reflects a loss of self-confidence which was at one time widespread in Islamic communities. The texts of the *Quran* are still and will always be valid, but we should understand them in the light of present knowledge. One of the great tasks facing religious scholars in our time is the re-examination of the jurisprudence of Islam in the light of reason and modern knowledge. Since Islam does not make a distinction between the secular and the religious, and since a large part of the Muslim world has but recently attained political independence and is now playing a significant role in world affairs, this re-examination of Islamic law is all the more urgently needed.

The relation between Islamic law and the law of the government is a pressing issue in modern times. In Turkey the national law is avowedly secular and evens the waqf funds are administered by secular authorities. In Egypt, Pakistan, and India the problem of the relation of Islamic and national law is the subject of frequent public discussion, and in Indonesia several political parties have grown up around this issue. Another problem is the relation between Islamic law and the customary law of a country, as has been noted in China and Indonesia in particular. This will inevitably continue to be a problem as Islam spreads throughout the rest of the world.

SECTS IN ISLAM

From the beginning, the basic sources of Islam have been the *Quran* and the Sunnah. Muslims have always looked to the *Quran* as their guide and have prayed and fasted and made pilgrimages as the Prophet did. For the details governing their lives, Muslims have relied upon their reason in applying the principles of the *Quran* and the Sunnah, and this has been the cause of the different schools of law, the various tendencies, and the sects which are found in Islam. Followers of the Hanafi School of law tend toward rationalism, such as is found among the Mu'tazilities; the Shafi'i school follows the moderate theology of the Ash'arites; the Malikites are predestinationist; and the Hanbalites tend to be literal in their interpretation of theology. These are theological tendencies, but not sectarian differences.

Among the Shi'as the three leading sects are the Ithna Ashariya, the Sab'iya, and the Zaidis. The Ithna Ashariya is the major group among the Shi'as, found primarily in Iraq and Iran; they accept the twelve Imams. The Sab'iya, sometimes called the Seveners because they broke away over the claim that Isma'il was the seventh Imam, are also known as the Isma'ilis. They have divided into several sects, of which the best known is the group which follows the Agha Khan, found in Pakistan, India, Iran, Syria, and East

Africa. The Zaidis, now found in Yemen, are a small Shi'a sect which has drawn closer to the Sunnis over the years.

The Kharijites, who rebelled against Ali, were originally Shi'a and have been somewhat influenced by Sunni thought. They are found in Oman and Muscat, and in North Africa where they are known as Ibadis. More than ninety per cent of the Muslims of the world are Sunnis, followers of the Sunnah. The only sects of any importance among the Sunnis are the Wahhabis, the reformist sect of Arabia, and the Qadiani sect of Pakistan which is generally looked upon as somewhat heretical - although its Lahori branch is not always so regarded. The various tendencies among the Sunnis have often led to differences in point of view, but not to the creation of new sects. The most widely accepted theological position is that of the Ash'arites. The rationalism of the Mu'tazilites at one time almost led to the formation of a recognizable sect, but today the rationalist point of view is only one of several tendencies among the Sunnis. Differences between the firmly orthodox and the modern reformist have not created a sectarian division.

The numerous Sufi orders cannot be classed as separate sects because they are made up of people who consider them to be Sunnis or Shi'as as well as Sufis. Sufi orders have been banned by the government of Turkey, but Sufism continues there as a powerful factor in the Islamic life of the country; both intellectuals and common people study the writings of their famous Sufis and continue their personal Sufi disciplines. The Sufi orders continue to be an important factor in Africa, though their influence in Egypt is declining. There is still, however, a strong interest in Sufi writings among the intellectuals in Egypt. The Shi'as has pronounced Sufi tendencies which have influenced the devotional life in Iran and Iraq as well as Pakistan and India. The Sufism of Pakistan and India has sometimes been influenced by the mysticism of Hinduism, leading on occasion to pantheistic tendencies there.

In Indonesia, as we have seen, Sufism plays a major role in the devotional life of the Muslims, both as organized orders among the common people and as a study and discipline among the intellectuals. Only in China do we find that Sufism has not been an important factor in the Muslim community. Sufism has been especially susceptible to the influences of Greek, Iranian, and Indian thought which have sometimes led it to excesses and fanaticism which were contrary to the real spirit of Islam. Some Sufis even denounced the Pillars of Islam and taught that union with God is the aim of Islam, a pantheistic doctrine which is heretical. Other Sufis have followed the teachings of Ghazali, combining the rituals of Islam with deep religious feeling. Such Sufis have made, and are making today, a valuable contribution to the religious life of the Muslim world.

CHARACTERISTIC ISLAMIC PRACTICES

Muslims are exhorted to follow the straight path of Islam in every detail of their daily lives, guided by the *Quran*, by the example of the life of the Prophet, and by the Hadith. The life of a Muslim should illustrate the teachings and example of the Prophet. When a Muslim baby is born, it is recommended that some one should whisper the call to prayer in his ear, "God is Most Great there is no God other than Allah. Muhammad is the Messenger of God... Welcome prayer.. Welcome good fortune... God is Most Great When the baby is one week old it is suggested that the parents sacrifice a sheep - one sheep for a girl and two for a boy - and distribute the meat among the poor. A baby should be given a good name on the seventh day. It is also recommended that boys should be circumcised, and girls also, for the sake of cleanliness.

The parents are urged to teach the children how to pray so that by the age of nine they should know everything about the prayers, including the proper ablutions to be done before prayers. The ablutions before prayer simply require the washing of the hands up to the wrist, washing the face and the head - a part of it is sufficient - and washing the feet up to the ankle. After any pollution or sexual intercourse, a Muslim must take an obligatory bath; in case there is no water, a symbolic action is necessary.

Muslims are required to pray five times a day, with two prostrations in the early morning before sunrise, four a little before midday, four in the afternoon when the shadow of a thing is as tall as the thing itself, three after sunset, and four about one hour later. Each prayer takes not more than five minutes, though it may be lengthened with optional prayers. It is recommended that the prayers be performed collectively or at least with one companion. In case a person is traveling, two prayers can be performed together and shortened by half. Shi'as customarily carry a small tablet made of the clay from Karbala which they place on the ground and touch with their forehead as they prostrate themselves in prayer.

All Muslims should attend the Friday midday prayer in the mosque and listen attentively to the address given by an Imam. Women may also go to the mosque, but they must pray behind the men. In practice, women either gather at a separate place in the mosque or do not attend the collective prayers at all. At the two major festivals, the Id al-Fitr at the end of the Ramadan fast and the Id al-Adha - or Id al-Qurban - at the end of the pilgrimage, Muslims are urged to perform additional congregational prayers, preferably in the open air, and to listen to the special address by the Imam. Before the prayers at the end of Ramadan they are urged to contribute food to the needy so no one may be hungry that day, and after the pilgrimage prayers they are exhorted to sacrifice a sheep, a cow, or a camel and distribute the meat to the needy.

There is no restriction on association between men and women in the Islamic community, the only reservation in the instructions being that there must be no occasion for misconduct. Thus, a woman must not meet a man alone, nor should a woman travel alone. She must protect her body decently but her face need not be covered. The practice of *purdah*, of veiling the face in public, which is followed in many Islamic countries, is only an exaggeration of the instructions enjoining modesty which has been deep-rooted in Islamic communities by long centuries of ignorance. When a young man wishes to marry he is allowed to see his prospective wife in order to assure the success of the marriage. The girl is protected by her parents, but they must ask her consent before giving her in marriage. If she is a widow, the consent must be explicit, and if she is a virgin tacit consent by silence is sufficient. The bridegroom must pay a dowry to the bride, which may be only a token. Two male witnesses are necessary for the marriage contract. A celebration after the marriage is recommended, but it should not be extravagant.

The husband must provide maintenance for the wife and children. Divorce is permitted only as a last resort. In case differences arise between a husband and his wife, relatives of both parties should serve as a committee of arbitration. Since divorce is a serious event "by which the throne of God is shaken," in the words of the Prophet, it must be delayed by two stages before it becomes final, and during that time the wife must receive maintenance.

A wife can also ask for a divorce on the grounds of cruel treatment, sexual defect, contagious disease, and like conditions which make the marriage intolerable. Polygamy is neither forbidden nor required. It may be called a necessary evil. If a man needs a son and his wife does not give birth to a male, for example, he might take a second wife. The question is still a subject of controversy among Muslim jurists, but there is general agreement that more than one wife is not permitted for the purpose of satisfying one's lust.

Mut'a, a temporary marriage which may be terminated after even one day upon payment of a gift, is permitted among the Shi'as. It was originally permitted by the Prophet, but later the permission was abrogated, according to the Sunnis. The Shi'a still maintain that there was no abrogation, but even those who claim that the permission continues are against the prevalent practice, which does not differ much from prostitution. Adultery is forbidden; if the evidence is sufficient, the prescribed penalty is flogging with eighty lashes or stoning to death if the offender is married. In case of death a man inherits from his wife or a wife inherits from her husband. The laws of inheritance are given in considerable detail but they follow the general principle that a man inherits twice as much as a woman.

This is because the man must bear the responsibility for maintenance of his wife and must provide dowry for the marriage, while a woman who marries will receive both dowry and maintenance. A dead person must be bathed and given ablution before burial and the community must pray for him. The prayer for a dead person is an obligation of the whole community. If it is neglected, the whole community is sinful, but if one person performs the prayer, the community is considered to have performed its duty. It is recommended that neighbors of the bereaved family should prepare food to be offered to the mourners and their visitors. It is also recommended that relatives should visit the grave from time to time to put flowers on it and to pray for the departed soul. Women, however, are urged not to go to the graveyard to pray for the deceased, since they are too sensitive.

Concerning food, Muslims are permitted to eat anything that is not explicitly forbidden. It is related that the Prophet said, "What God permits in His Book is permitted, and what He forbids is forbidden, and what is not mentioned is in favor, therefore take His favor. God does not forget." According to the *Quran*, Muslims are forbidden to eat a corpse, blood, pork, a pagan sacrifice, suffocated animals, animals killed other than by slaughtering, animals which died from a fall, animals killed by other animals, remnants of food eaten by a beast, food offered as a sacrifice to idols. All fish which live in the sea may be eaten, according to the ninety-sixth verse of the fifth Surah. All animals which live in the water and on land, such as frogs, crocodiles, turtles, and the like, are forbidden as food.

Of land animals, it is permitted to eat camels, cows, sheep, horses, and the like. It is forbidden to eat donkeys; beasts with claws such as lions, tigers, wolves, and bears; birds with talons, such as hawks and falcons; animals which the Prophet ordered killed, such as snakes, mice, crows; creatures which the Prophet forbade killing, such as ants and bees; animals judged to be dirty, and animals which live on dirt. In deciding what food can be eaten and what is forbidden Muslim jurisprudence accepts as guides the *Quran*, the Hadith, what the Prophet ordered to be killed and what he forbade killing, and the foods which are abhorrent to human feeling. The verses of the *Quran* make it clear that all kinds of drinks are permitted except wine. Wine is forbidden because it is intoxicating. On this point the Holy *Quran* is so clear that no other interpretation is possible. Thus, however small the quantity may be, the drinking of wine is absolutely forbidden. By wine is meant the fermented juice of grapes.

As to other fermented drinks, there is a difference of opinion among Muslim jurists. Some maintain that juices extracted from fruits other than grapes, such as apples or dates, are permitted. They base their opinion on some Traditions which say that Muhammad sometimes fermented dates for one or two days. A Muslim is forbidden to steal, and if he steals a certain amount deliberately the punishment prescribed is the cutting off of the hands. A Muslim must not gamble nor participate in lotteries. He must not deceive concerning measures or weights; he must not break a promise or go back on his word. He is forbidden to pay or receive interest when borrowing or lending money, but a debtor may present a token of gratitude to the creditor. These requirements and prohibitions, mentioned here only in general outline, are representative of the rules found in the *Quran* and Traditions which govern the lives of all Muslims.

ISLAMIC SOCIETY

To understand the role of Islam in society one must first realize that Islam is a universal religion in which all Muslims are brothers, regardless of differences in homeland, race, color, or rank. This brotherhood does not divide the world into Muslims and non-Muslims, for Muslims must be friendly toward non-Muslims so long as they are friendly, so long as they do not attack Islam. Islam has retained its unity and universal characteristics in the midst of such diverse cultures as those of Arabia, Greece, Rome, and Iran in ancient times, and later in the cultures of Africa, Egypt, Turkey, Central Asia, India, China, and Southeast Asia. Once more the universalism of Islam is being shown as it comes into contact with the new culture of the West.

In this interplay between Islam and the various cultures of the world it should be remembered that Islam has no master organization which requires conformity or organizes missionary programmes. The interplay is a spontaneous movement on the part of individual Muslims who seek to follow the straight path of Islam. These Muslims recognize no distinction between the religious and the secular; they try to follow in their social life the rules revealed to them in the *Quran* and the Sunnah and interpreted in Islamic law. For Islam, the present world is but a transitory existence to be followed by the Eternal World which is better by far, "And verily the latter portion will be better for thee than the former" (Surah XCIII, 4). This does not mean that we must neglect this world; on the contrary, Islam warns us against neglecting it, for the *Quran* says, "But seek the abode of the Hereafter in that which Allah hath given thee and neglect not thy portion of the world, and be thou kind even as Allah hath been kind to thee, and seek not corruption in the earth; lo! Allah loveth not corrupters" (Surah XXVIII, 77).

Islam recognizes the importance of life in the community in this world, but it warns the Muslim against considering this world as the end of existence. Moral and religious values must be seen to be higher than material values. The importance of social justice is constantly emphasized in Islam through the obligation of zakat and the distribution of gifts at the times of the great festivals. In the older Islamic countries this has been the origin of waqfs for all kinds of service to the community. The teachings concerning zakat stress the principle that the ownership of wealth is a privilege, not a right, and one which imposes obligations to the community. In the Traditions the Prophet exhorts us to give our servants the same food we eat and the same clothes we wear.

In Islam the merit of a person depends upon his deeds, not upon his words, nor his ancestors, nor his rank in the community. The *Quran* says, "There is nothing for the person but what he has done" (Surah LIII, 39) and again, "The highest among you is the most pious" (Surah XLIX, 13). The only recognized difference in rank in Islam is that which is merited by religious devotion and insight. Such recognition is accorded on the basis of deeds, not on the basis of office. Islam has no ordained clergy, no religious hierarchy with authority over their fellow Muslims. The ulama, the Shaikh, Mullah, Imam, Ahund, Mufti, Mujtahid, Hatib - all are only men like the others in the Muslim community, men who perform special services and are respected and elevated only on the basis of the Quranic principle that the highest is the most pious.

Slavery was customary at the time that Islam was revealed, but Islam prepared the grounds for its elimination. It encourages the emancipation of slaves by giving them the possibility of purchasing their freedom, it urges that part of zakat be given to slaves to help them free themselves, and it offers the possibility of atonement for certain sins, such as having sexual intercourse during fasting days, by releasing slaves. Women are given equality with men, in principle, for the *Quran* says, "Whoever, male or female, who is a believer, performs good actions, they will enter into Paradise" (Surah IV, 124), and again, "Men have reward for what they do, and women have reward for what they do" (Surah IV, 32). But we cannot deny that in general men are superior to women and consequently men have authority over women. The *Quran* says, "Men have authority over women" (Surah IV, 14).

With the rise of nationalism in the modern world, the relation of nationalism to Islam has become a problem which is frequently discussed. Many people think that since Islam is universal it must be against nationalism, but this is not the case. Universalism can begin with national loyalty, for nationalism is simply the result of the organization of a group of people in one political body, regardless of their differences in religion. Islam does not prohibit such political organizations so long as they do not jeopardize the essentials of Islamic teachings. Nationalism can unite or divide, and when it is guided by the universal principles of Islam it can lead men to unity rather than to divisions. In this regard it should be noted that the demand for the Caliphate, in the political sense, has greatly lessened in modern times. Pan-Islamism in our day is not a movement for one super-government over all Muslims, but for cooperation between Islamic nations.

Jihad, holy war, has sometimes been misunderstood as meaning that Muslims must declare war on non-Muslims until they accept Islam. This mistake arises from a misreading of the *Quran* without knowing the context of the verses and the circumstances in which they were revealed. The verses which call for war against unbelievers were revealed when pagans were still putting obstacles in the way of the activities of Muhammad even after opportunities for reconciliation had been given. War in Islam is only legitimate when it is declared in defense of religion, property, and prestige. The *Quran* says, 'Fight in the way of God those who wage war on you, and do not commit aggression. God does not like aggressors" (Surah II, 190).

Islam does not approve of hostility toward other religions. Rather, it proclaims freedom of religion and forbids coercion in religion. During his lifetime, Muhammad himself was very kind toward his neighbors and friends of other beliefs, Jews as well as Christians. He even married a Jewish woman, Safijah, and a Christian slave, Marie, who was given him by the ruler of Egypt. When the Emperor of Abyssinia died, Muhammad prayed for him in recognition of his help given to the Muslims who took refuge there in the early days of Islam. Islamic society has been greatly influenced, and the spread of Islam has been aided, by the educational opportunities offered through the mosques and religious leaders. The Prophet encouraged education by appointing many of his Companions as teachers in Arabia when Islam spread throughout the country. It was ruled that a poor man could marry a woman with a dowry of teaching her a chapter of the *Quran*.

As Islam spread to other lands, centers of study grew up at Baghdad, Kufa, and many other cities of the Muslim world. The system of education was simple, without organized programme or ceremony. Any pupil could approach a teacher and stay with him as long as he' continued to learn; then he might go on to other teachers, or receive a license to be a teacher himself. In the family the parents educated their children. The teachers did not form a special class but were at the same time landowners, merchants, or government officials. This system continues today in most Muslim countries. In addition, there have been in most countries the madrasas associated with the mosques, and special schools of higher learning. The oldest Islamic university is the Al Azhar in Cairo, founded in the fourth century (tenth century A.D.). Other centers for higher Islamic studies today are found at Fez in Morocco, at Zaitouna University in Tunisia, at Medina, at Istanbul and Ankara in Turkey, at Baghdad and Karbala in Iraq, at Tehran in Iran, at Lahore in Pakistan, at Lucknow and at Alighar and Usmania Universities in India, and at Jogjakarta in Indonesia.

In some of these centers the Islamic studies are associated with government-supported universities; there are also government universities in other countries which offer special courses in Islam, as is the case on Taiwan. Instruction in Islam is given in local languages at the lower levels, but for higher studies a good knowledge of Arabic is necessary and mastery of Persian and Turkish is required for any extensive research. Since art and music flourish in times of peace and prosperity, there was little time for them in the early days of the Prophet. Muhammad, however, approved of the music known in his day. He forbade the art which was prevalent in his time, consisting chiefly of human figures, since it was symbolic of idols and would have spread paganism. Because of that, the literal-minded jurists deduced that Islam opposed art and music, which is not correct. The better deduction would have been that we must be careful of the consequences of any kind of art. Art for art's sake is unknown in Islam. As long as art is useful as a means of heightening religion and morality, it is permitted; but if it leads to immorality, it is forbidden.

LATEST DEVELOPMENTS IN ISLAM

When the Mu'tazilite, or rational, movement was suppressed and the political organization of the Muslim world disintegrated, the Muslim people lost their vitality. They neglected the study of the *Quran* and the Traditions which are the original sources of Islam and instead adopted the teachings of the scholars. They thought that ijtihad was forbidden and that they must only imitate the four schools of law. Instead of making use of reason, they accepted the four schools of law as complete and unchanging and turned to mysticism and belief in the supernatural powers of saints, dead and alive. That gave rise to the worship of the graves of saints which is found today in all Islamic countries from North Africa to Indonesia.

The Wahhabi movement in Arabia was a reaction against the worship of saints, but it made use of force rather than arguments, and failed to establish a general reform. After the French occupied Egypt many scholars studied in Europe and a renaissance was started which culminated in the work of the great scholar, Muhammad Abduh, who brought new ideas to the people of Egypt. At about the same time the Muslims of India, led by such men as Sir Sayyid Ahmad Khan, who founded Alighar University, became conscious of their cultural importance and their national existence. Within the past half-century the greater ease of communication and travel has brought the peoples of the Muslim world into closer contact with each other and with the cultures of the rest of the world and made them aware of the need for a new evaluation of the ideas of the jurists and thinkers of the middle ages.

This is the period in which much of the Muslim world has attained political independence and the people have been preoccupied with political and international problems. Today the Muslims of Morocco, Tunisia, Egypt, the Levant, Turkey, Iraq, Iran, Pakistan, India, and Indonesia are vitally concerned with problems associated with the establishment of their new, independent governments. At the same time, the Muslims of Algeria and much of Africa, of the Soviet Union and of China, are struggling with political controls which are not encouraging to Islam and are often inimical. These political problems have been faced at the time when the impact of Western culture in the Muslim world has been most pronounced.

More than anything else, Islam today needs a period of peace in order that favorable conditions may develop for the growth of Islamic thought. Since the time of Ibn Khaldun, more than five centuries ago, no great thinker has arisen in the Muslim world. Now more than ever there is a need for a time of peace and intellectual freedom in which devout thinkers can interpret the *Quran* in the light of the progress of human knowledge. The rituals will remain as they are, the fundamentals will remain unchanged, but the understanding of Islam will be illuminated anew for our time. At the present time, there are four major tendencies in the Islamic world - orthodoxy, reform, Sufism, and Shi'a. The increase in commumcation and in education is bringing to the followers of each tendency a better understanding of the others. Significant progress is being made in Cairo in encouraging better understanding and reconciliation between Shi'a and Sunni. Orthodoxy is becoming less reactionary and the reformers less intolerant.

The Sufi orders are declining in influence at the same time that the devotional and mystical teachings of the Sufi masters are being studied more sympathetically by intellectuals. In Turkey, Egypt, and Indonesia in particular there are many evidences of a new vitality and interest in Islamic thought. Many books are being published, many students are engaged in Islamic studies, and new mosques are being built. Islam spread originally along the trade routes through North Africa, Iran, Central Asia, Indonesia, and China. As Muslim traders settled along those routes they married and established families which often became the nucleus for a new Muslim community. In spite of the diversities of cultures, they maintained the unity of Islam through the centuries. Today, with trade routes easily followed around the world, it is inevitable that the same process will be repeated and Islam will spread to new regions where it has not been known.

In this discussion of the unity and variety of Islam we have seen that divergences from the essential unity of Islam have occurred only when there is ignorance among the common people - a low level of education. It is the task of the present generation to provide training in the essentials of Islam, to know Islam deeply, for out of that knowledge of the straight path of Islam will come the unity of belief and practice which has been revealed to mankind in the *Quran* and the Sunnah.

"The story admits of being told up to this point,
But what follows is hidden, and inexpressible in words.
If you should speak and try a hundred ways to express it,
'Tis useless; the mystery becomes no clearer,
You can ride on saddle and horse to the sea-coast,
But then you must use a horse of wood (i.e. *a boat).*
A horse of wood is useless on dry land,
It is the special vehicle of voyagers by sea.
Silence is this horse of wood,
Silence is the guide and support of men at sea."

No one can approach the subject of this chapter-the state of the mystic who has reached his journey's end-without feeling that all symbolical descriptions of union with God and theories concerning its nature are little better than leaps in the dark.

How shall we form any conception of that which is declared to be ineffable by those who have actually experienced it? I can only reply that the same difficulty confronts us in dealing with all mystical phenomena, though it appears less formidable at lower levels, and that the poet's counsel of silence has not prevented him from interpreting the deepest mysteries of Sufism with unrivalled insight and power.

Whatever terms may be used to describe it, the unitive state is the culmination of the simplifying process by which the soul is gradually isolated from all that is foreign to itself, from all that is not God. Unlike Nirvana, which is merely the cessation of individuality, *fana*, the passing-away of the Sufi from his phenomenal existence, involves *baqa*, the continuance of his real existence. He who dies to self lives in God, and *fana*, the consummation of this death, marks the attainment of *baqa*, or union with the divine life. Deification, in short, is the Moslem mystic's *ultima Thule*.

In the early part of the tenth century Husayn ibn Mansur, known to fame as al-Hallaj (the wool-carder), was barbarously done to death at Baghdad. His execution seems to have been dictated by political motives, but with these we are not concerned. Amongst the crowd assembled round the scaffold, a few, perhaps, believed him to be what he said he was; the rest witnessed with exultation or stern approval the punishment of a blasphemous heretic. He had uttered in two words a sentence which Islam has, on the whole, forgiven but has never forgotten: "*Ana 'l-Haqq*"-"I am God."

The recently published researches of M. Louis Massignon, *Kitab al-Tawasin* makes it possible, for the first time, to indicate the meaning which Hallaj himself attached to this celebrated formula, and to assert definitely that it does not agree with the more orthodox interpretations offered at a later epoch by Sufis belonging to various schools. According to Hallaj, man is essentially divine. God created Adam in His own image. He projected from Himself that image of His eternal love, that He might behold Himself as in a mirror. Hence He bade the angels worship Adam (Kor. 2.32), in whom, as in Jesus, He became incarnate.

"Glory to Him who revealed in His humanity (*i.e.* in Adam) the secret of His radiant divinity,

And then appeared to His creatures visibly in the shape of one who ate and drank (Jesus)."

Since the 'humanity' (*nasut*) of God comprises the whole bodily and spiritual nature of man, the 'divinity' (*lahut*) of God cannot unite with that nature except by means of an incarnation or, to adopt the term employed by Massignon, an infusion (*hulul*) of the divine Spirit, such as takes place when the human spirit enters the body. {Massignon appears to be right in identifying the Divine Spirit with the Active Reason (*intellectus agens*), which, according to Alexander of Aphrodisias, is not a part or faculty of our soul, but comes to us from without. The doctrine of Hallaj may be compared with that of Tauler, Ruysbroeck, and others concerning the birth of God in the soul.} Thus Hallaj says in one of his poems:

"Thy Spirit is mingled in my spirit even as wine is mingled with pure water.

When anything touches Thee, it touches me. Lo, in every case Thou art I!"

And again:

"I am He whom I love, and He whom I love is I:

We are two spirits dwelling in one body.

If thou seest me, thou seest Him,

And if thou seest Him, thou seest us both."

This doctrine of personal deification, in the peculiar form which was impressed upon it by Hallaj, is obviously akin to the central doctrine of Christianity, and therefore, from the Moslem standpoint, a heresy of the worst kind. It survived unadulterated only amongst his immediate followers. The Hululis, *i.e.* those who believe in incarnation, are repudiated by Sufis in general quite as vehemently as by orthodox Moslems. But while the former have unhesitatingly condemned the doctrine of *hulul*, they have also done their best to clear Hallaj from the suspicion of having taught it. Three main lines of defence are followed:

Hallaj did not sin against the Truth, but he was justly punished in so far as he committed a grave offence against the Law. He "betrayed the secret of his Lord" by proclaiming to all and sundry the supreme mystery which ought to be reserved for the elect. Hallaj spoke under the intoxicating influence of ecstasy. He imagined himself to be united with the divine essence, when in fact he was only united with one of the divine attributes. Hallaj meant to declare that there is no essential difference or separation between God and His creatures, inasmuch as the divine unity includes all being. A man who has entirely passed away from his phenomenal self exists *quâ* his real self, which is God.

"In that glory is no 'I' or 'We' or 'Thou.'

'I,' 'We,' 'Thou,' and 'He' are all one thing."

It was not Hallaj who cried *"Ana 'l-Haqq,"* but God Himself, speaking, as it were, by the mouth of the selfless Hallaj, just as He spoke to Moses through the medium of the burning bush (Kor. 20.8-14).

The last explanation, which converts *Ana 'l-Haqq* into an impersonal monistic axiom, is accepted by most Sufis as representing the true Hallajian teaching. In a magnificent ode Jalaluddin Rumi describes how the One Light shines in myriad forms through the whole universe, and how the One Essence, remaining ever the same, clothes itself from age to age in the prophets and saints who are its witnesses to mankind.

"Every moment the robber beauty rises in a different shape, ravishes the soul, and disappears.

Every instant that Loved One assumes a new garment, now of eld, now of youth.

Now He plunged into the heart of the substance of the potter's clay-the Spirit plunged, like a diver.

Anon He rose from the depths of mud that is moulded and baked, and then He appeared in the world.

He became Noah, and at His prayer the world was flooded while. He went into the Ark.

He became Abraham and appeared in the midst of the fire, which turned to roses for His sake.

For a while He was roaming on the earth to pleasure Himself,

Then He became Jesus and ascended to the dome of Heaven and began to glorify God.

In brief, it was He that was coming and going in every generation thou hast seen,

Until at last He appeared in the form of an Arab and gained the empire of the world.

What is it that is transferred? What is transmigration in reality?

The lovely winner of hearts

Became a sword and appeared in the hand of 'Ali and became the. Slayer of the time.

No! No! for 'twas even He that was crying in human shape, *'Ana 'l-Haqq.'*

That one who mounted the scaffold was not Mansur {Hallaj is often called Mansur, which is properly the name of his father.}, though the foolish imagined it.

Rumi hath not spoken and will not speak words of infidelity: do not disbelieve him!

Whosoever shows disbelief is an infidel and one of those who have been doomed to Hell."

Although in Western and Central Asia-where the Persian kings were regarded by their subjects as gods, and where the doctrines of incarnation, anthropomorphism, and metempsychosis are indigenous-the idea of the God-man was neither so unfamiliar nor unnatural as to shock the public conscience very profoundly, Hallaj had formulated that idea in such a way that no mysticism calling itself Mohammedan could tolerate, much less adopt it. To assert that the divine and human natures may be interfused and commingled {*Hulul* was not understood in this sense by Hallaj, though the verses readily suggest such an interpretation. Hallaj, I think, would have agreed with Eckhart (who said, "The word *I am* none can truly speak but God alone") that the personality in which the Eternal is immanent has itself a part in eternity would have been to deny the principle of unity on which Islam is based. The subsequent history of Sufism shows how deification was identified with unification. The antithesis-God, Man-melted away in the pantheistic theory which has been explained above.

There is no real existence apart from God. Man is an emanation or a reflexion or a mode of Absolute Being. What he thinks of as individuality is in truth not-being; it cannot be separated or united, for it does not exist. Man *is* God, yet with a difference. According to Ibn al-'Arabi the eternal and the phenomenal are two complementary aspects of the One, each of which is necessary to the other.

The creatures are the external manifestation of the Creator, and Man is God's consciousness (*sirr*) as revealed in creation. But since Man, owing to the limitations of his mind, cannot think all objects of thought simultaneously, and therefore expresses only a part of the divine consciousness, he is not entitled to say *Ana 'l-Haqq*, "I am God." He is *a* reality, but not *the* Reality. We shall see that other Sufis-Jalaluddin Rumi, for example-in their ecstatic moments, at any rate, ignore this rather subtle distinction.

The statement that in realising the non-entity of his individual self the Sufi realises his essential oneness with God sums up the Mohammedan theory of deification in terms with which my readers are now familiar. I will endeavour to show what more precise meaning may be assigned to it, partly in my own words and partly by means of illustrative extracts from various authors. Several aspects of *fana* have already been distinguished. The highest of these-the passing-away in the divine essence-is fully described by Niffari, who employs instead of *fana* and *fani* (self-naughted) the terms *waqfat*, signifying cessation from search, and *waqif*, *i.e.* one who desists from seeking and passes away in the Object Sought. Here are some of the chief points that occur in the text and commentary.

Waqfat is luminous: it expels the dark thoughts of 'otherness,' just as light banishes darkness; it changes the phenomenal values of all existent things into their real and eternal values. Hence the *waqif* transcends time and place. "He enters every house and it contains him not; he drinks from every well but is not satisfied; then he reaches Me, and I am his home, and his abode is with Me"-that is to say, he comprehends all the divine attributes and embraces all mystical experiences. He is not satisfied with the names (attributes), but seeks the Named. He contemplates the essence of God and finds it identical with his own. He does not pray. Prayer is from man to God, but in *waqfat* there is nothing but God.

The *waqif* leaves not a rack behind him, nor any heir except God. When even the phenomenon of *waqfat* has disappeared from his consciousness, he becomes the very Light. Then his praise of God proceeds from God and his knowledge is God's knowledge, who beholds Himself alone as He was in the beginning. We need not expect to discover how this essentialisation, substitution, or transmutation is effected. It is the grand paradox of Sufism-the *Magnum Opus* wrought somehow in created man by a Being whose nature is eternally devoid of the least taint of creatureliness. As I have remarked above, the change, however it may be conceived, does not involve infusion of the divine essence (*hulul*) or identification of the divine and human natures (*ittihad*). Both these doctrines are generally condemned. Abu Nasr al-Sarraj criticises them in two passages of his *Kitab al-Luma'*, as follows:

"Some mystics of Baghdad have erred in their doctrine that when they pass away from their qualities they enter into the qualities of God. This leads to incarnation (*hulul*) or to the Christian belief concerning Jesus. The doctrine in question has been attributed to some of the ancients, but its true meaning is this, that when a man goes forth from his own qualities and enters into the qualities of God, he goes forth from his own will and enters into the will of God, knowing that his will is given to him by God and that by virtue of this gift he is severed from regarding himself, so that he becomes entirely devoted to God; and this is one of the stages of Unitarians. Those who have erred in this doctrine have failed to observe that the qualities of God are not God. To make God identical with His qualities is to be guilty of infidelity, because God does not descend into the heart, but that which descends into the heart is faith in God and belief in His unity and reverence for the thought of Him."

In the second passage he makes use of a similar argument in order to refute the doctrine of *ittihad*.

"Some have abstained from food and drink, fancying that when a man's body is weakened it is possible that he may lose his humanity and be invested with the attributes of divinity. The ignorant persons who hold this erroneous doctrine cannot distinguish between humanity and the inborn qualities of humanity. Humanity does not depart from man any more than blackness departs from that which is black or whiteness from that which is white, but the inborn qualities of humanity are changed and transmuted by the all-powerful radiance that is shed upon them from the divine Realities. The attributes of humanity are not the essence of humanity.

Those who inculcate the doctrine of *fana* mean the passing-away of regarding one's own actions and works of devotion through the continuance of regarding God as the doer of these actions on behalf of His servant." Hujwiri characterises as absurd the belief that passing-away (*fana*) signifies loss of essence and destruction of corporeal substance, and that 'abiding' (*baqa*) indicates the indwelling of God in man. Real passing-away from anything, he says, implies consciousness of its imperfection and absence of desire for it. Whoever passes away from his own perishable will abide in the everlasting will of God, but human attributes cannot become divine attributes or vice versa.

"The power of fire transforms to its own quality anything that falls into it, and surely the power of God's will is greater than that of fire; yet fire affects only the quality of iron without changing its substance, for iron can never become fire."

In another part of his work Hujwiri defines 'union' (*jam'*) as concentration of thought upon the desired object. Thus Majnun, the Orlando Furioso of Islam, concentrated his thoughts on Layla, so that he saw only her in the whole world, and all created things assumed the form of Layla in his eyes. Some one came to the cell of Bayazid and asked, "Is Bayazid here?" He answered, "Is any one here but God?"

The principle in all such cases, Hujwiri adds, is the same, namely:

"That God divides the one substance of His love and bestows a particle thereof, as a peculiar gift, upon every one of His friends in proportion to their enravishment with Him; then he lets down upon that particle the shrouds of fleshliness and human nature and temperament and spirit, in order that by its powerful working it may transmute to its own quality all the particles that are attached to it, until the lover's clay is wholly converted into love and all his acts and looks become so many properties of love. This state is named 'union' alike by those who regard the inward sense and the outward expression."

Then he quotes these verses of Hallaj:

"Thy will be done. O my Lord and Master! Thy will be done, O my purpose and meaning! O essence of my being, O goal of my desire, O my speech and my hints and my gestures! O all of my all, O my hearing and my sight, O my whole and my element and my particles!"

The enraptured Sufi who has passed beyond the illusion of subject and object and broken through to the Oneness can either deny that he is anything or affirm that he is all things. As an example of 'the negative way,' take the opening lines of an ode by Jalaluddin which I have rendered into verse, imitating the metrical form of the Persian as closely as the genius of our language will permit:

"Lo, for I to myself am unknown, now in God's name what must I do?

I adore neither the Cross nor the Crescent; I am neither a Giaour nor a Jew.

East nor West, land nor sea is my home, I have kin nor with angel nor gnome,

I am wrought not of fire nor of foam, I am shaped not of dust nor of dew.

I was born not in China afar, not in Saqsin and not in Bulghar;

Not in India, where five rivers are, nor 'Iraq nor Khorasan I grew.

Not in this world nor that world I dwell, not in Paradise, neither in Hell;

Not from Eden and Rizwan I fell, not from Adam my lineage I drew.

In a place beyond uttermost Place, in a tract without shadow of trace,

Soul and body transcending I live in the soul of my Loved One anew!"

The following poem, also by Jalaluddin, expresses the positive aspect of the cosmic consciousness:

"If there be any lover in the world, O Moslems, 'tis I.

If there be any believer, infidel, or Christian hermit, 'tis I.

The wine-dregs, the cupbearer, the minstrel, the harp, and the music,

The beloved, the candle, the drink and the joy of the drunken-'tis I.

The two-and-seventy creeds and sects in the world

Do not really exist: I swear by God that every creed and sect-'tis I.

Earth and air and water and fire-knowest thou what they are?

Earth and air and water and fire, nay, body and soul too-'tis I.

Truth and falsehood, good and evil, ease and difficulty from first to last,

Knowledge and learning and asceticism and piety and faith-'tis I.

The fire of Hell, be assured, with its flaming limbos,

Yes, and Paradise and Eden and the Houris-'tis I.

This earth and heaven with all that they hold,

Angels, Peris, Genies, and Mankind-'tis I."

What Jalaluddin utters in a moment of ecstatic vision Henry More describes as a past experience:

"How lovely" (he says), "how magnificent a state is the soul of man in, when the life of God inactuating her shoots her along with Himself through heaven and earth; makes her unite with, and after a sort feel herself animate, the whole world. He that is here looks upon all things as One, and on himself, if he can then mind himself, as a part of the Whole."

For some Sufis, absorption in the ecstasy of *fana* is the end of their pilgrimage. Thenceforth no relation exists between them and the world. Nothing of themselves is left in them; as individuals, they are dead. Immersed in Unity, they know neither law nor religion nor any form of phenomenal being. But those God-intoxicated devotees who never return to sobriety have fallen short of the highest perfection. The full circle of deification must comprehend both the inward and outward aspects of Deity-the One and the Many, the Truth and the Law.

It is not enough to escape from all that is creaturely, without entering into the eternal life of God the Creator as manifested in His works. To abide in God (*baqa*) after having passed-away from selfhood (*fana*) is the mark of the Perfect Man, who not only journeys *to* God, *i.e.* passes from plurality to unity, but *in* and *with* God, *i.e.* continuing in the unitive state, he returns with God to the phenomenal world from which he set out, and manifests unity in plurality. In this descent:

- "He makes the Law his upper garment
- And the mystic Path his inner garment,"

For he brings down and displays the Truth to mankind while fulfilling the duties of the religious law. Of him it may be said, in the words of a great Christian mystic:

"He goes *towards* God by inward love, in eternal work, and he goes in God by his fruitive inclination, in eternal rest. And he dwells in God; and yet he goes out towards created things in a spirit of love towards all things, in the virtues and in works of righteousness. And this is the most exalted summit of the inner life."

'Afifuddin Tilimsani, in his commentary on Niffari,

describes four mystical journeys:

- The first begins with gnosis and ends with complete passing-away (fana).
- The second begins at the moment when passing-away is succeeded by 'abiding' (baqa).

He who has attained to this station journeys in the Real, by the Real, to the Real, and he then is a reality (*haqq*). Thus travelling onward, he arrives at the station of the *Qutb*, which is the station of Perfect Manhood. He becomes the centre of the spiritual universe, so that every point and limit reached by individual human beings is equally distant from his station, whether they be near or far; since all stations revolve round his, and in relation to the *Qutb* there is no difference between nearness and farness. To one who has gained this supreme position, knowledge and gnosis and passing-away are as rivers of his ocean, whereby he replenishes whomsoever he will. He has the right to guide others to God, and seeks permission to do so from none but himself. Before the gate of Apostleship was closed {*I.e.* before the time of Mohammed, who is the Seal of the Prophets.}, he would have deserved the title of Apostle, but in our day his due title is Director of Souls, and he is a blessing to those who invoke his aid, because he comprehends the innate capacities of all mankind and, like a camel-driver, speeds everyone to his home.

In the *third* journey this Perfect Man turns his attention to God's creatures, either as an Apostle or as a Spiritual Director (Sheykh), and reveals himself to those who would fain be released from their faculties, to each according to his degree: to the adherent of positive religion as a theologian; to the contemplative, who has not yet enjoyed full contemplation, as a gnostic; to the gnostic as one who has entirely passed-away from individuality (*waqif*); to the *waqif* as a *Qutb*. He is the horizon of every mystical station and transcends the furthest range of experience known to each grade of seekers.

The *fourth* journey is usually associated with physical death. The Prophet was referring to it when he cried on his deathbed, "I choose the highest companions." In this journey, to judge from the obscure verses in which 'Afifuddin describes it, the Perfect Man, having been invested with all the divine attributes, becomes, so to speak, the mirror which displays God to Himself.

"When my Beloved appears,
With what eye do I see Him?
"With His eye, not with mine,
For none sees Him except Himself."

The light in the soul, the eye by which it sees, and the object of its vision, all is One.

We have followed the Sufi in his quest of Reality to a point where language fails. His progress will seldom be so smooth and unbroken as it appears in these pages. The proverbial headache after intoxication supplies a parallel to the periods of intense aridity and acute suffering that sometimes fill the interval between lower and higher states of ecstasy. Descriptions of this experience-the Dark Night of the Soul, as it is called by Christian authors-may be found in almost any biography of Mohammedan saints. Thus Jami relates in his *Nafahat al-Uns* that a certain dervish, a disciple of the famous Shihabuddin Suhrawardi, "Was endowed with a great ecstasy in the contemplation of unity and in the station of passing-away (*fana*). One day he began to weep and lament. On being asked by the Sheykh Shihabuddin what ailed him, he answered, 'Lo, I am debarred by plurality from the vision of Unity. I am rejected, and my former state-I cannot find it!' The Sheykh remarked that this was the prelude to the station of 'abiding' (*baqa*), and that his present state was higher and more sublime than the one which he was in before."

Does personality survive in the ultimate union with God? If personality means a conscious existence distinct, though not separate, from God, the majority of advanced Moslem mystics say "No!" As the rain-drop absorbed in the ocean is not annihilated but ceases to exist individually, so the disembodied soul becomes indistinguishable from the universal Deity.

It is true that when Sufi writers translate mystical union into terms of love and marriage, they do not, indeed they cannot, expunge the notion of personality, but such metaphorical phrases are not necessarily inconsistent with a pantheism which excludes all difference. To be united, here and now, with the World-Soul is the utmost imaginable bliss for souls that love each other on earth.

"Happy the moment when we are seated in the Palace, thou and I,

With two forms and with two figures but with one soul, thou and I.

The colours of the grove and the voice of the birds will bestow immortality

At the time when we come into the garden, thou and I.

The stars of heaven will come to gaze upon us;

We shall show them the Moon itself, thou and I.

Thou and I, individuals no more, shall be mingled in ecstasy,

Joyful and secure from foolish babble, thou and I.

All the bright-plumed birds of heaven will devour their hearts with envy

In the place where we shall laugh in such a fashion, thou and I.

This is the greatest wonder, that thou and I, sitting here in the same nook,

Are at this moment both in 'Iraq and Khorasan, thou and I."

Strange as it may seem to our Western egoism, the

prospect of sharing in the general, impersonal immortality of the human soul kindles in the Sufi an enthusiasm as deep and triumphant as that of the most ardent believer in a personal life continuing beyond the grave. Jalaluddin, after describing the evolution of man in the material world and anticipating his further growth in the spiritual universe, utters a heartfelt prayer-for what?-for self-annihilation in the ocean of the Godhead.

"I died as mineral and became a plant,
I died as plant and rose to animal,
I died as animal and I was man.
Why should I fear? When was I less by dying?
Yet once more I shall die as man, to soar
With angels blest; but even from angelhood
I must pass on: all except God doth perish.
When I have sacrificed my angel soul,
I shall become what no mind e'er conceived.
Oh, let me not exist! For Non-existence
Proclaims in organ tones, 'To Him we shall return.'"

8

Mysticism and Sufism

Sufism is generally understood to be the inner, mystical dimension of Islam. A practitioner of this tradition is generally known as a Sufi though some adherents of the tradition reserve this term only for those practitioners who have attained the goals of the Sufi tradition. Another name used for the Sufi seeker is dervish. Classical Sufi scholars have defined Sufism as "a science whose objective is the reparation of the heart and turning it away from all else but God." Alternatively, in the words of the renowned Darqawi Sufi teacher Ahmad ibn Ajiba, "a science through which one can know how to travel into the presence of the Divine, purify one's inner self from filth, and beautify it with a variety of praiseworthy traits."

The Sufi movement has spanned several continents and cultures over a millennium, at first expressed through Arabic, then through Persian, Turkish, and a dozen other languages. Sufi orders, which are either Shi'a or Sunni in doctrine, trace their origins from the Prophet of Islam, Muhammad, through his cousin Ali, or from Abu Bakr. Despite Sufi tradition long being rooted in Muslim culture and tradition, there are some factions of Islam — especially Salafism and Wahhabism — that consider Sufism heretical.

According to some modern proponents, such as Idries Shah, the Sufi philosophy is universal in nature, its roots predating the arising of Islam and the other modern-day religions; likewise, some Muslims feel that Sufism is outside the sphere of Islam.

ETYMOLOGY

The lexical root of Sufi is variously traced to "wool", referring either to the simple cloaks the early Muslim ascetics wore, or possibly to safa "purity". The two were combined by al-Rudhabari who said, "The Sufi is the one who wears wool on top of purity."

Others suggest the origin of the word Sufi is from Ashab as-suffa "Companions of the Porch", who were a group of impoverished Muslims during the time of Muhammad who spent much of their time on the veranda of the Prophet's mosque, devoted to prayer and eager to memorize each new increment of the Qur'ân as it was revealed. Yet another etymology advanced by the 10th century Persian historian Abû Rayhân al-Bîrûnî is that the word is linked with Greek word sophia "wisdom".

BASIC VIEWS

While all Muslims believe that they are on the pathway to God and will become close to God in Paradise — after death and after the "Final Judgment" — Sufis also believe that it is possible to draw closer to God and to more fully embrace the Divine Presence in this life.

The chief aim of all Sufis is to seek the pleasing of God by working to restore within them the primordial state of *fitra,* described in the *Quran* and similar to the concept of Buddha nature. In this state nothing one does defies God, and all is undertaken by the single motivation of love of God. A secondary consequence of this is that the seeker may be led to abandon all notions of dualism or multiplicity, including a conception of an individual self, and to realize the Divine Unity.

Thus Sufism has been characterized as the science of the states of the lower self (the ego), and the way of purifying this lower self of its reprehensible traits, while adorning it instead with what is praiseworthy, *whether or not* this process of cleansing and purifying the heart is in time rewarded by esoteric knowledge of God. This can be conceived in terms of two basic types of law (*fiqh*), an outer law concerned with actions, and an inner law concerned with the human heart. The outer law consists of rules pertaining to worship, transactions, marriage, judicial rulings, and criminal law – what is often referred to, a bit too broadly, as *shariah*. The inner law of Sufism consists of rules about repentance from sin, the purging of contemptible qualities and evil traits of character, and adornment with virtues and good character.

To enter the way of Sufism, the seeker begins by finding a teacher, as the connection to the teacher is considered necessary for the growth of the pupil. The teacher, to be genuine, must have received the authorization to teach (*ijazah*) of another Master of the Way, in an unbroken succession (*silsilah*) leading back to Sufism's origin with the Prophet Muhammad. It is the transmission of the divine light from the teacher's heart to the heart of the student, rather than of worldly knowledge transmitted from mouth to ear, that allows the adept to progress. In addition, the genuine teacher will be utterly strict in his adherence to the Divine Law.

Scholars and adherents of Sufism are unanimous in agreeing that Sufism cannot be learned through books. To reach the highest levels of success in Sufism typically requires that the disciple live with and serve the teacher for many, many years. For instance, Baha-ud-Din Naqshband Bukhari, considered founder of the Naqshbandi Order, served his first teacher, Sayyid Muhammad Baba As-Samasi, for 20 years, until as-Samasi died. He subsequently served several other teachers for lengthy periods of time.

The extreme arduousness of his spiritual preparation is illustrated by his service, as directed by his teacher, to the weak and needy members of his community in a state of complete humility and tolerance for many years. When he believed this mission to be concluded, his teacher next directed him to care for animals, curing their sicknesses, cleaning their wounds, and assisting them in finding provision. After many years of this he was next instructed to spend many years in the care of dogs in a state of humility, and to ask them for support.

As a further example, the prospective adherent of the Mevlevi Order would have been ordered to serve in the kitchens of a hospice for the poor for 1,001 days prior to being accepted for spiritual instruction, and a further 1,001 days in solitary retreat as a precondition of completing that instruction. Some teachers, especially when addressing more general audiences, or mixed groups of Muslims and non-Muslims, make extensive use of parable, allegory, and metaphor. Although approaches to teaching vary among different Sufi orders, Sufism as a whole is primarily concerned with direct personal experience, and as such has sometimes been compared to other, non-Islamic forms of mysticism (e.g., as in the books of Seyyed Hossein Nasr).

Sufism, which is a general term for Muslim mysticism, sprang up largely in reaction against the worldliness which infected Islam when its leaders became the powerful and wealthy rulers of multitudes of people and were influenced by foreign cultures. Harun al-Rashid, eating off gold and silver, toying with a harem of scented beauties, surrounded by an impenetrable retinue of officials, eunuchs and slaves, was a far cry from the stern simplicity of an Umar, who lived in the modest house, wore patched clothes and could be approached by any of his followers.

The typical early Sufi lived in a cell of in a mosque and taught a small band of disciples. The extent to which Sufism was influenced by Buddhist and Hindu mysticism, and by the example Christian hermits and monks, is disputed, but self-discipline and concentration on God quickly led to the belief that by quelling the self and through loving ardour for God it was possible to maintain a union with the divine in which the human self melted away.

In its early stages of development Sufism effectively referred to nothing more than the internalization of Islam. According to one perspective, it is directly from the *Quran*, constantly recited, meditated, and experienced, that Sufism proceeded, in its origin and its development. Others have held that Sufism is the strict emulation of the way of Muhammad, through which the heart's connection to the Divine is strengthened. From the traditional Sufi point of view, the esoteric teachings of Sufism were transmitted from the Prophet Muhammad to those who had the capacity to acquire the direct experiential gnosis of God, which was passed on from teacher to student through the centuries.

Some of this transmission is summarized in texts, but most is not. Important contributions in writing are attributed to Uwais al-Qarni, Harrm bin Hian, Hasan Basri and Sayid ibn al-Mussib, who are regarded as the first Sufis in the earliest generations of Islam. Harith al-Muhasibi was the first one to write about moral psychology. Rabia Basri was a Sufi known for her love and passion for God, expressed through her poetry. Bayazid Bastami was among the first theorists of Sufism; he concerned himself with *fanâ* and *baqâ*, the state of annihilating the self in the presence of the divine, accompanied by clarity concerning worldly phenomena derived from that perspective.

Sufism had a long history already before the subsequent institutionalization of Sufi teachings into devotional orders (*tarîqât*) in the early middle Ages. Almost all extant Sufi orders trace their chains of transmission (*silsila*) back to Prophet Muhammad via his cousin and son-in-law Ali. The Naqshbandi order is a notable exception to this rule, as it traces the origin of its teachings from the Prophet Muhammad to the first Islamic Caliph Abu Bakr. Different devotional styles and traditions developed over time, reflecting the perspectives of different masters and the accumulated cultural wisdom of the orders. Typically all of these concerned themselves with the understanding of subtle knowledge (gnosis), education of the heart to purify it of baser instincts, the love of God, and approaching God through a well-described hierarchy of enduring spiritual stations (*maqâmât*) and more transient spiritual states (*ahwâl*).

FORMALISATION OF DOCTRINE

Towards the end of the first millennium CE, a number of manuals began to be written summarizing the doctrines of Sufism and describing some typical Sufi practices. Two of the most famous of these are now available in English translation: the *Kashf al-Mahjûb* of Hujwiri, and the *Risâla* of Qushayri. Two of Imam Al Ghazali's greatest treatises, the "Revival of Religious Sciences" and the "Alchemy of Happiness," argued that Sufism originated from the *Quran* and was thus compatible with mainstream Islamic thought, and did not in any way contradict Islamic Law – being instead necessary to its complete fulfillment. This became the mainstream position among Islamic scholars for centuries, challenged only recently on the basis of selective use of a limited body of texts. Ongoing efforts by both traditionally-trained Muslim scholars and Western academics are making Imam Al-Ghazali's works available in English translation for the first time, allowing readers to judge for themselves the compatibility between Islamic Law and Sufi doctrine.

These remarks concern written sources. It is to be remembered that Sufism is transmitted from the heart of the teacher to the heart of the student, not through texts; and also, that texts may not convey everything, or may be read by different seekers on different levels. Therefore the notion of a "formalization of doctrine" in Sufism is not strictly correct.

GROWTH OF SUFI INFLUENCE IN ISLAMIC CULTURES

The spread of Sufism has been considered a definitive factor in the spread of Islam, and in the creation of integrally Islamic cultures, especially in Africa and Asia. Recent academic work on these topics has focused on the role of Sufism in creating and propagating the culture of the Ottoman world, and in resisting European imperialism in Africa and South Asia. Between the 13th and 16th centuries CE, Sufism produced a flourishing intellectual culture throughout the Islamic world, a sort of "Golden Age" whose physical artifacts are still present. In many places, a lodge (known variously as a *zaouia, khanqah,* or *tekke*) would be endowed through a pious foundation in perpetuity (*waqf*) to provide a gathering place for Sufi adepts, as well as lodging for itinerant seekers of knowledge.

The same system of endowments could also be used to pay for a complex of buildings, such as that surrounding the Süleymaniye Mosque in Istanbul, including a lodge for Sufi seekers, a hospice with kitchens where these seekers could serve the poor and/or complete a period of initiation, a library, and other structures. No important domain in the civilization of Islam remained unaffected by Sufism in this period.

CONTEMPORARY SUFISM

Sufism suffered many setbacks in the modern era, particularly (though not exclusively) at the hands of European imperialists in the colonized nations of Asia and Africa. The life of the Algerian Sufi master Emir Abd al-Qadir is instructive in this regard. Notable as well are the lives of Amadou Bamba and Hajj Umar Tall in sub-Saharan Africa, and Sheikh Mansur Ushurma and Imam Shamil in the Caucasus region. Sufism being the central organizing principle of many traditional Islam cultures, it is not surprising that colonial powers attacked Sufi masters as one means of undermining the forces of indigenous self-determination.

In spite of this recent history of official repression, there remain many places in the world with vital Sufi traditions. Sufism is popular in such African countries as Senegal, where it is seen as a mystical expression of Islam. Mbacke suggests that one reason Sufism has taken hold in Senegal is because it can accommodate local beliefs and customs, which tend toward the mystical. In South Asia, four major Sufi orders persist, namely the Chishti Order, the Qadiriyyah, the Naqshbandiyya, and the Suhrawardiyya. The Deobandis (i.e., adherents of the Darul Uloom Deoband) and Barelwi are two significant Islamic movements in this region whose followers often belong to one of these orders.

For a more complete summary of currently active groups and teachers, readers are referred to links in the site of Dr. Alan Godlas of the University of Georgia. A number of Westerners have embarked with varying degrees of success on the path of Sufism. One of the first to return to Europe as an official representative of a Sufi path, and with the specific purpose to spread Sufism in Western Europe was the Swedish-born wandering Sufi Abd al-Hadi Aqhili. The ideas propagated by such spiritualists may or may not conform to the tenets of Sufism as understood by orthodox Muslims, as for instance with G. I. Gurdjieff and Shawni. On the other hand, American- and British-born teachers such as Nuh Ha Mim Keller, Hamza Yusuf, and Abdal Hakim Murad have been instrumental in spreading messages that conform fully to the normative tenets of Islam. Other noteworthy Sufi teachers who have been active in the West in recent years include Nader Angha, Hazrat Inayat Khan, Riaz Ahmed Gohar Shahi, Muhammad Emin

Er, Nazim al-Qubrusi, Javad Nurbakhsh, and Muzaffer Ozak.

THEORETICAL PERSPECTIVES IN SUFISM

Traditional Islamic scholars have recognized two major branches within the practice of Sufism, and use this as one key to differentiating among the approaches of different masters and devotional lineages. On the one hand there is the path from the signs to the Signifier (or from the arts to the Artisan). In this branch, the seeker begins by purifying the lower self of every corrupting influence that stands in the way of recognizing all of creation as the work of God, as God's active Self-disclosure or theophany. This is the way of Imam Al-Ghazali and of the majority of the Sufi orders.

On the other hand there is the path from the Signifier to His signs, from the Artisan to His works. In this branch the seeker experiences divine attraction (*jadhba*), and is able to enter the path with a glimpse of its endpoint, of direct apprehension of the Divine Presence towards which all spiritual striving is directed. This does not replace the striving to purify the heart, as in the other branch; it simply stems from a different point of entry into the path. This is the way primarily of the masters of the Naqshbandi and Shadhili orders. Contemporary scholars may also recognize a third branch, attributed to the late Ottoman scholar Said Nursi and explicated in his vast Qur'ân commentary called the Risale-i Nur. This approach entails strict adherence to the way of the Prophet Muhammad, in the understanding that this wont, or *sunnah*, proposes a complete devotional spirituality adequate to those without access to a master of the Sufi way.

CONTRIBUTIONS TO OTHER DOMAINS OF SCHOLARSHIP

Sufism has contributed significantly to the elaboration of theoretical perspectives in many domains of intellectual endeavor. For instance, the doctrine of "subtle centers" or centers of subtle cognition (known as *Lataif-e-sitta*) addresses the matter of the awakening of spiritual intuition in ways that some consider similar to certain models of *chakra* in Hinduism. In general, these subtle centers or *latâ'if* are thought of as faculties that are to be purified sequentially in order to bring the seeker's wayfaring to completion. A concise and useful summary of this system from a living exponent of this tradition has been published by Muhammad Emin Er.

Sufi psychology has influenced many areas of thinking both within and outside of Islam, drawing primarily upon three concepts. Ja'far al-Sadiq (both an imam in the Shia tradition and a respected scholar and link in chains of Sufi transmission in all Islamic sects) held that human beings are dominated by a lower self called the *nafs*, a faculty of spiritual intuition called the *qalb* or spiritual heart, and a spirit or soul called *ruh*. These interact in various ways, producing the spiritual types of the tyrant (dominated by *nafs*), the person of faith and moderation (dominated by the spiritual heart), and the person lost in love for God (dominated by the *ruh*).

Of note with regard to the spread of Sufi psychology in the West is Robert Frager, a Sufi teacher authorized in the Halveti Jerrahi order. Frager was a trained psychologist, born in the United States, who converted to Islam in the course of his practice of Sufism and wrote extensively on Sufism and psychology. Sufi cosmology and Sufi metaphysics are also noteworthy areas of intellectual accomplishment.

SUFI PRACTICES

The devotional practices of Sufis vary widely. This is because an acknowledged and authorized master of the Sufi path is in effect a physician of the heart, able to diagnose the seeker's impediments to knowledge and pure intention in serving God, and to prescribe to the seeker a course of treatment appropriate to his or her maladies. The consensus among Sufi scholars is that the seeker cannot self-diagnose, and that it can be extremely harmful to undertake any of these practices alone and without formal authorization.

Prerequisites to practice include rigorous adherence to Islamic norms (ritual prayer in its five prescribed times each day, the fast of Ramadan, and so forth). Additionally, the seeker ought to be firmly grounded in supererogatory practices known from the life of the Prophet Muhammad (such as the so-called "sunna prayers"). This is in accordance with the words, attributed to God, of the following, a famous Hadith Qudsi:

> My servant draws near to Me through nothing I love more than that which I have made obligatory for him. My servant never ceases drawing near to Me through supererogatory works until I love him. Then, when I love him, I am his hearing through which he hears, his sight through which he sees, his hand through which he grasps, and his foot through which he walks.

It is also necessary for the seeker to have a correct creed (*Aqidah*), and to embrace with certainty its tenets. The seeker must also, of necessity, turn away from sins, love of this world, the love of company and renown, obedience to satanic impulse, and the promptings of the lower self. (The way in which this purification of the heart is achieved is outlined in certain books, but must be prescribed in detail by a Sufi master.) The seeker must also be trained to prevent the corruption of those good deeds which have accrued to his or her credit by overcoming the traps of ostentation, pride, arrogance, envy, and long hopes (meaning the hope for a long life allowing us to mend our ways later, rather than immediately, here and now).

Sufi practices, while attractive to some, are not a *means* for gaining knowledge. The traditional scholars of Sufism hold it as absolutely axiomatic that knowledge of God is not a psychological state generated through breath control. Thus, practice of "techniques" is not the cause, but instead the *occasion* for such knowledge to be obtained (if at all), given proper prerequisites and proper guidance by a master of the way. Furthermore, the emphasis on practices may obscure a far more important fact: The seeker is, in a sense, to become a broken person, stripped of all habits through the practice of (in the words of Imam Al-Ghazali words) solitude, silence, sleeplessness, and hunger.

DHIKR

Dhikr is the remembrance of God commanded in the *Quran* for all Muslims. To engage in dhikr is to practice consciousness of the Divine Presence (some would say "to seek a state of godwariness") according to a variety of means. Some types of dhikr are prescribed for all Muslims, and do not require Sufi initiation or the prescription of a Sufi master because they are deemed to be good for every seeker under every circumstance. Other types of dhikr require specific instruction and permission.

Dhikr as a devotional act includes the repetition of divine names, supplications and aphorisms from hadith literature, and sections of the *Quran*. More generally, any activity in which the Muslim maintains awareness of God is considered dhikr. Some Sufi orders stress and extensive reliance upon Dhikr and termed it the source to attain Divine Love likewise in Qadri Al-Muntahi Sufi tariqa, which was originated by Riaz Ahmed Gohar Shahi. This practice of Dhikr called Dhikr-e-Qulb(remembrance of Allah by Heartbeats). The basic idea of this practice is to visualize the Arabic name of God, Allah as having been written on the disciple's heart. Some Sufi orders engage in ritualized dhikr ceremonies, the liturgy of which may include recitation, singing, instrumental music, dance, costumes, incense, meditation, ecstasy, and trance.

MURAQABA

The practice of *muraqaba* can be likened to the practices of meditation attested in many faith communities. The word *muraqaba* is derived from the same root (*r-q-b*) occurring as one of the 99 Names of God in the *Quran*, al-Raqîb, meaning "the Vigilant" and attested in verse 4: 1 of the *Quran*. Through *muraqaba*, a person watches over or takes care of the spiritual heart, acquires knowledge about it, and becomes attuned to the Divine Presence, which is ever vigilant.

While variation exists, one description of the practice within a Naqshbandi lineage reads as follows:

He is to collect all of his bodily senses in concentration, and to cut himself off from all preoccupation and notions that inflict themselves upon the heart. And thus he is to turn his full consciousness towards God Most High while saying three times: "*Ilahî anta maqsûdî wa-ridâka matlûbî* — my God, you are my Goal and Your good pleasure is what I seek." Then he brings to his heart the Name of the Essence — Allâh — and as it courses through his heart he remains attentive to its meaning, which is "Essence without likeness." The seeker remains aware that He is Present, Watchful, Encompassing of all, thereby exemplifying the meaning of his saying (may God bless him and grant him peace): "Worship God as though you see Him, for if you do not see Him, He sees you." And likewise the prophetic tradition: "The most favoured level of faith is to know that God is witness over you, wherever you may be."

Sufi pilgrimages

In popular Sufism (i.e., devotional practices that have achieved currency in world cultures through Sufi influence), one common practice is to visit the tombs of saints, great scholars, and righteous people. This is a particularly common practice in South Asia, where famous tombs include those of Khoja Afâq, near Kashgar, in China; Sachal Sarmast, in Sindh, Pakistan; and the Darbar-e-Gohar Shahi in Kotri Sharif. Likewise, in Fez, Morocco, a popular destination for such pious visitation is the Zaouia Moulay Idriss II. Visitors may invoke blessings upon those interred, and seek divine favour and proximity.

ISLAM AND SUFISM

Sufism and Islamic law

Scholars and adherents of Sufism sometimes describe Sufism in terms of a threefold approach to God as explained by a tradition (*hadîth*) attributed to the Prophet Muhammad,*"The Shariah is my words, the tariqa is my actions, and the haqiqa is my interior states"*. Sufis believe the *shariah, tariqa* and *haqiqa* are mutually interdependent. The *tariqa,* the 'path' on which the mystics walk, has been defined as 'the path which comes out of the *Shariah,* for the main road is called *shar,* the path, *tariq.*' No mystical experience can be realized if the binding injunctions of the Shariah are not followed faithfully first. The path, *tariqa,* however, is narrower and more difficult to walk. It leads the adept, called *sâlik* (wayfarer), in his *sulûk* (wayfaring), through different stations (*maqâmât*) until he reaches his goal, the perfect *tawhîd,* the existential confession that God is One.

TRADITIONAL ISLAMIC THOUGHT AND SUFISM

The literature of Sufism emphasizes highly subjective matters that resist outside observation, such as the subtle states of the heart. Often these resist direct reference or description, with the consequence that the authors of various Sufi treatises took recourse to allegorical language. For instance, much Sufi poetry refers to intoxication, which Islam expressly forbids. This usage of indirect language and the existence of interpretations by people who had no training in Islam or Sufism led to doubts being cast over the validity of Sufism as a part of Islam. Also, some groups emerged that considered themselves above the Sharia and discussed Sufism as a method of bypassing the rules of Islam in order to attain salvation directly. This was disapproved of by traditional scholars.

For these and other reasons, the relationship between traditional Islamic scholars and Sufism is complex and a range of scholarly opinion on Sufism in Islam has been the norm. Some scholars, such as Al-Ghazali, helped its propagation while other scholars, such as Ibn Taymiyyah, opposed it. W. Chittick explains the position of Sufism and Sufis this way:

In short, Muslim scholars who focused their energies on understanding the normative guidelines for the body came to be known as jurists, and those who held that the most important task was to train the mind in achieving correct understanding came to be divided into three main schools of thought: theology, philosophy, and Sufism. This leaves us with the third domain of human existence, the spirit. Most Muslims who devoted their major efforts to developing the spiritual dimensions of the human person came to be known as Sufis.

TRADITIONAL AND NON-TRADITIONAL SUFI GROUPS

The traditional Sufi orders, which are in majority, emphasize the role of Sufism as a spiritual discipline within Islam. Therefore, the Sharia (traditional Islamic law) and the Sunnah (customs of the Prophet) are seen as crucial for any Sufi aspirant.

One proof traditional order assert is that almost all the famous Sufi masters of the past Caliphates were experts in Sharia and were renowned as people with great Iman (faith) and excellent practice. Many were also Qadis (Sharia law judges) in courts. They held that Sufism was never distinct from Islam and to fully comprehend and practice Sufism one must be an observant Muslim.

In recent decades there has been a growth of non-traditional Sufi movements in the West. Examples include the Universal Sufism movement, the Golden Sufi Center, the Sufi Foundation of America, the neo-sufism of Idries Shah, and Sufism Reoriented. Rumi has become one of the most widely read poets in the United States, thanks largely to the translations published by Coleman Barks.

The use of the title *Sufi* by non-traditional groups to refer to themselves, and their appropriation of traditional Sufi masters (most notably Jalaluddin Rumi) as sources of authority or inspiration, is not accepted by Muslims who are Sufi adherents. Some traditional Sufis also object to interpretations of classical Sufis texts by writers who have no grounding in the traditional Islamic sciences and therefore no prerequisites for understanding such texts. These are considered by certain conventional Islamic scholars as beyond the pale of the religion. This being said, there are Islamic Sufi groups that are open to non-Muslim participation.

RECEPTION

CRITICISM WITHIN ISLAM

Riaz Ahmed Gohar Shahi was heavily criticized by orthodox theological scholars in Pakistan and abroad. Shahi's books were banned by the Government of Pakistan. Public meetings are not allowed to his followers and no press coverage is allowed to either Gohar Shahi or to his followers due to charges of blasphemy law violations. Many attempts were made on Shahi's life including a petrol bomb attack, thrown into his Manchester residence, and an attack with a hand grenade during the discourse at his home in Kotri, Pakistan.

Gohar Shahi was booked in 1997 on alleged charges of murdering a woman who had come to him for spiritual treatment; Gohar Shahi, and many of his followers were later convicted under Islamic blasphemy laws by an antiterrorist court in Sindh. Gohar Shahi was convicted in absentia—as then he was in England—resulting in sentences that totaled approximately 59 years. Gohar Shahi died abroad, prior to any decision on appeals filed with the High Court of Sindh.

PERCEPTION OUTSIDE ISLAM

Sufi mysticism has long exercised a fascination upon the Western world, and especially its orientalist scholars. Figures like Rumi have become household names in the United States, where Sufism is perceived as quietist and less political. The Islamic Institute in Mannheim, Germany, which works towards the integration of Europe and Muslims, sees Sufism as particularly suited for interreligious dialogue and intercultural harmonisation in democratic and pluralist societies; it has described Sufism as a symbol of tolerance and humanism – undogmatic, flexible and non-violent. The Indian government has likewise praised Sufism as the tolerant face of Islam though many believe that Sufis like Naqshbandis have been fanatical and that some of the Sufi traditions like dancing, copied from native Indian traditions help in camouflaging Islamic extremism.

THE INFLUENCE OF SUFISM ON JUDAISM

A great influence was exercised by Sufism upon the ethical writings of Jews in the middle ages. In the first writing of this kind, we see "Kitab al-Hidayah ila Farai'd al-Kulub", Duties of the Heart, of Bahya ibn Pakuda. This book was translated by Judah ibn Tibbon into Hebrew under the title "Hobot ha-Lebabot". The author says: "The precepts prescribed by the Torah number 613 only; those dictated by the intellect are innumerable." This was precisely the argument used by the Sufis against their adversaries, the Ulamas.

The arrangement of the book seems to have been inspired by Sufism. Its ten sections correspond to the ten stages through which the Sufi had to pass in order to attain that true and passionate love of God which is the aim and goal of all ethical self-discipline. It is noteworthy that in the ethical writings of the Sufis Al-Kusajri and Al-Harawi there are sections which treat of the same subjects as those treated in the "$obot ha-Lebabot" and which bear the same titles: e.g., "Bab al-Tawakkul"; "Bab al-Taubah"; "Bab al-Mu%asabah"; "Bab al-Tawa

u'"; "Bab al-Zuhd". In the ninth gate Ba%ya directly quotes sayings of the Sufis, whom he calls "Perushim. "However, the author of the "$obot ha-Lebabot" did not go so far as to approve of the asceticism of the Sufis, although he showed a marked predilection for their ethical principles.

The Jewish write Abraham bar $iyya teaches the asceticism of the Sufis. His distinction with regard to the observance of Jewish law by various classes of men is essentially a Sufic theory. According to it there are four principal degrees of human perfection or sanctity; namely:

1. Of "Shari'ah," i.e., of strict obedience to all ritual laws of Islam, such as prayer, fasting, pilgrimage, almsgiving, ablution, etc., which is the lowest degree of worship, and is attainable by all,
2. Of "Tarikah," which is accessible only to a higher class of men who, while strictly adhering to the outward or ceremonial injunctions of religion, rise to an inward perception of mental power and virtue necessary for the nearer approach to the Divinity,
3. Of "Hakikah," the degree attained by those who, through continuous contemplation and inward devotion, have risen to the true perception of the nature of the visible and invisible; who, in fact, have recognized the Godhead, and through this knowledge have succeeded in establishing an ecstatic relation to it; and,
4. Of the "Ma'arifah," in which state man communicates directly with the Deity.

IN POPULAR CULTURE

IN MOVIES

The movie Bab'Aziz (2005) directed by Nacer Khemir tells the story of an old and blind dervish who must cross the desert with his little granddaughter during many days and nights to get to his last dervish reunion celebrated every 30 years. The movie is full of Sufi mysticism and even contains quotes of Rumi and other Sufi poets and shows an ecstatic Sufi dance.

IN MUSIC

Madonna on her record Bedtime Stories (1994) sings a song called Bedtime Story that talks about getting in a high unconsciousness level. The video for the song shows an ecstatic sufi ritual with many dervishes dancing around, Arabic calligraphy and some other Sufi elements. In the year 1998 she recorded the song Bittersweet in which she recites Rumi's poem by the same name. In the year 2001 Madonna sang the song Secret during her Drowned World Tour showing rituals from many religions including a Sufi dance. Singer/song writter Loreena McKennit on her record *The Mask and Mirror* (1994) has a song called The Mystic's Dream clearly influenced by Sufi music and poetry. *The Band, me without You,* has made references to Sufi parables, including the name of their upcoming album "it's all crazy! It's all false! It's all a dream! It's alright!" (2009) Lead singer, Aaron Weiss, claims this influence comes from his parents who are both Sufi converts.

The Sufis are not an ethnic or religious group, but a mystical movement that is found all over the Islamic world and that still has a deep influence on the varied populations of the Middle East. Sufism grew historically as a reaction against the rigid legalism of the orthodox religious leadership and as a counterweight to the growing worldliness of the expanding Muslim empire. One source of Sufism is to be found in the twofold presentation of God in the *Quran*: on the one hand he is described as the almighty creator, lord and judge, and on the other hand he is seen as abiding in the believer's heart and nearer to man than his own jugular vein.

Sufism searches for a direct mystical knowledge of God and of his Love. Its goal was to progress beyond mere intellectual knowledge to a mystical (existential) experience that submerged limited man in the infinity of God. It used Jewish, Christian, Gnostic, Hellenistic, Zoroastrian and Hindu traditions that were brought into Islam by converts from the many conquered populations. The name Sufi is derived from the Arabic word Suf which means wool. Early Sufis wore simple coarse woollen garments similar to those of Christian monks.

Sufism believed that the *Quran* and Hadith have secret, esoteric, meaning and symbolism (Batin). In opposition to the literal method of interpretation (Tafsir), Sufism used an allegorical method (Ta'wil) which looked for the hidden meaning and symbols in the holy texts. Sufism had an important part in the formation of Muslim societies as it educated the masses and met their felt needs, giving spiritual meaning to their lives and channeling their emotions. Sufis were also great missionaries who converted new regions to Islam.

Its cultural contribution was a rich poetry in Arabic, Persian, Turkish, Urdu, Sindi, Pashto and Punjabi, which spread its mystical ideas all over the Muslim world and enriched local literature and identity. Several techniques were developed to achieve the goal of a blissful union with Ultimate Reality. They were known as Dhikr (remembrance, mention of God) and Sama' (hearing). In the Dhikr Sufis would recite the many names of God and sing hymns of praise. Special forms of breathing were supposed to aid concentration and help them attain to an ecstatic state in which they actually felt they had reached union with God.

During the Sama', poetry, music and dance were used as an aid to reaching the ecstatic state.

These informal groups later crystalized into Sufi brotherhoods gathered around famous leaders. In some countries even today most Muslims belong to one order or another. Around the Muslim world there are hundreds of orders and they are an important religious and political force. Sufism is found amongst both Sunnis and Shi'a, being a movement within orthodox Islam. However it has many links with Isma'ilism and other extreme Shi'a sects (Ghulat) as it developed in similar times and circumstances.

Sufism developed in the 8th and 9th centuries in three major centres: 1. The cities of Basra, Kufa and Baghdad in Iraq. 2. The city of Balkh in the Khorasan district of Persia. 3. Egypt.

Muhammad is regarded as the first Sufi master who passed his esoteric teachings orally to his successors who also received his special grace (barakah). An unbroken chain of transmission of divine authority is supposed to exist from Muhammad to his successor 'Ali and from him down to generations of Sufi masters (Sheikhs, Pirs). Each order has its own Silsilah (chain) that links it with Muhammad and 'Ali.

FIRST STAGE - ASCETICISM

Under the Umayads (661-749) there was a growing tendency to compare the wealth and luxury of the ruling class with the simple lifestyle of the first Caliphs. Devout believers were shocked by the worldliness and opulence of court life and they reacted with a growing concern for reality in their own personal relationship with God.

Outward observance of the Shari'a laws could not satisfy their growing spiritual hunger, and they started to imitate Christian hermits who had discovered asceticism and poverty as a way to develop a close relationship with God.

The first Sufis were ascetics who meditated on the Day of Judgement. They were called "those who always weep" and "those who see this world as a hut of sorrows." They kept the external rules of Shari'a, but at the same time developed their own mystical ideas and techniques. "Little food, little talk, little sleep," was a popular proverb amongst them. Mortification of the flesh, self denial, poverty and abstinence were seen as the means of drawing near to God, and this included fasting and long nights of prayer.

Some Early Sufis

Hasan of Basrah (d.728) was one of the first Sufi ascetics. He exhorted his followers against attachment to this evil world and encouraged them to reject it and to follow a path of poverty and abstinence. Ibrahim b. Adham (d. 777) of Balkh in Khorasan taught his disciples the importance of meditation and of silence in worship.

Shaqiq of Balkh (d.810) taught that only a rigid system of self-discipline could lead to absolute trust in God (tawakkul) and to the mystical state (hal). Al-Muhasibi (d.837 in Baghdad) taught that self-discipline and self-examination were the needed preparation for fellowship and union with God. Dhu an-Nun of Egypt (d.859) taught that Ma'rifah (inner knowledge, enlightenment, Gnosis) was necessary to attain real union with God.

Abu Yazid al-Bistami (d. 874) taught that union with God is achieved through the annihilation of self (Fana'). This is done by a total stripping away of a person's attributes and personality and by rigorous mortification of the flesh. He was the first "intoxicated" Sufi who in his ecstatic state felt that God had replaced his own ego and now dwelt in his soul. This caused him to exclaim: "Glory to me! How great is my majesty!"

Junaid of Baghdad (d.910), stressed the importance of wisdom and sobriety in achieving both fana' (dying to self, extinction of self) and baqa' (abiding in God). The first great

Sufi martyr was Hallaj who was crucified in 922 in Baghdad for blasphemy. His offence was the statement "I am the Truth" which signified that he had attained union with God who now dwelt in his body instead of his own self. He saw Jesus as his great example of a holy man in whom God was incarnate.

SECOND STAGE - MYSTICISM OF LOVE

A woman from Basrah in Iraq, Rabi'a al-Adawiya (d.801) introduced the theme of Divine Love into Sufism. She yearned to love God only for Himself, not for hope of any reward (paradise) nor out of fear of judgement (hell). Following her death the love theme became a dominant feature of Sufism. It expressed the Sufi's yearning for the development of a love relationship with God that would lead to an intimate experience of God and finally to a total union with God.

The love theme found its main expression in Sufi poetry in which the relations between God the Divine Lover and the man searching for his love were symbolically described. Early Sufi poems in Arabic express the soul's deep yearning for union with the beloved.

Persian poetry often compared the soul's love relationship with God to that between a man and a beautiful youth. In Indian poetry the loving wife yearning for her husband symbolised the soul's yearning for God. Later poets developed the long mystical poems called Mathnawis (Masnawis) which expressed in symbolical verse the manifold emotions of love to God and of unity with him.

Persia had the greatest flourishing of Sufi poetry, and most of its classical poetry has a Sufi content. One example is the Mathnawi "Mantiq al-Tair" (speech of the birds) by Farid al-Din 'Attar, an allegory which portrays the mystic on his pilgrimage from asceticism through illumination to union with God. Jalal ad-Din Rumi (1207-1273), named "Mawlana" - our Lord or Teacher - was the greatest Persian mystical poet. His famous Mathnawi of 26,000 rhythmic couplets is a real encyclopaedia of Sufi allegorical and mystical thought and experience.

Persian Sufis regard it as next to the *Quran* in holiness. Rumi also founded the Mawlawi (Mevlevi) order of whirling dervishes. Sufi poetry uses the symbols of wine (God's intoxicating love), the wine cup (the Sufi's heart) and the cup bearer (the spiritual guide). The wine house is the religion of love and it is compared to the religion of law symbolised by the mosque. Learning the many Sufi symbols and their meaning is essential to an understanding of this kind of poetry.

THIRD STAGE - SUFI APOLOGETICS

Early Sufi masters gathered informal circles of disciples and transmitted their teachings orally. At first, the orthodox religious authorities were very suspicious of the Sufis and accused them of heresy and blasphemy. This led some Sufis in the 10th century to defend Sufism by writing handbooks of their teaching and practice in the hope of proving their orthodoxy. Al-A'rabi (d.952), Makki (d.996), Sarraj (d. 988), Kalabadhi (d.1000) and Hujviri (d.1057) were such masters who wrote in defence of Sufism. They also published histories and biographies of Sufism, trying to prove that it was based on the practice (Sunnah) of the Prophet and his companions.

Al-Qushairi (d. 1072) defended Sufism against the accusations of antinomianism (lawlessness). In addition to writing biographies of Sufi saints he wrote "Risala", a book in which he defined Sufi doctrines and terms. He defined the mystical stations (maqamat, a result of the Sufi's own labours), and states (ahwal, mystical states bestowed by God's grace). Abu Hamid al-Ghazali (d.1111), called Hujjat al-Islam - Proof of Islam, was a great Muslim thinker who found no satisfaction in his extensive study of theology and law. Turning to Sufism he found in it the certainty of God he had yearned for and failed to find in his previous studies. In his book "The Revival of the Religious Sciences" (Ihya' 'Ulum ad-Din) he attempted to reconcile Sufism with orthodoxy. It was immensely popular and finally guaranteed Sufism an official place in orthodox Islam alongside Law and Theology.

FOURTH STAGE - PHILOSOPHICAL-MYSTICAL SYSTEMS (THEOSOPHY)

Theosophy is any mystical system of religious philosophy that claims a direct intuitive insight into God's nature. Theosophical speculations on the nature of God and man were introduced into Sufism by Sahl al-Tustari (d.896) and at-Tirmidi (d 898). The greatest of all Sufi theosophical writers in Arabic was Ibn al-'Arabi (d.1240) who was born in Spain. He travelled to Tunis and Mecca and finally settled in Damascus. In his 500 books he teaches that all existence is but a manifestation of God, the one ultimate divine reality which is totally "other", an undifferentiated unity, but in whom the archtypes of all potential beings exist. This is the "unknown God" from whom emanates a hierarchy of divine beings (Names, Lords) the lowest of whom is the Lord of revelation and creation who is also called the First Intellect.

The emanations are the mediating link between the unknowable, transcendent God and the created world. This teaching was the basis of the Sufi concept of the Unity of Being (Wahdat al-Wujud). The First Intellect, an emanation of the God was also called the "idea of Muhammad". He is the archtype through whom man was made. This emanation is incarnated in a Perfect Man in every generation - the perfect Sufi. This man most fully manifests the nature of God and he is the pole (Qutb, axis) around which the cosmos revolves. Ibn al-'Arabi saw himself as a "pole" and he called himself the seal (the most perfect) of the saints.

Another theosophical system that of illumination was developed by Shihab al-Din Suhrawardi (executed in

Aleppo in 1191). He taught that all things exist as varying degrees of light, beginning with the Absolute Light, the Light of Lights who is God himself. Light then spreads out from God in ever weaker degrees (angels), each reflecting the light above it to those beneath it. The whole world of being is composed of innumerable angels of light spreading out in geometrical patterns. Indian Sufis were influenced by Hindu mysticism and strayed far from Islamic orthodoxy in their speculations. The Naqshbandi order founded in the 13th century in Central Asia to preserve true Islam from the ravages of the Mongol invasions, succeeded in keeping them within orthodoxy. Ahmad Sirhindi (d.1624) taught that the Unity of Being was a subjective experience occurring only in the Sufi's mind - not the Hindu concept of total annihilation of the personal in the infinite.

FIFTH STAGE - THE RISE OF SUFI ORDERS

Sufi orders began to form in the 12th and 13th centuries centering around a master founder and stressing companionship (Suhbah, fellowship) as essential to the Sufi spiritual path. This was the time of the terrible Mongol invasions when the 'Abassid Caliphate in Bagdad was overthrown. Sufism was one of the forces that helped prevent the downfall of Islam. It helped convert the conquerors and had a stabilising influence on the community during those troubled times. This period was actually Sufism's golden age.

In its first stages Sufism had been the prerogative of a limited spiritual elite. From the twelfth century onwards it succeeded in involving the Muslim masses on a large scale in its network of orders. Sufi hospices, (Zawiyas in Arabic, Khanagas in Iranian, Ribat in the Maghreb and Tekkes in Turkish) were founded all over the Muslim world from Morocco to Central Asia. The Sheikh of each order, a successor of the original founder, presided over the hospice.

In this centre he taught his disciples (Murids) and performed with them the Sufi rituals of Dhikr and Sama'.

There was an elaborate initiation ritual for the disciple when he was admitted into full membership (usually after three years). In this ceremony he received from the Sheikh a special cloak (Khirqa) which symbolised poverty and devotion to God. Sufis had no rule of celibacy and most were married. The orders received endowments from sympathetic rulers and rich citizens and some eventually became fabulously wealthy. Sufi orders had an extensive missionary outreach into Africa and into Southeast Asia where they are still very influential.

Each order developed its own specific set of techniques for its Dhikr and Sama', used by its members to attain to the ecstatic state. These rituals also had a social function, helping to unify people from widely varying backgrounds into a spiritual brotherhood. The orders were thus a unifying force in society, drawing members from all social classes to their Dhikr and Sama' ceremonies as well as to their joyous celebrations of the anniversaries of the deaths of their founder ('Urs). They provided the masses with a spiritual and emotional dimension to religion which the hair splitting legalists could not supply. The orders also established trade and craft guilds and provided hospices for travellers and merchants which were located along the great trade routes (such as the famous Silk Road). Between the 13th and the 18th century most Muslims belonged to some Sufi Tariqah.

SOME FAMOUS ORDERS

There are more than two hundred known Sufi orders. Some are local, others universal. Some are rural and others are urban.

The Qadiriyah – It is the oldest and most widespread order. It has branches all over the world loosely tied to its centre at Baghdad. It was founded in Baghdad by 'Abd al-

Qadir Jilani (d.1166), considered being the greatest saint in Islam. It later became established in Yemen, Egypt, Sudan, the Maghreb, Central Asia and India. The Qadiriya stresses piety, humility, moderation and philanthropy and appeals to all classes of society being strictly orthodox. It is governed by a descendant of al-Jilani who is also the keeper of his tomb in Baghdad which is a pilgrimage centre for his followers from all over the world.

The Jilaliya - A Qadiri branch in the Maghreb which worships al-Jilani as a supernatural being, combining Sufism with pre-Islamic ideas and practices.

The Naqshbandiya – It was founded in Central Asia in the thirteenth century in an attempt to defend Islam against the ravages of the Mongol invasions. It later spread to the Indian subcontinent. The Naqshbandis tried to control the political rulers so as to ensure that they implemented God's will. They were politically and culturally active; the great poet Mir Dad (d.1785) belonged to this order. They were also connected to trade and crafts guilds and held political power in the 15th century in Central Asia and in Moghul India. A Naqshbandi branch, the Khaltawiyah, had an important part in efforts to modernise the Ottoman Empire during the 18th and 19th centuries.

The Naqshbandiya developed mainly as an urban order with close links to the orthodox hierarchy. They recite their Dhikr silently, ban music and dance, and prefer contemplation to ecstasy. Their "middle way" between extreme asceticism and extreme antinomianism seemed acceptable to the orthodox hierarchy. They have been involved in underground movements against Soviet rule in Central Asia and supported the Afghan Mujahedin against the Russians.

The Mawlawiyah - This order was founded by Jalal al-Din Rumi (d.1273, called Mawlana), the greatest Sufi poet who wrote in Persian. Their rituals are aesthetically sophisticated, and their Sama' is famous for its exquisite combination of music, poetry and whirling dance (in the West they are called "Whirling Dervishes") which transports them into the trace like state. The Mawlawiya were especially attractive to the educated elite of the Turkish Ottoman Empire and were widespread in Anatolia where they had close links with the authorities.

The Bektashiya - A syncretistic order whose ritual and beliefs are a mixture of Shi'ism, Orthodox Christianity and gnostic cults. By the sixteenth century the Bektashis were the order of the famous Janissary corps, the elite military unit of the Ottoman Empire. Their magic-like rituals appealed to the illiterate masses of Anatolia. Their clergy were celibate, they practiced ritual confession and communion and had a trinitarian concept of God similar to that of the 'Alawis.

The Tijaniya – It was founded by al-Tijani in 1781 in Fez, Morocco, extended the borders of Islam towards Senegal and Nigeria and founded great kingdoms in West Africa. They taught submission to the established government and their influence is still an important factor in these countries where it is associated with conservative businessmen.

The Daraquiya – It was founded in the early 19th century by Mulay 'Arabi Darqawi (d. 1823) in Fez in Morocco. It was the driving force behind the Jihad movement which achieved mass conversions to Islam in the mixed Berber-Arab-Negro lands of the Sahel. It is influential today in Mali, Niger and Chad and still widespread in Morocco.

The Khalwatiya – It was founded in northwest Persia in the 13th century and spread to the Caucasus and to Turkey. It was closely associated with the Ottoman Sultans and had its headquarters in Istanbul. It has also spread to Egypt and Indonesia.

The Suhrawardiya – It was started in Iraq by al-Suhrawardi (d.1234) who stressed serious training and teaching. They have many adherents in the Indian subcontinent. They were very involved politically in Iraq and Iran during the Mongol threat, seeking to ensure the survival of Islam.

The Rifa'iya – It was founded in the marshlands of southern Iraq by al-Rifa'i (d.1187). They stress poverty, abstinence and mortification of the flesh, and are also known as the "Howling Dervishes" because of their loud recitation of the Dhikr. They focus on dramatic ritual and bizarre feats such as fire eating, piercing themselves with iron skewers and biting heads off live snakes.

The Shadiliya – It was started by al-Shadili (d.1258) in Tunis. It flourished especially in Egypt under ibn-'Ata Allah (d.1309) but also spread to North Africa, Arabia and Syria. It is the strongest order in the Maghreb where it was organised by al-Jazuli (d. 1465) and has sub-orders under other names. The Shadiliya stress the intellectual basis of Sufism and allow their members to remain involved in the secular world. They are not allowed to beg and are always neatly dressed. They appealed mainly to the middle class in Egypt and are still active there. It is said that the Shadiliya were the first to discover the value of coffee as a means of staying awake during nights of prayer!

The Chishtiya - It was founded by Mu'in al-Din Chishti in Ajmer, India. His teaching was simple and the order is known for its fervour and hospitality. They helped in the islamisation of the Indian subcontinent.

The Sanusiya – A military brotherhood started by al-Sanusi (d.1837) in Libya with political and military as well as religious aims. They fought against the colonising Italians and the former King of Libya was head of the order.

The Ni'matulahiya: Developed first in Persia and then in India as a specifically Isma'ili oriented Sufi order.

The Ahmadiya – It is the leading order in Egypt with its centre at Tanta. It was founded by Ahmad al-Badawi (d. 1276).

The orders helped spread Islam and their Sufi concepts in frontier lands such as India, Central and Southeast Asia, Sudan, Morocco and sub-Saharan Africa.

SIXTH STAGE - THE DECLINE AND REVIVAL OF SUFISM

The Sufi orders grew steadily in wealth and in political influence, but their spirituality gradually declined as they concentrated on saint worship, miracle working, magic and superstition. The external religious practices were neglected, morals declined and learning was despised. In many areas Sufi orders succeeded in ruling the ignorant masses through a well organised and power hungry hierarchy.

Their local saints were revered by the populace and worshipped after their death as mediators and intercessors. Pilgrim's flocked to the Saint's tombs, willing to pay for a share in the Sheikh's Baraka. The orders became rich and powerful, and both politicians and theologians feared to oppose them and preferred to share in the profits.

Some sincere mystics still rose above the general decline. In Egypt, al-Shar'ani (d.1565) lived at the time of the Ottoman conquest and was a serious and comprehensive scholar. In Iran Sadr al-Din Shirazi (d.1640), also known as Mulla Sadra, was a great thinker who continued to develop the theology of illumination founded by Suhrawardi and integrated it with Ibn-'Arabis Unity of Being. His impact is still felt on theologians and philosophers in Iran today.

In India in the 18th century Shah Wali-Allah of Delhi tried to integrate the various schools of Sufi thought, whilst Mir Dard contributed much to the formation of Urdu poetry. In Iran the Safavid order gained political power for two centuries (1499-1720). The Sheikhs of this order claimed descent from 'Ali and they were favourably treated by both the Mongol and the Timurid dynasties. Based in Ardabil in Azerbaijan the order became a local power in the 15th century as it alternatively allied itself with and fought against the rulers of the Turkmen tribal confederations (Ak-Koyunlu, the White Sheep and Kara- Koyunlu, the Black Sheep).

The Turkmen Safavids of Anatolia and Azerbaijan were called Kizilbash (Redheads) from the red headgear they wore. In 1501 the Safavid Sheikh Ismail I defeated the Ak-Koyunlu and took the old Mongolian capital of Tabriz where he proclaimed himself as Shah. Later he instituted Twelver Shi'ism as the state religion of Persia and imposed it by force on the population. Many Sunni 'Ulama' and Sheikhs of other Sufi orders were executed.

The Sunni Ottomans felt threatened by Shi'a Persia, and in the ensuing centuries of warfare between these two powers they evolved an aggressive Sunnism within their own Empire. The Sultan Selim I massacred all the Shi'ites that he could lay his hands on, and until modern times the Kizilbash of Anatolia and other Shi'a groups collectively called "Alevis" by the Ottomans were forced to exist as an underground movement. Alevis still number some 8 million people in modern Turkey but they are officially ignored as non-existent by the authorities.

In Arabia the Wahabi puritan revival was extremely anti-Sufi, seeing their practices and doctrines as later pagan additions to pure Islam. Colonialism, nationalism and secularisation had a negative impact on Sufism in the 19th and 20th centuries. The modern revival of Islamic learning was accompanied by a violent reaction against the superstitions of Sufism.

It was accused as being the cause of the Islamic world's backwardness compared to the West. The two great Muslim reformers of the 19th century, Jamal al-Din al-Afghani and

Muhammad 'Abduh, both campaigned successfully against Sufi orders helping to diminish their influence.

In Turkey, Kemal Ataturk abolished the Sufi orders in 1925 and confiscated their lands and property. He saw them as corrupt and backward forces that hindered the modernisation of Turkish society. In other countries too post-colonial independent central governments were often suspicious of the orders.

They were suspected of being cells of political unrest and revolution that held the loyalty of the masses by their superstitions, religious emotionalism and outmoded power structures.

Despite religious and political attempts to eliminate them, the Sufi orders continued to exist, often underground. With the resurgence of fundamental Islam in the second half of the 20th century came also a Sufi revival. Sufism still flourishes in North Africa, Egypt, Sudan, Iran, Central Asia, Pakistan, India and Indonesia. In Soviet Central Asia their underground networks helped Islam survive until the reforms of the late eighties. The disintegration of the Soviet Union has allowed them to return to full public activity in the new republics. Sufism today is still a formidable force in the Islamic world. It still touches and transforms the lives of Muslim people, giving them meaning and emotional support in a world that is increasingly unstable and full of economic woes, suffering and confusion.

SUFI PRACTICE

INITIATION

Initiation into a Sufi order is seen as a necessary ritual that transmits the spiritual grace (barakah, spiritual power) of the guide (murshid) to the disciple (murid). This special grace goes back in an unbroken line to the Prophet himself.

In Sufi thought it is likened to a seed planted in the initiate's soul, the equivalent of Christian baptism or new birth. At the initiation ceremony the Master who has experienced union with God and annihilation of self, in addition to giving the disciple the special garment also gives him a secret word or prayer to help him in his meditation.

Sufis also believe in Spiritual Guides who reveal themselves to the Sufi in visions or dreams and help him on his path. Al-Khidr is one well known such guide who is sometimes identified as the prophet Elijah. The initiate has to learn spiritual poverty (faqr) which means emptying the soul of self in order to make room for God. The illusion of the individual ego must be erased by humility and love of one's neighbour. This is attained by a rigid self discipline that removes all obstacles to the revelation of the Divine Presence.

THE PATH OR PILGRIMAGE

Sufism is seen as a spiritual path of self knowledge that leads to knowledge of God. God is seen by the "eye of the heart", not by intellectual knowledge or legalistic customs. The outward form of religion is a mere shell which hides the kernel inside it. The kernel is the real Truth, the Sufi's goal on his spiritual path. The Sufi path contains many stages (Maqamat) and states (Ahwal). It begins with repentance when the seeker joins the order and prepares him for initiation. The guide (Sheikh, Pir) accepts the seeker as his disciple by the ritual of initiation when he imparts his grace, gives him strict ascetic rules to follow and a certain secret word for meditation. The disciple's path is one of continuous struggle against his lower soul. He passes through a number of spiritual stations and states clearly defined by Sufi teaching.

These are the Sufi stations: 1. detachment from the world (zuhd). 2. patience (sabr). 3. gratitude (shukr), for whatever God gives. 4. love (hubb). 5. pleasure (rida) with whatever God desires. Linked to these stations are specific moods or emotions (ahwal) such as fear and hope, sadness and joy, yearning and intimacy, granted to the pilgrim by God's grace for a while with the goal of leading him to on to Ma'rifah (esoteric knowledge, Gnosis), Mahabbah (Love) and to the ultimate goal which is annihilation of personality and unity with God.

Beyond this stage the Sufi then enters the state of Baqa', or perseverance in God. He returns from his state of intoxication (Sukr) back into the world completely transformed - reborn. The Sufi path has three ways: Makhafah, the way of fear of God leading to purification, Mahabbah, the way of love leading to sacrifice and Ma'rifah, the way of intuitive knowledge leading to illumination.

DHIKR AND SAMA'

Dhikr and Sama' were based on words attributed to the Prophet: "Whenever men gather together to invoke Allah, they are surrounded by Angels, the Divine Favour envelops them, the Divine Glory (as-Sakinah) descends upon them, and Allah remembers them in His assembly." The hospices became centres where lay people from the countryside would gather together with the members of the order to obey the Quran's injunction to remember God often.

This was done in the celebration of the Dhikr, which involved the communal rhythmic repetition of a phrase, usually from the *Quran,* in which one of the names of God appears. Breathe control and body movements were also used as techniques to aid in achieving concentration and control over senses and imagination. The rosary with 99 or 33 beads was used since the 8th century as an aid to counting the many repetitions (it entered Christian Churches from Sufism via the Crusades). This concentrated meditation can lead to a mystical trance and enlightenment which transforms man's whole being.

Sama' was first developed in the mid 9th century in Baghdad. It is another communal ritual practice, defined as a concert of music, poetry recital, singing and dance, which leads the participants to a mystical experience where they seem to hear the music of the heavenly spheres and the voice of God Himself. It attunes the heart to communion with God and is thought to remove all veils hiding God from man's inner vision. Drugs were used by some as an aid to reaching the ecstatic state, coffee by the Shadiliya in the 14th century.

SUFI SAINTS AND FOLK ISLAM

Sheikhs who had reached the highest mystical stage of union with God, were revered by the masses as saints (Awliya') upon whom God had bestowed miraculous supernatural powers and grace. A cult of living and of dead saints developed around them influenced by pagan customs. They were seen as miracle workers, healers, and intercessors for others before God. Their tombs became pilgrimage centres visited by many in order to partake of the Saint's Baraka (blessing, supernatural power) to meet their needs for healing and other help. They would make vows and pray for the saint's intercession on their behalf. Special celebrations which developed into folk festivals were held on the anniversary of their deaths ('urs). They were seen to be mediators between God and man, God answering their prayers on behalf of the supplicants.

Bibliography

Ali, Syed Ameer. *The Spirit of Islam: A History of the Evolution and Ideals of Islam,* with *a Life of the Prophet*. London: Chatto & Windus, 1978.

Bloom, Jonathan and Sheila Blair. *Islam: A Thousand Years of Faith and Power.* New Haven, CT: Yale University Press, 2002.

Booth, E. *Aristotelian Aporetic Ontology in Islamic and Christian Thinkers.* Cambridge, 1983.

Bowker, John. *What Muslims Believe.* Oxford, UK: Onewworld, 1999.

Burrell, D. *Knowing the Unknowable God: Ibn Sina, Maimonides, Aquinas* (Notre Dame: 1986).

Cook, Michael. *The Koran: A Very Short Introduction.* Oxford, UK: Oxford University Press, 2000.

Corbin, H. *History of Islamic Philosophy,* trans. L. Sherrard. London, 1993.

Craig, E. (ed.), *Routledge Encyclopedia of Philosophy.* London, 1998.

Davidson, H.A. *Proofs for Eternity, Creation and the Existence of God in Medieval Islamic and Jewish Philosophy.* Oxford, 1987.

Elias, Jamal J. *Islam.* Upper Saddle River, NJ: Prentice Hall, 1999.

Fakhry, M. *A History of Islamic Philosophy* , 2nd ed. New

York, 1983.

Gibb, Hamilton A.R. and J.H. Kramers, eds. *Shorter Encyclopedia of Islam.* Leiden: E.J. Brill, 1997 (reprint ed.).

Hodgson, Marshall G.S. *The Venture of Islam,* 3 Vols. Chicago, IL: University of Chicago Press, 1974.

Keller, Nuh Ha Mim, trans. *Al-Nawawi's Manual of Islam.* Cambridge, UK: The Islamic Texts Society, 1996.

Leaman, O. *An Introduction to Classical Islamic Philosophy.* Cambridge, 2002.

Marmura , M.E. (ed.), *Islamic Theology and Philosophy.* Albany, 1984.

Nasr, Seyyed Hossein. *The Heart of Islam: Enduring Values for Humanity.* San Francisco, CA, Harper San Francisco, 2002.

Newby, Gordon D. *A Concise Encyclopedia of Islam.* Oxford, UK, Oneworld, 2002.

Peters, F.E. *A Reader on Classical Islam.* Princeton, NJ: Princeton University Press, 1994.

Qadir , C.A. *Philosophy and Science in the Islamic World.* London, 1990.

Renard, John, ed. *Windows on the House of Islam: Muslim Sources on Spirituality.* Berkeley, CA: University of California Press, 1998.

Renard, John. *Seven Doors to Islam: Spirituality and the Religious Life of Muslims.* Berkeley, CA: University of California Press, 1996.

Ruthven, Malise. *Islam in the World.* New York: Oxford University Press, 2nd ed., 2000.

Schimmel, Annemarie. *Islam: An Introduction.* Albany, NY: State University of New York Press, 1992.

Schuon, Frithjof. *Islam and the Perennial Philosophy.*

London: World of Islam Festival Publ. Co., 1976.

Sharif, M.M. *A History of Muslim Philosophy,* 2 vols. (Wiesbaden: 1963-6).

Stern, S.M. *Medieval Arabic and Hebrew Thought* , ed. F. Zimmermann, London, 1983.

Stern, S.M., Hourani, H. and Brown, V. (eds.), *Islamic Philosophy and the Classical Tradition*. Oxford, 1972.

Waines, David. *An Introduction to Islam.* Cambridge, UK: Cambridge University Press, 1995.

Watt, M.W. Islamic Philosophy and Theology. Edinburgh, 1962, revised ed. 1985.

Watt, William Montgomery. *The Formative Period of Islamic Thought.* Oxford, UK: Oneworld,1998.

Watt, William Montgomery. *What is Islam?* London: Longman, 1970.

Williams, John Alden, ed. *The Word of Islam.* Austin, TX: University of Texas Press, 1994.

Wolfson, H.A. *Studies in the History of Philosophy and Religion* , ed. I. Twersky, G.H. Williams, in 2 vols. Cambridge, MA, 1973, 1977.

Wolfson, H.A. *The Philosophy of the Kalam.* Cambridge, MA, 1976.

Ziai, H. "Islamic Philosophy," in *The Oxford Companion to Philosophy,* ed. T. Honderich. Oxford , 1955.

Index